TEACHING IN A PLURALISTIC SOCIETY

TEACHING IN A PLURALISTIC SOCIETY
Concepts, Models, Strategies

RICARDO L. GARCIA
The University of Utah

1817

HARPER & ROW, PUBLISHERS, New York

Cambridge, Philadelphia, San Francisco
London, Mexico City, São Paulo, Sydney

Sponsoring Editor: George A. Middendorf
Project Editor: Jo-Ann Goldfarb
Designer: T. R. Funderburk
Production Manager: William Lane
Photo Researcher: Mira Schachne
Compositor: Maryland Linotype Composition Company, Inc.

Art Studio: Vantage Art, Inc.
Cover and part opening photographs: Paul Conklin, Monkmeyer

TEACHING IN A PLURALISTIC SOCIETY: Concepts, Models, Strategies

Copyright © 1982 by Harper & Row, Publishers, Inc.

Library of Congress Cataloging in Publication Data

Garcia, Ricardo L.
    Teaching in a pluralistic society.

    Includes index.
    1. Intercultural education—United States.   2. Minorities—Education—
United States.   I. Title.
LC1099.G37   371.1'02   81–6530
ISBN 0–06–042233–5   AACR2

To my wife, Sharon, and the twins,
Shane and Maria, for their patience.

Contents

Part III   EXERCISES AND ACTIVITIES   189

Preface

We live in a pluralistic society. Before you finish your teaching career, you will more than likely teach all kinds of students—black, Spanish-speaking, Native American, Asian, Appalachian, white ethnic —to name a few. They may represent most social classes, religious affiliations, and regions of the country. The challenge will be to make a difference in their lives: to teach them all that they are capable, unique individuals, who have a right to be respected by others and a responsibility to respect others. If you can embrace the idea that ethnic diversity is an asset rather than a liability, and if you can grapple with your values and biases regarding ethnic diversity, then you can make a difference in the lives of students. This book examines the roles that culture and ethnicity play in American society and focuses specifically on teaching and learning in U.S. public schools.

While the text stresses how culture and ethnicity influence teaching and learning, it is not the final word on teaching in a pluralistic society.

Rather, it offers a set of theoretical and practical premises that serve as means of exploring this issue. First, the text highlights the philosophic posture of cultural relativism, explaining what the posture means and how it applies to pluralistic teaching and learning. Second, the text provides an overview of fundamental cultural and ethnic concepts both as social realities and as theoretical constructs. Third, it focuses on broad communal theories, and school and community relationships. Fourth, it examines two specific instructional models, ethnic studies and bilingual education, and two instructional strategies, human rights and intergroup relations. The text ends with a synthesis and a forecast on pluralistic teaching.

The text is divided into three parts. Part I describes basic socio-cultural concepts necessary for an analytical approach to pluralistic teaching and learning. Part I attempts to clarify objectively the notions of culture, ethnicity, community, assimilation, racism, and discrimination—all potent, volatile realities not usually discussed in teacher education programs and often difficult to assess analytically. Yet, as educators interested in providing equal educational opportunities for all students, we are professionally bound to deal with these notions in a more than superficial manner.

Part II describes two instructional models, ethnic studies and bilingual education, and two instructional strategies, human rights and intergroup relations, that can be employed to provide equal educational opportunities. The models and strategies are described historically, conceptually, and practically; that is, after discussion of where they come from and how they work, concrete suggestions about how they can be used in the classroom are provided. They are pertinent to all democratic U.S. public school classrooms, irrespective of ethnic or cultural complexion. The models and strategies are not intended solely as recipes for teaching ethnic minority students. Instead, these models and strategies provide teachers with means to teach about U.S. pluralism while concurrently teaching in a pluralistic classroom if the situation exists.

Part III provides various role-playing and critical-thinking exercises. These can be used in teacher education programs to stimulate thought and insight into issues that arise in pluralistic teaching.

One of the text's goals is to help teachers approach pluralistic teaching analytically and rationally. Rather than acting on moralistic impulses about what seems to be right, I feel that teachers should act on well-conceived, rational decisions about what is right for students. The text can be used for these purposes: (1) pre-service multicultural education; (2) in-service multicultural education; (3) pre- or in-service education that attempts to comply with the NCATE multicultural education standards; (4) human relations, equal opportunity, or desegregation workshops and institutes.

The text is introductory, and it encourages a thoughtful approach to pluralistic teaching and learning. It should help teachers make reasoned judgments about the many difficult issues that arise, but provides no pat answers for specific situations. No recipes for teaching ethnic minority students are given. Teaching these students, like teaching any kind of student, is a changing, ongoing process for which recipes are inappropriate. I have avoided statements like "Black students are. . . ." or "Japanese American students tend. . . ." because such assertions serve to perpetuate rather than diminish cultural stereotypes. What makes good teaching difficult is that there are few consistent, pat answers.

Good teachers should develop sophistication in cross-cultural teaching. If they teach in white, suburban schools, I believe they should teach their students about the diversity of American society, even though their schools may appear monolithic. If they teach in the ghetto, the barrio, or on a Native American reservation, I believe they should build upon the cultural differences of their students rather than treat differences as deficiencies to be ignored or purged. I also expect teachers to consider the ethnicity of all types of students, including those from white Catholic, Protestant, Jewish, Islamic, Hindu, Buddhist, and other religious-cultural backgrounds; they all have histories and cultures worth knowing.

Certainly, sensitivity about a student's ethnicity is central to good teaching. And certainly, some sensitivity about and concern for students from American ethnic minority groups is long overdue. Ultimately, this text calls for a cultural sophistication not yet reached in the education profession, especially among teachers, guidance counselors, curriculum specialists, and administrators. These prefatory remarks, I hope, express "where I'm coming from" as a teacher. I hope they help you as a teacher understand where you are going.

ACKNOWLEDGMENTS

I am indebted to colleagues who assisted and encouraged me as I wrote this text. I want to thank especially those patient colleagues who read and critiqued the original draft. Some of them remain anonymous, as they did not identify themselves with their critiques; in particular, I wish to thank the colleague who informed me of the works of Merton and van den Berghe, and who otherwise so thoroughly reviewed my work. James Banks, James Boyer, Carlos Córtes, and Johanna Lemlech made excellent suggestions for improvement and changes in the manuscript. Thanks to Luther Wilson, University of Oklahoma Press editor, and George Henderson, professor of human relations, whose support was extremely helpful. And thanks to Jodie Anderson, who patiently typed and prepared the text. I am especially grateful to my wife, Sharon, for her concern and counsel as I prepared the manuscript.

Ricardo L. Garcia

Part I
CONCEPTS

Part I describes sociocultural concepts basic to effective pluralistic teaching, such as assimilation, acculturation, culture, equal-status contact, community, cultural relativism, desegregation, discrimination, ethnic groups, ethnocentrism, ethnicity, nationality, prejudice, racism, socialization, self-fulfilling prophecy, and cultural stereotyping as basic teaching and learning concepts. Also discussed are the relationships between the school, the community, and informal communal living theories. These relationships are described as dynamic human forces which influence teaching and learning because the forces are manifestations of the text's basic concepts.

Chapter 1
The Ethnic Factor

Imagine that you are a good literature teacher. Your ninth-grade class has just finished reading a series of short stories on liberation themes. As the group leader, you have led the class through the labyrinth of personal, human struggles for liberation from hunger, poverty, racism, sexism, and political and religious suppression. As a final project the class members want to organize into small groups and, using magazine and newspaper clippings and pictures, construct a collage that summarizes the human struggle for liberation. "Why not?" you think. "That's a creative way to have the students show they understand the themes." Okay, you'll permit it. The next day, students bring their material. You provide scissors and glue, help organize the groups, and set a deadline. Halfway through the project, one male student hollers, "Aw, hell! This stinks! Cutting paper dolls is girl's stuff! I won't do it!" He takes the collage from his group, tears it up, and throws it on the floor.

So what's the problem? Forty years ago you could beat the youngster for his deviant behavior. Ten years ago you could paddle him, and now you could beat or paddle the youngster. Now, of course, you'll have to face a law suit. But if you really are a good teacher, you will approach the whole situation differently. You will treat each classroom experience, planned or unplanned, as a learning experience for students and a teaching experience for you.

In this case, what is being taught and learned by the young man's protest? Have you somehow created a climate in your classroom that discourages or encourages dissent? Is this good? Bad? Is the student's self-concept threatened? Has he learned from his cultural background that there are distinct role behaviors for men and women? Is cutting pictures for a project synonymous with cutting paper dolls to him? Or did you, in your zeal to teach about the liberation of the poor, the religious, and women, unintentionally teach that the oppressor in American society is the white male? Did the youngster, an American white male, find no positive white males in the liberation literature and thereby infer that his kind was responsible for all of the oppression in American society? Did you mean to teach the inference? If so, is the inference that white males are responsible for all religious, social, and racial oppression valid, given a rigorous study of American social history? If the inference is valid, how does it relate to the angry young man in your class? What rights does he have? Does he have the right to dissent? The right to sex-role stereotype? Do you have a responsibility to change the student's attitudes or values, especially if the student has a cultural or ethnic reason why the project threatens his self-concept? What about the rights of other students? Do they have to listen to foul language? Do they have property rights in the torn collage?

And then, you ask, just what are you teaching? Literature? Liberation? Democratic living? The answer is that you are teaching all three, because you are a good teacher who knows that you have a responsibility to transmit more than data about literature—to provide your students basic literary skills and to socialize them to live and work in a democratic, pluralistic society. So, as a good teacher, what do you do about the angry young man whose self-concept is threatened by your assignment, and who, in turn, violates some of the rights of his peers? You can ignore the problem, hoping that in some vague way someone will teach your students their rights and responsibilities within the human community. Or, you can seriously weigh and consider the role that ethnicity, race, and culture play within the daily dynamics of teaching and learning, and then act accordingly. Do teachers really make a difference in the lives of students? No doubt some great leaders and technicians once had teachers who influenced them. Yet, most of the prisoners in American jails, including corrupt political leaders, had a few teachers in their lives. Did teachers perversely influence the latter just as they positively influenced great leaders and good citizens?

The question defies an answer. I believe that teachers can make a difference, and while they do not deliberately lead students to lives of crime or political corruption, they may forget to take the active role in the socialization of students that could circumvent criminal tendencies.

Teaching is a challenging profession, a difficult task, and a poorly rewarded one. What you must keep in mind is that teaching in the public schools is an exceedingly complicated task that is worth doing. Everything about teaching is always changing. Each group of students is new. Faculties, social conditions, and curriculum goals change. Parents, school boards, administrators, professional education organizations, teacher educators, and civic groups inundate the teacher with their views on the nature of students, learning, teaching, and the good life. Usually, the views conflict. Teaching complexities are not new, but they are real. There is nothing simple about teaching. Even on a daily basis, students and teachers are influenced by factors such as the day of the week, the time of day, the weather, and the seasons. There are constant, general factors central to the teaching-learning situation. The quality of classroom management and instructional strategies and the student's and the teacher's self-concepts are important in good teaching practices. For teaching in a pluralistic society such as the United States, consideration of *cultural* and *ethnic* differences is fundamental to good teaching (see Figure 1.1).

The ethnic factor is not just another teaching-learning complication. Cultural and ethnic differences have always existed in classrooms. At one time, the function of a good teacher was to melt away ethnic

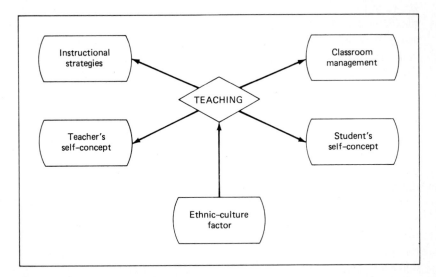

Figure 1.1   The Ethnic-Culture Factor

differences. To Americanize and homogenize students of immigrant families, teachers discouraged any indications of ethnic heritage and ancestral ties. English-only laws were enacted, prohibiting the use of any language other than English in the public classroom. Students could be and were punished for speaking a non-English language. Teachers could lose their certification, go to jail, and be fined. Later, it was fashionable to ignore ethnic differences, to claim that, "I treat all my students *as though* they were alike." Ignoring ethnic differences by pretending they didn't exist served to submerge rather than purge ethnic differences in the classroom, and ignored the students' fundamental humanity.

All classroom activities and factors—classroom management techniques, instructional strategies, and, of course, self-concepts—operate on assumptions which are embedded in cultural values, attitudes, and beliefs. There is no such thing as a culturally neutral or culturally free teaching activity. The search for culturally free techniques, curriculum materials, or tests is in vain. Teaching activities spring from unconscious assumptions one makes: they are based on one's cultural and ethnic perspectives. Likewise, students' learning and behaving are influenced by their cultural and ethnic perspectives. What students learn and what teachers teach are ultimately filtered and strained through their cultural sieves. Understanding the ethnic-culture factor creates the consciousness necessary to perceive that transmitting culture and socializing students are inherent in classroom teaching and learning.

It's true that "when you're waist-deep in a swamp filled with alligators, it's easy to forget your initial goal was to drain the swamp." It's easy to forget, once you begin analyzing and evaluating the complexities of teaching and learning in a pluralistic society, who or why anyone would teach. Keep in mind that we live in a global society. Nations, cultures, and peoples throughout the world are interdependent even though at times certain cultures and nations consider themselves aloof from the global society. The fact is that we inhabit one planet, breathe the same air, and depend on the same sun. We are challenged with a new image, the image of global citizens within a pluralistic world. Remember that all cultures, nations, and peoples have in common the enemies of ignorance, disease, famine, and poverty. Even in our affluent society, there are undernourished, hungry, sick, and illiterate people. If you as a teacher determine to liberate your students —even only one student—from one of these common enemies, you will achieve the respect given only to excellent teachers. I am not referring to some pie-in-the-sky liberalism or some missionary zeal. Rather, I mean that a good teacher must be committed to making a difference in the lives of students.

Students, for the most part, are captive audiences with little real say in who will teach them or what they will be taught. Essentially, students in the classroom are sentenced (compulsory education) to attend and their teachers are mandated (equal educational opportunity) to teach any and all students. This being the case, teachers must accept the reality of their students and the sociocultural milieus from which the students emerge. One teacher who did this was Sylvia Ashton-Warner, who made a difference in the lives of her students by committing herself to eliciting excellence. In her book, *Teacher*,[1] she tells of her experiences teaching English among New Zealand Maori infants. Rather than pouring the English language into her students, Ashton-Warner activated students to generate language and content from their individual cultural perspectives. To make a difference in the lives of students, you as a teacher must liberate yourself from provincial and narrow conceptions about people, teaching, learning, and yourself and try to elicit excellence within the context of the students' own cultural perspectives.

DEFINITION OF BASIC TERMS

To insure communication, I will provide a definition of the key terms that will be referred to throughout the text, as follows:

Ethnicity: the values, perceptions, feelings, assumptions, and physical characteristics associated with ethnic group affiliation or membership. It influences one's sense of space and time and refers to a sense of belonging to an ethnic group.

Culture: a system of beliefs, values, customs, and institutions that when combined serves as a cluster to provide a person meaningful ways for survival.

Cultural group: some human group that provides a person a *way of life* or *living*. The group may be occupational (e.g., college professor or truck driver), or it may be an ethnic group such as Jewish American. Thus, a person may identify first with a cultural group (e.g., "I'm a coal miner" or "I'm a Protestant minister"), and second with an ethnic group ("I'm a Greek Orthodox minister").

Pluralism/pluralistic: the condition of human diversity. In this context, *pluralism* refers to the ethnic diversity of U.S. society and includes white ethnic and racial minority groups. While allusions will be made to other groups, for example, poverty groups, the focus herein will be on ethnic groups, or what Gordon calls "ethclass" groups,[2] that is, a confirmation of ethnic-group affiliation and social-class membership.

American society: the total composite of all human groups living in the United States, including the groups living in U.S. territories, former territories (Hawaiian Islands), and commonwealth (Puerto Rico). The term *American* to denote U.S. society is admittedly ethnocentric, as it originally denoted all of both American continents and included all the inhabitants of what is now called North, Central, and South America. It is a revealing fact that U.S. society has expropriated the term as though the entire hemisphere were its exclusive domain. For example, the "American World Series" of baseball includes only teams from the United States, and until only a few decades ago, only United States whites were allowed on the world series teams.

Multiethnic instruction: teaching activities, strategies, and techniques based on the goal of preparing students to live harmoniously in an ethnically diverse society with focus on the United States. The goal is accomplished by instruction that (1) reflects in school curricula, classroom practices, and environments the ethnic diversity of American society, fostering what Banks calls "ethnic literacy"[3]; (2) deals directly with American ethnic-group similarities and differences; (3) provides students with experiences and opportunities to understand their ethnic heritage and the ethnic-cultural heritage of others; (4) counters racism and ethnic bias in school curricula, classroom environments, climates, and practices; and (5) fosters respect for all ethnic groups and peoples with an abiding respect for the uniqueness of all human beings.

Multiethnic instruction differs from international instruction and multicultural instruction.

International instruction directly counters U.S. societal provincialism by teaching about non-U.S. cultures and nations. When non-U.S. cultures are compared and contrasted to U.S. culture(s), *comparative instruction* occurs. When non-U.S. cultures and U.S. culture(s) are compared in a search for universal, transcending values and institutions (e.g., every known culture has a taboo against incest), *intercultural* or *transcultural* instruction occurs. When all cultures are viewed as interdependent, *global education* occurs.

Multicultural instruction directly counters elitism, sexism, and racism in American public school teaching and learning. Multicultural instruction is the generic term for a broad-based educational encounter with unjust, exclusive, and exclusionary educational policies, programs, and practices. *Multiethnic instruction* is a subcomponent of multicultural instruction.

The term *pluralistic teaching and learning* will be used as synonymous with multiethnic instruction. Because multiethnic education, like multicultural education, is a term currently in vogue, I wish to emphasize that teaching in a pluralistic society such as the United States is a serious professional activity that should not go out of fashion even though certain terms such as multiethnic education may. Whatever the popular or fashionable educational trends of the next decades, public school teachers will be faced with teaching ethnically and culturally diverse students.

Generic concepts such as *ethnic studies, bilingual instruction, intergroup relations instruction, human rights*, are defined in the text. I tend to refer more often to Mexican American culture and the cultures and experiences of certain other ethnic minority groups because of my familiarity with these groups. My intent is to provide a reality base for my perceptions and opinions, not to imply that ethnicity is the exclusive domain of these particular ethnic minorities. I hope not to offend any group by omission or lack of reference to it. Rather, I would like references to particular groups to serve a heuristic purpose, providing some parameters within which multiethnic instruction can succeed.

CULTURAL RELATIVISM AND TEACHING

To teach in a pluralistic society, in my view, one must take the position that all cultures and ethnic groups should be examined relatively, that is, looked at from the vantage point of the group under consideration. Rather than viewing the value of a certain culture or ethnic group from the perspective of one's own culture, a teacher in a pluralistic society should develop the ability to see how other cultural and ethnic groups perceive their social reality. Not an easy task! Most of us have been taught to think that our cultural or ethnic-group ways are better than others—ethnocentrism—and the idea that other groups may differ does not always seem to convince us that our way may be good only for our group. Nevertheless, we are faced with cultural and ethnic-group differences and cultural relativism in a pluralistic society.

Difficult ethical problems exist with cultural relativism. Some might argue that violence is a basic value in their culture, and thus they have a right to inflict violence on others. (In fact, few known cultures condone violence for the sake of violence. Because violence begets violence, it is, in the final analysis, self-destructive and contrary to group survival.) Violence *qua* violence in the classroom would not only disrupt learning activities but would violate the students' right to personal safety. Further, some teachers might argue that their culture supports racist attitudes toward racial minority students, and because of cultural relativism, racist teachers have a right to promote their brand of racism. This problem is compounded by the fact that we live in a democratic society, which allows academic and individual freedom of opinion. In this context, cultural relativism would encourage racist teachers to make a negative difference in the lives of students.

Subsumed in the preceding arguments is the attitude that ethical anarchy or ethical neutrality prevails in a cultural relativist classroom. Clearly, the attitude is unacceptable. Teachers are legally and morally bound to manage a classroom that protects the fundamental right of all students to equal educational opportunity. As such, teachers are mandated to assert equitable leadership in the classroom. Ethical anarchy and neutrality can be destructive of human survival. In other words, there are times when teachers have to judge and prohibit certain behavior as inimical to the rights of students. This is predicated on the faith that teachers can assume ethical leadership in the classroom. (Chapter 9, which deals with human rights and classroom management, analyzes the issue in detail.) My hope is that teachers will use cultural relativism to enhance the teaching-learning process and to better understand the many cultural and ethnic differences that exist within the United States.

There is a parallel between what I am proposing and what the astronomer Copernicus proposed many centuries ago. Until the time of Copernicus, European scholars accepted the Ptolemaic view of the physical universe which placed the earth at the center. This was a simple, cozy, and stable viewpoint. Elaborate but easily comprehensible theological systems of beliefs were based on the view. Still, it limited human knowledge of the earth itself and of an even greater universe filled with immense constellations and galaxies. Copernicus proposed that the earth was not the center of the universe and that, in fact, the earth revolved around the sun. Although religious leaders proclaimed Copernicus's view as heretical because it challenged established religious beliefs about the order of nature and God, time and history have verified the truth of the Copernican view.

In the cultural universe of teaching and learning in U.S. public schools there still persists a Ptolemaic view. In the Ptolemaic view of the teaching and learning universe, the values, attitudes, and beliefs of white, middle-class Americans have prevailed, seeming to reflect the nature of all students and presuming to provide standards of that culture as the final criteria of right and wrong. In this synoptic view, white, middle-class culture sits at the hub of the teaching-learning universe; other cultures are far removed or nonexistent. The presumption is that only one model citizen exists,[4] and variations from this white, middle-class model are perceived as deviancies requiring remediation. This is not meant to demean white, middle-class culture, but rather to place it in perspective within the myriad of other American cultures. The Ptolemaic, geocentric view of teaching and learning is simple, stable, and cozy; it is also dysfunctional. It limits our view of the cultural universe available for our classrooms. Thus, we fail to benefit from the ethnic and cultural diversity of American society.

Time and history will verify the validity of a Copernican view of teaching and learning. Once freed from the Ptolemaic view, we can see the teaching universe from a Copernican perspective. The astronomer Copernicus transcended the myopic vision of the Ptolemaic view and opened our vision to a universe of innumerable galaxies and infinite space. The Copernican view broadened our horizons and revealed an endless array of planets, stars, and possibly other worlds. A Copernican view of teaching—the view that the universe of teaching and learning consists of vast galaxies of cultures and human groups— abandons the fiction that the hub and center of the teaching universe is the white, middle-class American culture. The Copernican view calls for a radically different perspective based on the ethnic diversity of American society. It calls for viewing all cultures as coexistent and equally valid, abandoning paradigms that speak of cultures as "underdeveloped," "overdeveloped," and "primitive." It discards educational labels that describe nonwhite, non-middle-class students as "culturally deprived," "disadvantaged," or "culturally deficient." Bilingualism becomes an asset rather than a liability and Black English becomes another dialect of American English rather than substandard English. Embracing a Copernican reorientation to the universe of teaching and learning can serve to liberate teachers and assist them in transcending the narrow confines of their cultures.

Once committed to a Copernican view of the cultural universe of teaching and learning, consider the idea that there exist in the teaching-learning universe many progressive cultures, each rich, complex, and worthy of knowing. A caveat is necessary here. The words "progress" and "progressive" connote positive developments in white, middle-class culture. They imply growth and development, but they also create confusion because what is viewed as progress or progressive in one culture may be perceived as decadence in another. Rather than getting caught in the semantics of what is progressive cultural development, it would be better to free cultures from the notion of industrial progress, keeping in mind that all cultures, if they are to grow and develop continuously, must adapt and change according to present exigencies while yet conserving aspects of their past. All cultures, if they are to remain viable, must constantly strive toward self-improvement by balancing forces of change and conservation. Within any cultural group, there will be people of change and conservation. Within any cultural group, there will be people who advocate change as a means to improve and adapt the culture to meet current and future situations. Within the same cultural group there will be people who oppose or resist change, arguing that conservation of present and past practices or customs will serve to meet current and future situations. Too much conservation of the past can lead to decadence and ultimately to cultural decay. Yet too much change can lead to instability and ultimately to cultural chaos. "Progressive" cultural development requires an equilibrium between the forces of change and conservation. Any cultural group that maintains an equilibrium between these forces, changing by degrees and conserving by degrees, will constantly improve within its own context as a cultural group.

Cultural development should not be viewed in an industrial format, with cultures evolving from the primitive, to the medieval, and then to the "modern" stages of industrial development. The industrial progression theory—the notion that cultures progress in a linear thrust and can be compared according to their degree of progress toward industrialization—pervades European and American thinking.[5] This progress theory posits that cultures progress from so-called primitive food gathering or hunting stages to more advanced agricultural and economic stages. Industrialized cultures, such as the United States, are somehow the most advanced and modern. But what practices are more advanced? Examine the customs dealing with the elderly in Eskimo and middle-class American cultures. In the Eskimo culture—a "primitive" hunting culture according to the progress theory—when elders are too old to help with fishing, hunting, or housekeeping, they are given a position of social eminence within the family and are then sought for advice and guidance. Eventually, when they no longer feel of use to the younger family members, they leave the household to freeze to death on the Alaskan ice plains. In white, middle-class culture—a "modern" industrial culture according to the progress theory —elders are often placed in an "old folks' home" when they are no longer useful to the family. Many times, they do not choose to go to the homes but are compelled to confinement because they are perceived as a burden to the family. In the rest home, the elders are further demeaned by inane, time-killing activities. Their knowledge and experience are for naught. Like broken-down machines, the elders are discarded to finish their lives among other discards. They cannot choose when, where, or with whom to die, and so must die slowly among other dying strangers. Which culture is more advanced? More modern? Which preserves human dignity and conserves the wisdom that comes with age and experience? According to the progress theory, the "modern" industrialized culture is more complicated and therefore "progressive"; the "primitive" hunting culture is ostensibly less complicated and therefore "less progressive" than the industrialized culture. Which culture is more advanced in its treatment of the elderly? The answer is apparent.

As a person who may have been influenced by the progress theory, can you view cultures as different without making judgments about the differences? Can you reconcile the differences of other cultures with your cultural orientations and be comfortable? Obviously, you need to understand yourself as a member of some cultural or ethnic group. As you read this book, ask the questions: From my cultural perspective, how do I feel about the particular values and issues that are raised? Why do I feel this way? From his perspective (the author's), how does he feel about these values and issues? Why does he feel that way? To start the task of understanding you and your cultural group, try to develop an in-group/out-group perspective about yourself. In other words, how do you appear to someone outside your cultural group? How do you think you appear as an insider in your group? For example, how might the much maligned "Dick and Jane" reading stories appear to an Eskimo child? As an outsider to middle-class, white America, the Eskimo child might wonder about that cute but useless dog named Spot. In the story, Spot runs and barks a lot. Spot doesn't do any work. In the child's Eskimo culture, the dog is an important and extremely useful member of the group who works a lot. Also, the father is curiously dressed in a white shirt and tie. Perhaps the white shirt is worn to reflect the intense sunlight? Why is the shirt tied around the neck? Wouldn't that make the father warmer? Maybe the climate is cold? Why then the white shirt? A darker shirt would absorb whatever rays. . . . As an insider to the middle-class, white American group, why do Dick and Jane have a dog only for a pet? Why does the father wear a white shirt and tie?

To better understand cultural relativism, contrast the nonrelativistic Ptolemaic view and the relativistic Copernican view of the teaching-learning universe. The Ptolemaic view takes the posture of cultural monism and the Copernican view takes the posture of cultural relativism toward teaching and learning. Table 1.1 describes the two types of postures by contrasting students' responses to some patterns of monistic teaching with responses to analogous patterns of relativistic teaching. Considering that monism represents a philosophic belief that all reality is a unified whole (i.e., there is a single correct answer to any question) and that relativism represents a philosophic belief that all of reality is a diversified whole (i.e., there are differing correct answers to any question), effective teaching and learning in a pluralistic society require individuals who can assume a posture of cultural relativism.

Table 1.1 MONISTIC AND RELATIVISTIC PATTERNS COMPARED

CULTURAL MONISTIC UNIVERSE OF TEACHING AND LEARNING	CULTURAL RELATIVISTIC UNIVERSE OF TEACHING AND LEARNING
TEACHER AS BANKTELLER Add knowledge to student's data bank; charges interest or otherwise punishes for data deficits.	TEACHER AS LEADER Provides sets of circumstances that lead students to explore the full parameters of their curiosity, imagination, and creativity.
STUDENT RESPONSE Ingests knowledge from teller's treasury and pearls of wisdom; loses interest in self-discovered knowledge.	STUDENT RESPONSE Explores and discovers knowledge; gains insight into self and others through exploration and discovery.
TEACHER AS ALL-KNOWING TELLER Owns all important ideas and knowledge; anything teacher does not know is unimportant.	TEACHER AS FACILITATOR Reduces obstacles and identifies resources that enhance knowledge acquisition.
STUDENT RESPONSE Depends on owner of knowledge to give knowledge and wisdom.	STUDENT RESPONSE Independent of teacher's knowledge yet able to use teacher's knowledge as springboard to discovery and acquisition of knowledge.
TEACHER AS MONISTIC TELLER Views own accounting (cultural values) system as superior, as it is presumed to be the central system within the teaching-learning universe.	TEACHER AS RESPECTER OF DIFFERENCES Views own cultural value system in context of a pluralistic society; respects the student's right to differing cultural value system.
STUDENT RESPONSE Accepts teller's views and accommodates them by ignoring or rejecting own cultural view; or rejects the teller's view and suffers the consequences, e.g., loses interest or suffers knowledge deficit.	STUDENT RESPONSE Explores and learns about own ethnicity as well as the ethnicity of others.

CULTURAL RELATIVISM AND TEACHING MYTHS

There are some myths, if not outright misconceptions, about teaching and teachers that need to be dispelled. *Roll over Copernicus and tell Ptolemy the news.* Teachers need not be charismatic. Among the folklore about teachers is the myth that good teachers have charisma, all too often perceived as personal attraction and magnitude. I think a charismatic person will not necessarily make a good teacher. So-called charismatic teachers are led to believe that students respond to those who they sense are committed to liberation of the mind. Now if charisma involves having an insatiable curiosity—that is, an inquiring mind, and a burning desire to share the inquiry—and if charisma involves the desire and ability to help others develop an inquiring mind, then it is essential to teaching that liberates. But if charisma merely means being a "nice guy," then charismatic teachers are expendable.

One can have an inquiring mind about many things. The football coach and the elementary math teacher who are self-compelled searchers for new patterns and combinations and who can share this quality with students so they too can develop such compulsions are on the path to releasing students' curiosities. Releasing students' minds to probe the unconventional and to explore the dimensions of their curiosities is vastly different from holding over students a charismatic power which allows one to deposit data in their minds. Freire calls this the "banking method"[6] of teaching. In regular installments, a teacher places knowledge in the students' data banks. From time to time, students record the installments by taking a test or in some manner demonstrating that they have memorized the data in their banks. Teachers own all the data and make deposits as the occasion permits. Students are used as depositories who are expected to store the data but are not expected to use it in any way. Holding this type of charismatic power over students creates a dependence upon you, the teacher; rather than freeing students from impoverished minds or bodies, the teacher makes them subjects.

Ultimately, you cannot liberate students, per se. Liberation is an act of self-assertion, a leap of faith that students will take when you have created the correct set of conditions and circumstances for them. Consider the mother and father robins who care for and feed their fledglings, creating the correct set of circumstances for them. One day as the fledglings approach the brink of the nest, the mother and father robins encourage the fledglings to take a leap, spread their wings, and fly. And they do.

Roll over Copernicus and tell Ptolemy the news. A teacher need not know everything about ethnicity in a pluralistic society. Actually, a teacher can't possibly know everything about ethnic groups. Further, to admit ignorance about ethnicity is the first step toward understanding, and the willingness to make such an admission is assurance that you *can* eventually understand ethnicity and pluralism.

Rather than seeing teachers as transmitters of knowledge (the banking method) about ethnicity and pluralism, consider them leaders or facilitators who assist students in their pursuit of understanding ethnicity and pluralism. As a teacher-leader, one initiates action, maintains the teaching-learning process, sets individual and group guidelines, assures equalitarian individual and group relations, and evaluates the students' experiences and products. As the teacher-leader, you confront the problem of leading your students to a goal that you desire and value. I am not referring to subtle, covert manipulative maneuvers which program students to pursue your interests. Rather, I am referring to an open, unhidden agenda of values that you clearly explain to students. If you value pluralism and are committed to the goal of preparing students to live in a pluralistic society, it is critical that you explain this to your students and then commence to lead them toward the goal, learning with them about the diversity of U.S. society.

Before you can create correct sets of conditions and circumstances —before you can bring students to the brink of knowledge or encourage them to make a guess, take a position, follow up on a hunch, expand their knowledge, and explore the vast panorama of speculation and creation—you must liberate your mind from a provincial, Ptolemaic view of teaching and learning.

A PARADIGM FOR TEACHING IN A PLURALISTIC SOCIETY

Teachers can make a difference in the lives of students. To make a difference in a pluralistic society, a teacher should understand how the ethnic factor impinges upon teaching and learning. Teachers should keep their focus first on transcending problems that are common in important ways to all cultures, nations, and students—ignorance, poverty, disease, hunger—and second on the cultural differences manifest in their students' learning styles and ways of behaving. A posture of cultural relativism, which views ethnic and cultural groups from their own vantage point, can assist the teacher with the awesome task of dealing with and teaching in a pluralistic society.

Cultural relativism takes the attitude that cultures are different but not necessarily inferior or superior. In fact, cultures differ because groups of people develop them to accommodate unique physical, demographic, political, and economic situations. Cultural relativism requires that we perceive cultures and the people who hold them from their own unique perspectives rather than solely from the perspective of the white, middle-class American. Some may argue that cultural relativism is amoral or that "anything goes." For example, do the cultures of groups who advocate violence for the sake of violence have to be respected? Or, do extreme racial theories such as bigotry and biological racism have to be accepted under cultural relativism? These questions defy answers. The purpose of cultural relativism is to foster positive attitudes about cultures and groups in the United States that have been historically and economically oppressed. Cultural relativism provides a climate of acceptance for the cultures of ethnic minorities and the poor; it allows public schools a way to incorporate these cultures in the schools. Therefore, cultural relativism should not be perceived as a philosophy of nihilism where "anything goes" but rather as a way of building acceptance of the cultures of ethnic minorities. Cultural relativism is not amoral. It does not endorse political or religious philosophies that suppress the dignity of human life. Philosophies, policies, or practices that suppress the dignity of human life are alien to cultural relativism.

A paradigm serves the purpose of giving conceptual clarity to the thrust and parameters of an idea. I end this chapter with a paradigm placing the basic ideas discussed into a teaching and learning perspective:

1. *Who should be taught to live in a pluralistic society?* All students irrespective of ethnic, cultural, religious, or socioeconomic background should be prepared to live in a pluralistic society.

2. *Who should teach in a pluralistic society?* Anyone who is committed to cultural relativism and pluralism, and who is otherwise intellectually competent, should teach. Ethnic minority teachers should be encouraged to teach where they are most comfortable, sharing their cultural understanding with their students. Nonminority teachers should be encouraged to do likewise; they should also be encouraged to study their own ethnic heritage as well as the heritage of others so as to develop an appreciation of the pluralism of American society.

3. *What should be taught in a pluralistic society?* The ethnic and cultural pluralism of American society should be taught. Students should be taught their own ethnic heritage as well as the heritages of others. Also, students should be taught to respect cultural and ethnic differences, especially as these differences exist in U.S. society.

4. *How should ethnic and cultural pluralism be taught?* Ethnic and cultural pluralism should be taught as the basic model of American society. Thus, multiethnic experiences should permeate the entire school curriculum.

Notes

1. Sylvia Ashton-Warner. *Teacher.* New York: Simon & Schuster, 1963; see also, Herbert Kohl. *Thirty-six Children.* New York: New American Library, 1967.
2. Milton Gordon. *Assimilation in American Life.* New York: Oxford University Press, 1964, pp. 51–54.

3. James Banks. *Teaching Strategies for Ethnic Studies*. Boston: Allyn & Bacon, 1975, pp. 18–22.
4. Robert Howsam, et. al. *Educating a Profession*. Washington, D.C.: American Association of Colleges for Teacher Education, 1976, pp. 23–24.
5. Melvin Rader. *Ethics and the Human Community*. New York: Holt, Rinehart and Winston, 1964, p. 231.
6. Paulo Freire. *Pedagogy of the Oppressed*. New York: Seabury Press, 1978, pp. 53–56.

Chapter 2
Sociocultural Factors
for Pluralistic Teaching

"Cultural relativism," you might say, "is such an ethereal view of the teaching-learning universe. How can I understand this view when I really don't know even more basic concepts, such as what a culture is?" This chapter will describe the fundamental sociocultural factors which impinge upon teaching and learning in a pluralistic society. My concern is that beginning teachers and, all too often, experienced teachers are unaware of the sociocultural forces which affect the classroom experience. In the many human relations and cultural awareness workshops and courses I have taught, I found that while teachers and student teachers are eager to make differences in the lives of their students, they are not prepared to analyze in any meaningful and thorough manner the impact of a pluralistic society on teaching and learning. Also, they are eager to jump across the sociocultural factors and dive into methods for teaching ethnic minority students. My feeling is that teachers cannot use such methods effectively without a firm grasp of the impact of sociocultural factors on teaching and learning. And, having gained an understanding of the impact of sociocultural factors, teachers need a rational conceptual approach to countering those which are pernicious. Part II of this text provides such conceptual models and strategies.

I have emphasized that teaching and learning in a pluralistic society require a posture of cultural relativism, which in turn requires understanding one's own culture and that of others. We are now ready to examine the fundamental sociocultural factors that affect the classroom. I am calling these factors "concepts." They are descriptive of social, group, and human phenomena, such as "culture" or "community." The concepts consist of generalizations about some social phenomena; subsumed in the generalizations are "elements" or "components" which can be verified empirically.[1] For example, one element of the concept of "culture" is a value and belief system. That a group of people who have a certain culture hold certain beliefs or values can be verified in a variety of ways, such as by examining the group's religious literature. Yet, when persons analyze their values and beliefs in order to understand their cultures, they experience difficulty as they attempt to empiricize their values and beliefs. Social concepts make distinctions and delineations among different people and groups, but people and groups, in the meantime, are organic—changing, diffusing, and emerging.

Social concepts are empirical frames of reference that enable us to analyze and group phenomena; they are not "eternal verities" or "truths." Rather, they are attempts to make sense of humans and groups, who as dynamic phenomena are in constant flux. Consequently, the concepts discussed below are generalized ideas about the interaction of humans and groups. The degree to which the concepts fit any individual's life experience is, in the final analysis, an assessment each individual must make. My concern is that individuals should consider how the concepts fit them rather than how they fit the concepts. Once understood, the concepts can be used to analyze the complex social dynamics of a pluralistic society and the impact these dynamics have upon teaching and learning.

CULTURE AND ETHNIC-GROUP MEMBERSHIP

Every student has a culture. Every student belongs to some ethnic or cultural group. Without a culture or an ethnic group, a student could not exist; such group affiliation is essential to human survival.

Fifteen years ago, it was popular to label students from ethnic minority or low socioeconomic backgrounds "culturally deprived." The cultural deprivation theories were based on the assumption that because ethnic minority and poor students did not exhibit in school the cultural characteristics of middle-class white youngsters, they were deprived of a valid culture. Without a valid culture, the theories reasoned, it was difficult for these students to compete and succeed in school. Subsumed in the cultural deprivation theories was the notion that "culturally deprived" students were also linguistically deprived because they did not speak school English. Speakers of nonschool English were described as alingual, that is, without a legitimate language, and their dialects were perceived as adulterations of school English. Using the jargon of behavioral modification, elaborate methods were developed to extinguish these so-called dialects; once cleansed of their deviant dialects, students were programmed with school English.

The cultural deprivation theories spawned a myriad of compensatory education programs. These programs attempted in various ways to provide the ethnic minority and poor students the background, experiences, and replacement dialects necessary for succeeding in middle-class school English. Compensatory programs attempted to transform ethnic minority and poor students into middle-class, white, school-English-speaking students.[2] Some compensatory programs failed to improve educational achievement substantially. They were not successful because they were based on the faulty assumption that ethnic minority and poor students have invalid languages and cultures. The programs ignored the reality of ethnicity; they ignored the fact that ethnic minority and poor students have cultures, languages, and ethnic group heritages that cannot easily be replaced by those of another culture.[3]

We now realize that all students, regardless of race, color, creed, and ethnic group affiliation, come to school as culturally whole persons with a culture and a language and concomitant values, attitudes, beliefs, and knowledge. What we now need to know is how to understand the student's cultural and ethnic background and experiences so we may utilize them productively in the teaching-learning process. We need to understand that all students have a cultural and/or ethnic group.

One myth about culture that must be dispelled is that it is elitist. This belief views culture as a characteristic that only a few people attain, such as those who listen to opera or read only Shakespearian plays and poetry. While great poetry, plays, and operas are products of cultural activities, the elitist view of culture limits a culture to a small group of people. Another myth is that culture is esoteric. This belief views culture as a phenomenon that existed in the past or, if in the present, exists in the backwoods of dense jungles where exotic music and rites are performed. This view, like the elitist view, limits culture to a few groups of people. Both views ignore the reality that all people must have a culture in order to live and work. Ralph Linton classified these mythic views of culture and leads us to a workable definition. Culture, he wrote, refers to the total way of life of any society, not simply to those parts of this way which the society regards as higher or more desirable. . . . It follows for the social scientist there are no uncultured societies or even individuals.[4]

Anthropologists define culture as the totality of learned attitudes, values, beliefs, traditions, and tools shared by a group of people to give order, continuity, and meaning to their lives.[5] Culture is not merely an abstraction, nor is it a mysterious entity acting outside the realm of human existence. Rather, it is central to human and group existence; it is invented and transmitted by the individual in a group, and by individuals acting as a group. Individuals take action, influencing other individuals, and collectively these individuals internalize a pattern or system for daily activities. Because human action takes place in time, the past undoubtedly influences present action. Thus, each group has a history which percolates into the present, influencing perceptions, opinions, and, ultimately, decisions about how to live in the present. The total history of a group, combined with its present modes of living, coalesces to form its culture.

A group's culture can be defined as a distinctive way of life. This is a holistic definition; it includes the total group's history, current practices, traditions, material products, tools, and attitudes and beliefs. One of the earliest definitions of culture, written by anthropologist E. B. Tylor in 1871, stated:

> Culture . . . is that complex whole which includes knowledge, belief, art, law, morals, customs, and any other capabilities and habits acquired by man as a member of society.[6]

Much later, in 1929, the anthropologist Ruth Benedict wrote that a group's culture consists of "that complex whole which includes all the habits acquired by man as a member of society."[7] These two definitions are actually representative of definitions given by many other anthropologists, all of whom stress culture as the sum total or the totality of a group's past and present experiences. Culture, as conceived by these definitions, focuses on the accumulated products and experiences of a particular group. The problem with these definitions is that they do not specify aspects, components, or elements of culture well enough to make culture understandable in human terms. What follows, then, are more workable descriptions of culture. They include:

Culture as having discrete elements.
Culture as a process that functions at varying levels of explicit and implicit realities.
Culture as a process that is learned and taught.
Culture as a process of shared gratification.

DISCRETE ELEMENTS OF CULTURE

A culture can be construed as an intragroup experience that has discrete components or elements. Of the various definitions which describe culture, that of anthropologist Frank Boas has withstood the test of time and explicit criteria:

> Culture may be defined as the totality of the mental and physical reactions and activities that characterise the behavior of the individuals composing a social group. . . . It also includes the products of these activities and their role in the life of the group.[8]

What is good about Boas's definition is its explanation of three discrete cultural components: (1) behavior of individuals in a group; (2) the individual's reactions or behaviors as influenced by customs; and (3) material or tangible products determined by the customs or habits. While the definition explicitly describes three cultural components, it does not mention the implicit aspects of culture—values, attitudes, beliefs. Under Boas's definition, the individual's mental reactions most nearly approach the implicit level of culture. Nevertheless, the definition establishes a basis from which culture can be understood. On the explicit level of cultural reality, it is the stuff of customs combined with the individual's reactions and products that tangibly reflect a culture.

LEVELS OF CULTURE

A group's culture operates at two levels of reality, explicit and implicit. The explicit level consists of overt, standardized ways of behaving, reacting, and feeling. The implicit level consists of covert, unstated, and largely unconscious values, attitudes, and assumptions. Verbal and nonverbal behavior and language mediate the culture for a group. For example, in one ethnic group direct eye contact between individuals is a presumed signal of trust and respect, and yet in another ethnic group such eye contact is presumed to be a signal of defiance and disrespect. What is important to understand is that one must carefully interpret the explicit actions of a group's culture from the group's perspective, a perspective based on the implicit meaning the group gives certain overt acts. This requires knowledge, sensitivity, and an understanding of the group's values, beliefs, and attitudes—all of which are affected by its history as well as its current status and condition. In short, to really know a group's culture, one must know it at the implicit level of reality.

"But," you ask, "how in the world can I know a group's implicit culture without knowing anything about the people who constitute the ethnic group?" This is a good question, and the answer is that the more one studies a group's culture, from every possible dimension, the better one can understand the culture. The question deserves a much better answer, and it will be treated in depth when the ethnic studies model is discussed later in the book. So before enrolling in too many ethnic studies and cultural awareness courses, a word of caution is necessary: from a strictly existential point of view, no one can truly know someone else's experiences. No one can know what it felt like when I was a teenager who experienced discrimination because of my Mexican American ethnic-group affiliation. Nor can I truly understand what it feels like to be a poor white in an affluent and dominantly white society. What I can understand are the details and generalizations about the poor white group's history and current status (which are based on its explicit cultural components). From these historical and current details and generalizations I can begin to infer something of the group's implicit culture, keeping in mind that I must perceive this culture from the group's vantage point.

Because of the importance of implicit culture, I would like to present another illustration. Consider the ubiquitous western movie which shows the "Injuns" attacking a wagon train of "harmless pioneer families." Why would the Native Americans attack a group of pioneers who were crossing the land in peace? The pioneers, one might comment, were simply trespassing on Native American land. One is tempted to infer, on the basis of the Native Americans' explicit acts, that they were in those days a violent and barbarous group. Yet, before making that inference, consider the explicit action from the perspective of the Native Americans. More than likely, the situation was that the Native Americans had signed with the U.S. government a treaty which defined this particular tribe's territorial boundaries. Further, the treaty prohibited any non-Indian settlement or crossing on the land. Yet, as was the case with many treaties between the U.S. government and Native Americans, pioneering expeditions were not informed of the treaty's settlement and crossing agreements. Some pioneers had already settled in the Indian territory and others crossed without obtaining permission. From the Native American perspective, an attack on the wagon train was necessary to defend the Native Americans' homes. The seemingly violent and barbarous attack on the wagon train was actually nothing more than people defending their own homes. What at first view appears to be a morally reprehensible act, at second view appears to be the expected behavior of a rational group of people who are defending their homeland. In this example, a true understanding of the Native Americans' action necessitates recognition of the implicit beliefs and values of the Native Americans.

A true understanding of any ethnic or cultural group requires an understanding of the group's perceptions. Everyone has perceptions that have been forged, hammered, and molded by one's culture. Consequently, we all perceive life experiences from our own cultural perspectives. Cultural perceptions are the key to understanding how individuals and groups view their social realities.

TEACHING AND LEARNING A CULTURE

Culture is learned. Everyone is born into a culture, but the culture is not inborn, innate, or inherent.[9] Rather, once born into a culture, the individual goes about the task of learning the culture. Family members, especially parents and siblings, go about the task of teaching the culture to the new member. Of course, this is not an overtly conscious effort. Instead, the parents and siblings simply do different things to protect and nurture the new child. The things that they do—for example, cuddle the child, feed the child, sing to the child—are habits and activities once learned and now transmitted to the child. Thus, the process of socialization begins.

Socialization is the process used by parents, siblings, and other significant persons to transmit their culture and prepare the new member for living. Essentially, the new member of a group is taught the group's values, behaviors, and language(s). Socialization activities are not formal tasks taught to the child; they are just things parents and siblings do as a matter of course. What is important to understand is that socialization activities and tasks are not instinctive. Rather, they are tasks that have been taught in some way to the parents and siblings. In like manner, the new member catches many attitudes, values, and beliefs in the process of growing up in a family. The child is constantly catching attitudes and values by the tone of the voices, the vocabulary, and sundry other parts of the surrounding human environment.

Notice in this scenario how two young girls from different groups "catch" different attitudes about ownership of property:

MARY MARTIN'S DOLL

MARY: Mom, have you seen my Barbie doll?
MOM: No, honey. See if your sister Judy has it.
MARY: What? How come? I told her not to use *my* doll. Did you let her use it?
MOM: Oh, Mary, I . . .
MARY: But, it's my doll!
MOM: Well, defend what's yours! Take it up with her!
MARY: Okay. (Mary seeks out Judy.)

Maria Martinez's Doll

MARIA: Mama, have you seen my Barbie doll?

MAMA: No, honey, see if your sister Anita has it.

MARIA: When did she get it? I had it in the room last night.

MAMA: She must have taken it this morning before you were up.

MARIA: I wish she would just tell me she was going to take it.

MAMA: Why don't you play with the Bionic Woman? Use Barbie later?

MARIA: But Carlos has the bionic doll.

MAMA: Well, take turns with Anita and Carlos. Or, play together.

MARIA: Okay. (Maria seeks out Anita and Carlos.)

In both scenarios, the girls felt ownership of their dolls, but Mary Martin was encouraged by her mother to feel that the doll was Mary's exclusive personal possession. Maria Martinez's mother, on the other hand, encouraged Maria to think of the doll as the communal property of hers and her brother and sister. Neither girl was explicitly taught these differing attitudes toward ownership, yet if small incidents such as these were to occur over and over again, each girl would acquire a different patterned attitude toward ownership of property and thereby internalize her attitude as the "natural" way to think of ownership.

Notice in this scenario how two young boys from different groups "catch" different attitudes about crisis management:

Jimmie Echohawk and the Snake

JIMMIE: Daddy!! Daddy!! There's a snake outside! Go kill it!

DADDY: What color is the snake?

JIMMIE: I don't know!

DADDY: Does it have rattles?

JIMMIE: I don't know!

DADDY: Jimmie, you must learn to look carefully at it.

JIMMIE: But daddy?

DADDY: If the snake has no rattles, or if it has no diamonds on its back, it's probably a bull snake.

JIMMIE: But, it's still a snake.

DADDY: No, Jimmie. Bull snakes never bite people. They eat rattlers. But even rattlers aren't bad. They will rattle and run from you unless you step too near them. Now go watch the snake carefully. Then, if it tries to get in the house, tell me.

Jimmie MacNigh and the Snake

JIMMIE: Daddy!! Daddy!! There's a snake outside! And . . .

DADDY: I'll get my shot gun! You watch it!

JIMMIE: But, Dad . . .

DADDY: You get over to the window and watch it! (Scurries to gun rack for gun.) Now, I've got my gun loaded! Where's the snake?

JIMMIE: I tried to tell you, Daddy! Joe brought it over! It's dead!

DADDY: Oh, heck! Why didn't you say so?

JIMMIE: I did, but . . .

DADDY: Okay, okay. Let's forget about it.

In both scenarios the boys were excited about the snake. Jimmie Echohawk's father, who may have been equally excited, emphasized the attitude that snakes have a place in the ecosystem and that they are to be respected in that place. The father insisted that Jimmie learn to first observe the possible "crisis" and then act accordingly. Jimmie MacNigh's father took the "shoot and then ask questions" attitude. He reacted immediately by getting and loading his gun to kill the snake. He emphasized through his behavior that the snake was an enemy, part of the "untamed" wilderness that had to be tamed. Both sons caught different attitudes toward snakes, toward the human relationship to nature as well as the way to solve problems. Yet, neither father realizes that he is teaching and his son is unconsciously catching attitudes that reflect his respective cultural values.

Many of the prejudices about black Americans that children learn in white families are caught rather than explicitly taught.[10] Parents transmit their attitudes, biases, and beliefs through their tones of voice or the unconscious connotations of their vocabulary. References to the color black as a negative or evil influence are replete in American English vernacular. Common conversational expressions, from "he got blackballed," or "he got blacklisted" to more subtle expressions such as "she's in a dark mood," serve to transmit negative attitudes toward blackness and black people.

The culture is taught by family members. As children grow, friends, teachers, rabbis, priests, ministers, and others teach their cultural roles. A child is taught to watch adults acting out, or living within, certain roles, and then by modeling after one or some of those roles, the child begins to learn a role in the cultural group.[11] As one is taught a role in the cultural group, a self-concept develops—a global attitude and idea about who and how important one is. In other words, we are taught that others in the cultural group are like a mirror which reflects to some extent what we look like. This is the "looking glass" notion of cultural group participation developed by social psychologists such as Kurt Lewin and George Mead.[12]

Imagine what happens to the self-concept of a Native American youngster. She is born into a Comanche tribe and taught the folklore and ways of the Comanche people. She notices that her brothers and sisters, parents, and grandparents are dark in skin color, have black hair and eyes. She learns the Comanche language; she learns rhymes and songs in the language. Then she attends an American public school. There she notices that the teacher speaks only English, and that her classmates are of different skin colors, but primarily they are off-white in color. She is taught that these off-white colored people brought civilization and culture to the "untamed" wilderness, and that these same people had to fight against barbarous, savage dark-skinned tribes who did not want to be tamed. She notices that dark-skinned people, especially those whose tribes were rooted in Africa, had to be enslaved so they could be tamed and civilized. When she goes home at night, she again sees dark-skinned people, her people. Yet, it's true—they have language and beliefs like those people who resisted civilization, who were like the "untamed" wilderness. What kind of self-concept will this youngster learn? She is taught two opposite lessons: be a Comanche, but don't be a dark-skinned savage. But her parents and her teachers mean no harm. Her teachers are just teaching American history from the white colonial point of view.[13] Nevertheless, she experiences difficulty because there is no consonance between what the parents are teaching and what the teachers and the school are teaching. If the school's point of view prevails, she will develop a negative self-concept. The research on Native American students (as well as other culturally different students) reports that the experience of schooling can be detrimental to their self-concepts.[14]

LANGUAGE AND CULTURE

Culture is learned through both imitation and language. Through imitation of parents, siblings, and sometimes grandparents, uncles, and aunts youngsters learn the family's or parents' culture. By imitation, youngsters assume attitudes, beliefs, and values about religion, politics, economics, and people. Further, the content of the culture is learned through the parents' language. The language youngsters inherit, imitate, and eventually speak serves to form perceptions and attitudes about their human and physical environments.

Language develops in youngsters at an early age. Exactly when language begins in infants has not been determined. However, by 2½ years of age, infants exhibit babbling and other streams of sounds which resemble the inflections of full, natural sentences. By age 4, most U.S. youngsters exhibit control over basic sentence patterns and most sounds of American English. When youngsters begin kindergarten or first grade (ages 5–7), they exhibit control over the fundamental rules, sentence patterns, and sounds of their parents' language. In short, youngsters begin school with basic control of their language.

Further, anthropologists Sapir and Whorf[15] reported in their studies on language and perception that a person's language serves to form one's world view and perceptions of reality. Thus, children begin school with a language which serves to form their perceptions and world views.

The notion that some youngsters begin schooling speaking a substandard dialect or language is a misconception about their dialect. In fact, the language of their parents is the standard they have learned to imitate: black urban children, for example, who speak a form of Black English, adhere to the standards and rules of the language taught by their parents and family.[16] They do not enter school speaking a substandard language. Rather, they may enter school speaking a nonschool standard brand of English or a different standard of English. To take the position that these children speak a substandard brand of English is a blatant imposition of school English as the only standard brand of English capable of use for learning, which is an untenable, ethnocentric position unsupported by linguistic research. The natural language research of Labov,[17] Baratz,[18] Garcia,[19] has affirmed that all dialects and languages are capable of abstract reasoning, mathematic reasoning, and human communications. In short, all language and dialects are equally valid systems of cognition and communications.

In American public schools, teachers have traditionally attempted to ignore or eradicate languages and dialects which deviate from the standard taught in schools. Rather than accepting the language of youngsters who speak different dialects and building from their language bases, teachers have attempted to remediate the language through behavioral modification and English-as-a-sound-language techniques which have not been optimally successful. The attempt has caused the youngsters innumerable cognitive and emotional problems because of the disorientation caused by the language remediation thrust. Students have a right to their particular dialects, and teachers have a responsibility to use that language as a means to expand the students' perceptual, cognitive, and emotional development. The students' language, after all, is as intimate as their mothers' love, and any educational practice that seeks to strip away this language is morally and humanly reprehensible. Yet all students have the right to expect the school to teach them mainstream English literacy.

CULTURE AS SHARED GRATIFICATION

A culture is shared. People form a culture to enhance their survival. Then they share it with group members. Sharing a culture requires cooperation and interdependence among group members. When a member is not cooperative, or when he or she is deviant, the group applies certain sanctions. The sanctions range from mild physical punishment (e.g., spankings) to withholding of affection or ostracism from the group. The sanctions are based on *norms*, or what is considered normal behavior by the group. The norms spring from the behaviors valued by the group.

People from different cultural groups may not apply the same norms to assess deviant behavior. A teacher may see as deviant a child who is acting normally within his or her cultural perspective. For example, in some Mexican American families a child is expected to show respect for elders and anyone in a position of authority. The youngster is also taught to think independently, but to think of the feelings of others, especially those who may be older and wiser. The child's teacher, on the one hand, may encourage all students to disagree with him as a way of learning to be independent thinkers. To the child, disagreeing with the teacher—like disagreeing with a grandparent— is deviant behavior, behavior not valued by the child's group. Thus, this child's attempt to show respect by refusing to disagree may confuse the teacher, who may think of the child as "passive," "introverted," or "disinterested" and "unmotivated" to learn. In this instance, the student and the teacher do not share the values of a common culture and unconscious cultural conflict occurs. The teacher means the student no harm, and the student means the teacher no disrespect. Neither is conscious that a basic cultural problem exists. For the student this unawareness is acceptable; for the teacher who is responsible for teaching and learning, it is unacceptable.

A culture is gratifying. In other words, a culture must fill certain biological and emotional needs of the group members. For example, every culture has a customary behavior for fulfilling basic biological needs. Every culture provides infants some kind of family: adults whose major responsibilities are care and feeding of the infants. Every culture has a customary behavioral pattern for fulfilling sexual drives. Thus, courtship and marriage rituals determine how, when, and with whom sexual drives (along with other needs such as love, security) will be consummated. The culture is the mechanism by which political and economic as well as social needs are fulfilled. Systems of government and (ways to make a living) are developed by the people within the culture. When a particular need is not filled, then individuals within the group look for ways to change their behavior so as to better fulfill the need. Currently in American society, for example, citizens are demanding a change in government spending and a change in wage and price controls because of an inflationary spiral that is making it more and more difficult for the middle- and lower-income groups to purchase homes, cars, groceries, and other staples.

As you can see, a culture consists of values, behaviors, and products which become manifest when humans organize a group to enhance their survival. Group members learn and teach each other their culture by sharing it, and when a particular aspect of the culture does not meet the group's needs, then a change is required. A culture, then, both preserves and conserves the group's values, behaviors, and products. Herein lie the essential dynamics of a culture: the push of history and the pull of the present into the future. To make sense of these dynamics, I am going to explain them within the context of an ethnic group. Examples of ethnic minority group behavior in current U.S. society will be used, but the dynamics are universal and applicable to any ethnic group. The key ideas here are that culture is learned and is shared by individuals within a group or within a society. People are born almost as clean slates, devoid of culture. The instant of birth introduces infants to their cultures whether that be an abrupt slap on the bottom or a thump on the ground. From birth till death, people learn their cultures.

ETHNIC-GROUP MEMBERSHIP

An ethnic group is a unique type of human group. Banks and Gay provide a comprehensive definition of an ethnic group:

> A cultural ethnic group is an ethnic group which shares a common set of values, experiences, behavioral characteristics, and linguistic traits which differ substantially from those of other ethnic groups within the society.[20]

Banks and Gay are careful to point out that their definition of an ethnic group represents an ideal-type construct, and that in actuality ethnic-group members will exhibit in varying degrees the ethnic-group characteristics they have identified. A trait among humans is to form an ethnic group centered on common interests, needs, and aspirations. The group develops patterns of behavior, systems of belief, communication networks, a language or languages, and the technology and tools to promote survival. Established patterns become tradition; established beliefs become a group's *ethos* and *mores*. An *ethos* is the totality of a group's commonly held values and *mores* are its taboos, norms, or moral restrictions.

The ethos and mores of the group control individual behavior by prescribing social parameters and constraints which guide an individual's behavior, helping one conform to the group's standards. The group does not impose total conformity upon the individual. Total conformity would stifle creativity, innovation, and change. The group must tolerate a certain amount of deviancy to survive. This principle of tolerable deviation is a change mechanism. It allows the group an

adaptive means. Central to group survival, it allows group heterogeneity, intragroup diversity, and individual development. It also prevents oppressive conformity, monolithic thinking, and suppression of
individuality. The principle allows diversity, and while it prescribes
normative parameters, it prevents the suffocating group conformity
imposed by totalitarian ideologies such as those portrayed in Aldous
Huxley's *Brave New World* or George Orwell's *1984*. For example, the
Mexican American ethnic group is bound together by a common language, Spanish, general Roman Catholic Christian moral precepts,
liberal political doctrines (influenced by Mexican socialism), and
deeply felt family ties. Individually, Mexican Americans differ vastly.
Not all speak or think in Spanish; some use English only; others speak
various dialects of Spanish. Not all are Roman Catholics; some are
Protestants but of different sects. Not all are Democrats; many are
conservative Democrats; others are Republicans. Still others belong to
splinter parties, such as the Chicano party, La Raza Unida. Not all
have strong family ties, although some have nuclear families and
others have extended families including grandparents, *compadres* (godparents), and third-generation grandchildren.

An ethnic group must allow for intragroup diversity. Or, in other
words, an ethnic group cannot force all its members to be alike. For
example, among black Americans in the United States, there exists a
great amount of diversity among blacks living in various parts of the
country. Dialects, traditions, attitudes, and beliefs differ. Further, even
within the various subgroups, differences exist regarding traditions,
attitudes, and beliefs. What holds an ethnic group together is the
cohesion that a pervasive sense of peoplehood provides. Black Americans may refer to each other as "soul brothers" or "soul sisters" to
connote a sense of peoplehood, or a feeling of belonging and identify-
ing with the black American group. This cements the ethnic group,
giving it a sense of common interests and destinies.[21]

An ethnic group transmits its culture through customary patterns,
a language or languages, and social institutions. In preindustrial
western European societies, the family transmitted the ethos, mores,
traditions, and technical skills necessary for group perpetuation.
Socialization began at birth and extended beyond puberty. At puberty,
the individual was inducted into the group by some rite of passage.
Cultural transmission was the education of youth; it was the family's
essential function and the parent's primary responsibility after biological needs were met. In current western European societies and in
the United States, the family has delegated educational responsibilities
to other institutions. Education of youth is a responsibility shared with
the church, schools, and mass media. We expect the teacher and other
school personnel to act *in loco parentis* to the degree that we wish

them to share in the technical and spiritual education of our youth. Thus, cultural conflict occurs in the schools when the teacher's and the ethnic group's socialization practices vary.

Is a nationality group the same as an ethnic group? In some cases, the two are the same. Technically, nationality is one's official country of citizenship. For example, anyone who is a legal citizen of Canada is a Canadian regardless of race, color, or religious creed. U.S. citizens, including citizens of the Commonwealth of Puerto Rico and other U.S. territories, regard their nationality as American. For some Americans, their sense of peoplehood, their allegiance and loyalty, is to their nationality rather than to a specific ethnic group. For other Americans, allegiance and loyalty to both the country as a whole (nationality) and to their ethnic group are not considered mutually exclusive. In times of national crisis, priority may be given to the national needs and ethnic group considerations subordinated. In times of national calm, priority is given to ethnic group considerations. In the United States, one can be an ethnic and a citizen of a pluralistic nation. One's ethnic group, as a human cultural group, is identified by race, religion, or national origin. In Figure 2.1, note the ways some ethnic groups are identified in the United States.

One's ethnic group in American society is not synonymous with one's language or nationality. In nineteenth-century Europe, a person's ethnic group was also his or her nationality. Many times, the ethnic, national, and language group was the same. A Spaniard (ethnic group) was Spanish (nationality) and spoke Spanish (language

Ethnic Group	National Origin	Religion	Race
Black			X
Irish	X		
Jews		X	
Chinese*	X	X	X
WASP	X**	X	X

* "Chinese Americans" are viewed as non-Christians from China of the mongoloid race.
** "Anglo-Saxon" refers to England.

Figure 2.1 Differing Ethnic-Group Identifications

group). Yet, Jews in Spain were described as Sephardic Jews. They spoke Spanish and considered themselves Spanish Jews. Citizens of the United States call themselves Americans and perceive their national allegiance to be to the United States of America. One can have an American nationality, a particular ethnic group such as Greek American, and speak an American variety of English. Some people can trace their ethnic heritage to various national origins and identify as members of transnational ethnic groups; some members of transnational groups are not sure they have an ethnic group. Many will say they have no ethnic group and that they are "Heinz 57" variety, that is, of mixed national origins.

A dominant ethnic group in American society is the much maligned white, Anglo-Saxon Protestant (WASP). The power of the white, Anglo-Saxon Protestant heritage of the United States is still potent, manifested in people's attitudes and behaviors. The WASP group is so embedded in American society that its customs and beliefs are perceived by some to be the American core culture. I use the WASP acronym to describe and not to disparage this ethnic group. The acronym has come to imply entirely negative notions such as "bigot" and "redneck." The implications are clearly unfair and grossly incorrect because bigotry, racism, and other human vexations are not monopolized by any group. The WASP group is an ethnic majority group because of its political and economic power, and the acronym identifies its ethnic heritage, cultural orientations, and religious influences.

Ethnic-group membership is primarily involuntary, but ethnic-group affiliation is voluntary. We are born into some ethnic group. We do not choose parents or our ethnic-group membership. At some time, we may choose to leave our ethnic group of birth. Persons of mixed ancestry may at some time in their lives choose to affiliate with an ethnic group. In the final analysis, a lucky person is one born into a caring family. The family may belong to some traditionally defined ethnic group such as Jewish American, or into a family of mixed or lost national origin: the family may also belong to some cultural, social, or religious group. It is the family that teaches values and beliefs that are the basis for human action. Therefore, while ethnic-group affiliation is ultimately voluntary, as you will see in the next chapter, voluntary choices about ethnic-group affiliation are conditioned by one's social circumstances.

Culture is central for all human activities, including learning. Acknowledging that all students have a valid culture places emphasis on the notion that all students are learning beings who have learned and will continue to learn a culture.[22] As such, all students are educable. A student's culture provides a means to perceive and function within different groups and in the greater society. While culture is not innate or inborn, it is learned and transmitted so unconsciously that students consider their culture as the "natural" way of perceiving and believing. Students learn their culture through their families and associates. They also learn their culture through the broader social and ethnic milieu into which they are born, reared, and thrust. The next chapter will examine the broader social milieu of U.S. society as a means to understand better how students acquire their culture.

Notes

1. Talcott Parsons. *The Structure of Social Action*. New York: McGraw-Hill, 1937, pp. 27–36.
2. Thomas J. Labelle. "What's Deprived About Being Different," from Julius Merracher and Erwin Pollack, *Emerging Education Issues: Conflicts and Contrasts*. Boston: Little, Brown, 1974, p. 175.
3. Labelle, "What's Deprived," p. 175.
4. Ralph Linton. *The Cultural Background of Personality*. New York: Prentice-Hall, 1945, p. 30.
5. Al Kroeber and Clyde Kluckhohn. *Culture, A Critical Review of Concepts and Definitions*. Cambridge, Mass.: Peabody Museum of American Archeology, 1952.
6. E. B. Tylor, quoted in Kroeber and Kluckhohn, *Culture*, p. 43.
7. Ruth Benedict, quoted in Kroeber and Kluckhohn, *Culture*, p. 43.
8. Franz Boas. *The Mind of Primitive Man*. New York: Macmillan, 1938, p. 159.
9. Kimball Young. *Sociology: A Study of Society and Culture*. New York: American Book, 1949, p. 35; see also, Charles W. Morris. *Signs, Language, and Behavior*. New York: Braziller, 1955, p. 204.
10. Kenneth B. Clark. *Prejudice and Your Child*. Boston: Beacon Press, 1962, pp. 29–31.
11. Paul F. Secord and Carl Backman. *Social Psychology*. New York: McGraw-Hill, 1964, pp. 454–459.
12. Kurt Lewin. *A Dynamic Theory of Personality*. New York: McGraw-Hill, 1935.
13. Jack Forbes. "Teaching Native American Values and Cultures," in James Banks, *Teaching Ethnic Studies*. Washington, D.C.: National Council for the Social Studies, 1973, pp. 201–205.
14. U.S. Commission on Civil Rights. *Teachers and Students*, Report V, Washington, D.C.: U.S. Government Printing Office, March 1973; see also, U.S. Commission on Civil Rights. *Ethnic Isolation of Mexican Americans in the Public Schools of the Southwest*, Report I, Washington, D.C.: U.S. Printing Office, April 1971; see also, Theresa Chang, "Asian American Identity and the School Curriculum," in Boyer and Boyer, *Curriculum and Instruction After Desegregation*. Manhattan, Kan.: Ag Press, 1975, pp. 99–105; see also, Robert Havighurst and Bernice Neugarten. *American Indian and White Children*. Chicago: University of Chicago Press, 1955.

15. Edward Sapir. *Culture, Language, Personality*. Berkeley: University of California Press, 1958; see also, B. L. Whorf. *Language, Thought and Reality*. New York: Wiley, 1956.

16. Janet Catro. "Untapped Verbal Fluency of Black School Children," in Eleanor Leacock, ed., *The Culture of Poverty, A Critique*. New York: Simon and Schuster, 1971; see also, Martha Word. *Them Children: A Study in Language Learning*. New York: Holt, Rinehart and Winston, 1971.

17. W. Labov. "The Logic of Nonstandard English." In F. Williams, ed., *Language and Poverty*. Chicago: Markam, 1970, pp. 153–189.

18. J. Baratz. *Language Abilities of Black Americans—Review of Research: 1966–1970*. Unpublished manuscript, Washington, D.C.: Education Study Center, 1973.

19. Ricardo Garcia. *Identification and Comparison of Oral English Syntactic Patterns of Spanish-English Speaking Hispanos*. Unpublished dissertation, University of Denver, 1973; see also, Carolyn Kessler. *The Acquisition of Syntax in Bilingual Children*. Washington, D.C.: Georgetown University Press, 1971.

20. James Banks and Geneva Gay. "Ethnicity in Contemporary American Society: Toward the Development of a Typology," *Ethnicity*, 1978, *5*: 244.

21. Milton Gordon. *Assimilation in American Life*. New York: Oxford University Press, 1964, pp. 23–29.

22. Maurice Levitas. *Marxist Perspectives in the Sociology of Education*. Boston: Routledge & Kegan Paul, 1974, p. 10.

Chapter 3
Social Theories on
Communal Living

Going beyond basic concepts of culture and ethnicity, how do people develop a social identity? "Who am I?" is largely dependent upon what other people say I am. Because of their social status and power, the more powerful and influential people surrounding me have much to say about who I am. The question is also dependent upon early family influences and broader sociocultural notions about "the American way." Most U.S. citizens find themselves caught between the general moral values of American society—for example, equality, justice, and liberty for all—and the more specific value systems of their regional, religious, racial, or cultural groups.

How have people in the United States gone about the business of living together? The way people live together in a community is a result of social and historical forces as well as regional and local circumstances. Children growing up in the many different communities in the United States acquire their family's culture as well as the regional culture that pervades their community. Also, because the public schools teach a universal culture—allegiance to free enterprise, individualism, and self-reliance—students are taught a core, economic American culture. In my view, the culture taught by the family has the greatest impact upon students; the culture taught by the region has the least impact, with the school culture falling in between. This chapter attempts to answer the question of how people develop a social identity by describing and evaluating the various social theories which have been used to describe "the American way." Particular attention will be given to how the theories deal with the relationships between ethnic and minority peoples and the so-called American creed.

THE AMERICAN CREED

The "American creed" is the general theory of social living in the United States. It is a feeling intertwined with general Christian notions which hold that all people are brothers and sisters under the skin, that all peoples are equal in the eyes of the law.[1] Implicit in the creed is the Protestant work ethic: work is one's salvation, and if one works hard, spends wisely, takes advantage of opportunities, and leads a clean life, salvation will be at hand.[2] Material gain, such as money in the bank, a new house, and two cars, is tangible proof that one is saved. The American creed basically holds that any person in American society can prosper materially by capitalizing on the opportunities offered in the society. This is sometimes called the "bootstrap theory," from the adage, "if you want to succeed, you must pull yourself up by the bootstraps." The creed assumes that all persons are equal under the law, and with this general protection, all persons can prosper on their own merit. Those who do not prosper, according to the creed, fail because they do not capitalize on opportunities provided them. They fail, therefore, because of some character flaw, such as laziness or slovenly living, rather than a flaw or breakdown in the workings of the creed. Circumstances of birth, such as the social class or racial or ethnic group one inherits, are considered irrelevant.

The American creed has been expressed eloquently in the *Declaration of Independence*, "we hold these truths to be self evident: that all men are created equal; that they are endowed by the Creator with inherent and inalienable rights. . . ." Abraham Lincoln succinctly expressed the creed when he said in his *Gettysburg Address*: ". . . our fathers brought forth on this continent a new nation, conceived in liberty, and dedicated to the proposition that all men are created equal. . . ." In our time, Martin Luther King, Jr., reaffirmed the American creed, calling for all Americans to join him when he delivered his "I Have a Dream" speech at the end of a historic march on Washington, D.C.

While the American creed provides general ethical guidelines for how people should live together in American society, it does not provide specific guidelines for living together on a day-to-day basis in a pluralistic society. Ethnic, social class, economic, political, and religious realities impose upon people the responsibility of working out a daily ethic by which they somehow reconcile their daily behavior with the American creed. People left to themselves to work out a daily ethic have developed through their behavior and customary ways of living varying theories of communal living. I have culled communal theories from various sources and specifically give credit to three classic texts in the field: Milton Gordon's *Assimilation in American Life*,[3] Isaac Berkson's *Theories of Americanization*,[4] and James Banks's *Teaching Strategies for Ethnic Studies*.[5] What follows is an analysis of six theories of communal living which are currently in use among people and groups in American society.

MELTING POT I: ANGLO-CONFORMITY

Melting Pot I, the Anglo-Conformity assimilation theory, developed from the eastern colonial American belief that all immigrants should renounce their former ethnic and national culture and adopt the ways of the English (Anglo) cultural groups living in the Atlantic seaboard colonies. Melting Pot I was conceived for white Europeans; black and Native Americans were not to be melted into the Anglo-conformity pot. Blacks were to serve the society as slaves. The institution of slavery clearly defined blacks' role in colonial society. Native Americans were considered people of different nations. They were to be kept out of the society by treaties that placed them west of the eastern seaboard states. Treatment of Native Americans as separate nations rather than as assimilable human groups clearly defined their role.

The French scholar, Alexis de Tocqueville, noted in his study[6] of the emerging American republic that exclusion of Native Americans and slavery of blacks threatened the unity and stability of the republic. Since the white groups considered Native Americans unmeltable, de Tocqueville felt that Native Americans had only the options of war with the American republic or withdrawal to the west. If the Native Americans attempted to remain within the republic, de Tocqueville predicted that the whites would resist, isolate, and eventually expel them. For blacks, de Tocqueville thought emancipation or expatriation to Africa was inevitable. He also predicted that if blacks were emancipated, whites would remain hostile to them for years to come; assimilation of blacks into the Anglo-conformity melting pot, according to de Tocqueville, would not inevitably follow emancipation.

MELTING POT II: ETHNIC OR BIOLOGICAL FUSION

This theory envisioned a biological fusion or ethnic synthesis of all white Americans regardless of religious affiliation or national origin. From this merger would emerge a new American culture. The theory was popularized by Israel Zangwill's play, *The Melting Pot*. Melting Pot II emerged from the large-scale immigration of people from southeastern and central Europe in the years 1880 to 1914. The notion of racial fusion of American whites can be traced to 1756 in a letter by Jean de Crevecoeur,[7] who wrote that in the eastern colonies individuals were being melted into a new race. Melting Pot II did not require complete renunciation of ethnic background or culture; rather, one could adopt aspects of other cultures, abandon some parts of one's own culture, and maintain other parts.

The notion of Americanization countered Melting Pot II.[8] Americanization required renunciation of one's culture and complete adoption of the older Anglo-Saxon culture. Thus, the Americanization notion was the Melting Pot I Anglo-conformity notion in disguise. Americanization rose out of the fears of older immigrant groups whose American roots were in the Atlantic seaboard colonies. They feared that the so-called Nordic American race would be diluted, especially by Jewish, Polish, Italian, and other dark-skinned immigrants.

Concurrent with the emergence of Americanization, a popular racial theory emerged which categorized people into two races, the white and the colored.[9] People were then subdivided into a hierarchy within the two races. In the hierarchy of the white race, the "Nordic" or "Aryan" strain was the purest strain, consisting of the older German and English immigrant groups, who were ostensibly tall, blond, blue-eyed people. The "Alpine" strains were less pure, consisting of the darker, eastern European immigrants who were the in-between strains; the lowest white strains were the Mediterranean, consisting of the dark-haired southern Europeans. The colored race, "people of color," was at the bottom. People of color were members of the "yellow" races (Chinese, Japanese, etc.), the "red" races (Native Americans), and the black race. All were considered unmeltable into the white race.

One other melting pot theory that merits citation is the frontier melting pot of historian Henry J. Turner.[10] Turner's thesis was that the frontier exigencies and experiences of white pioneers forged a type of cultural synthesis in the American West. In the frontier West, pioneers of all nationalities were compelled to merge by the austere social and physical environment, according to Turner. Irrespective of past status in Europe or on the eastern U.S. seaboard, on the frontier all were equalized by their ability to contribute to human survival. The forced merger of all national groups in the frontier's crucible fused a new American nationality, the transnational white Americans, with their unique frontier values and beliefs. The frontier melting pot is fundamentally the same as Zangwill's urban melting pot, with the important difference that Zangwill described the ideal communal desires of urban European immigrants, and Turner described similar desires for rural European immigrant pioneers.

CULTURAL AND RELIGIOUS PLURALISM

This theory called for the economic and political integration of white ethnics into U.S. society, but called also for retention of their languages, cultures, and religions. Berkson called this notion the community theory:

> The Community Theory differs from the Americanization and Melting Pot theories in that it refuses to set up as ideal such a fusion as will lead to the obliteration of all ethnic distinction.[11]

For Berkson, ideal cultural pluralism would allow people to select ethnic or cultural communities compatible with their ethnic preferences. These communities would be home base, the source of sustenance, retreat, and renewal. People could voluntarily select their ethnic affiliation and enclave. On this point, Berkson and the recognized originator of cultural pluralism, Horace Kallen, disagreed. Kallen[12] felt that ethnic-group affiliation was involuntary, that people could not change their past heritage and their parents would inevitably socialize them according to their past ethnic heritage. Thus, people really had no choice about their ethnic group, as they were thoroughly indoctrinated with it before reaching adulthood. In later years, Kallen softened his stance, conceding that adults could possibly select ethnic-group affiliation if accepted by a particular ethnic group.

Because Kallen's writings were the beginning of cultural pluralism, let us examine his three basic themes. The first was that almost everyone had an ethnic group. Considering that Kallen wrote in the early twentieth century, the theme made sense. At that time, most people could identify some ethnic or national group as their own. Also, Kallen thought that most people had no choice but to belong to their ethnic group of birth: that is, most people inherited a family which belonged to some ethnic group, and the family would socialize its youth into that ethnic group. Kallen's second theme was that cultural pluralism was in agreement with the democratic, American way. Because it allowed people to be different and yet be American, the theory allowed people to define themselves freely. Third, Kallen emphasized a unity-within-diversity theme. He argued that it was possible for a society to be diverse as well as unified. Further, he argued that the society could benefit from diversity.

The cultural-religious pluralism theory emerged as a reaction to the Melting Pot II theory which, according to cultural pluralism proponents, was an undemocratic Anglo-conformity melting pot in disguise. The cultural-religious pluralism theory evolved into what Herberg called "the triple melting pot."[13] In his study on the sociology of American religions, Herberg found that in the first four decades of this century Americans tended to marry within their religious group—Protestants, Catholics, and Jews. In other words, interreligious marriages occurred in relatively small numbers. The study also revealed that within religious groups, minimal intermarriage occurred between ethnic minorities and whites: black and white Protestants rarely married, and Mexican American or Puerto Rican Catholics rarely married white Catholics. Glazer and Moynihan's similar study conducted in New York City, *Beyond the Melting Pot*,[14] reaffirmed Herberg's thesis. The limitation of the triple melting pot concept is that the role of non-Christian religions is not treated. Nevertheless, the triple melting pot thesis does point to the tenacity of religious plurality and ethnic stratification in American society.

Cultural pluralism is often described with the salad bowl analogy. In a salad bowl, each ingredient adds to the overall taste and flavor of the salad, yet each retains its individual identity. A society based on cultural pluralism is like a salad bowl in that each ethnic group retains its identity while contributing to the overall society. The salad would not be complete without the participation of all ingredients; under cultural pluralism, the society would not be complete without the involvement of all ethnic groups. Another analogy is that of the orchestra. In an orchestra, each instrument belongs to a group that retains its identity; each group is interdependent with other instrument groups, and each instrument group contributes to the overall orchestral harmony. In a culturally pluralistic society each group retains its group identity, is interdependent with other groups, and contributes to the overall social harmony.

RACIAL SEPARATION: AMERICA FOR WHITES ONLY

The racial separation theory is attributed to the early American colonial and nativist belief that racial minorities could not be assimilated into American society. The belief was predicated on the presumed genetic inferiority of racial minorities, as well as the presumed excessive prejudice and discrimination racial minorities would experience at the hands of whites if an attempt were made to assimilate them. Some

U.S. Presidents practiced the racial separation theory to varying degrees.[15] Thomas Jefferson, Andrew Jackson, Abraham Lincoln, and Franklin D. Roosevelt implemented policies and programs to isolate, relocate, or export blacks, Native Americans, and Japanese Americans.

Thomas Jefferson proposed that all blacks be educated in a trade or craft. At the age of 18 for females and 21 for males, they would be freed and exported to some other country or to the western United States. He believed that blacks were biologically inferior and could not be amalgamated into the eastern colonies. He felt, too, that white prejudices and discrimination against blacks would intensify if attempts were made to assimilate them.[16] Andrew Jackson made his reputation as an Indian fighter. Once President, he supported the southern states righters who wanted to export all Native Americans from the South to the Oklahoma Indian Territory. When his removal activities were declared unconstitutional by the U.S. Supreme Court, Jackson reportedly said about the Chief Justice of the Supreme Court, "John Marshall has made his decision, now let him enforce it." Thus, in violation of the U.S. Constitution, President Jackson exported almost all Native Americans from the South.[17]

President Abraham Lincoln vacillated between colonizing blacks in other countries and emancipating blacks within the United States. Between 1862 and 1864, Lincoln experimented with colonization of blacks on Cow Island, off Haiti. The experiment ended in failure. Lincoln was aware of the American Colonization Society which advocated colonization and exported blacks from the United States. It was founded in 1817 to establish colonies in Africa for black Americans, sending them to live in Sierra Leone and Liberia. Supporters of this "back to Africa" society were prominent political leaders, including James Monroe, James Madison, John Marshall, and Henry Clay; however, it was not supported by the black leadership because it was viewed as an expatriation ploy. Before the society's demise after the Civil War, more than 15,000 blacks had been expatriated to Africa.[18] Lincoln knew that the colonization movement was opposed by the black leadership and that it failed to attract a significant number of blacks. He thus supported both black exportation and emancipation.[19] President Franklin Roosevelt developed a pro-civil rights record while acting as president, but signed the executive order (Executive Order 9066) that dispossessed some 112,000 Japanese Americans of their property. U.S. armed forces then relocated them from the west coast to concentration camps in the interior United States.[20]

The racial separation theory evolved and existed concurrently with the melting pot and pluralistic theories. Gunnar Myrdal in *The American Dilemma* calls the theory the "anti-amalgamation doctrine" which coexisted with the American creed doctrine. Racial minorities could not be assimilated into American society without diluting it. Therefore, it was necessary to segregate, relocate, or export racial minorities as a means of preserving the racial and ethnic purity of white American society, the only society for which the American creed was intended, according to the racial separation theory.

SEGREGATION-DESEGREGATION-INTEGRATION THEORY

This theory is based on the belief that segregated public facilities, businesses, and schools are inherently unequal and detrimental to both whites and racial minorities. The theory sprang from the civil rights movement of the 1950s and '60s and from various U.S. Supreme Court decisions, primarily the *Brown* v. *Topeka Board of Education* decision, which declared that schools segregated on the basis of race were inherently unequal. Segregated minority schools tended to be under-funded and understaffed; they were not "separate but equal." The decision and subsequent civil rights laws and legislation have provided legal authority to dismantle the residue of institutions formed on the basis of the racial separation theory.[21] Thus, miscegenation (anti-interracial marriage) laws and Jim Crow laws, which allowed official discrimination against racial minorities, were abrogated.[22]

But the segregation-desegregation-integration theory did not spring suddenly from the civil rights movement; it underlies the legal changes ethnic and racial minorities have historically struggled to bring about in American society. Aware that U.S. society was legally segregated and that they were legally impeded from full participation in American society, minorities have striven through legal and democratic channels to abolish the segregation laws and thereby desegregate formal institutions such as schools, the armed forces, and federally financed corporations.

Once formal segregation was made illegal, the second phase of the process, desegregation, began, ultimately leading to the third phase, integration into American society. The civil rights movement of the fifties and sixties sought to abrogate formal and legal societal segrega-tion, which then began the desegregation phase of the process. To a large extent, legal segregation has been ended, and the desegregation phase has been engaged and continues to operate, although recent reverse discrimination lawsuits, such as the *Bakke* case, will no doubt impede the progress. The third phase, integration, is yet to come, ac-cording to the theory. Until the segregation and desegregation phases are successfully completed, integration is not possible because it is more than mere elimination of legal segregation and discrimination; it is the condition of full participation for ethnic and racial minorities in all realms of American life. To set the stage for integration, according to the theory, the current desegregation phase must successfully wipe out the racist traditions, folkways, and beliefs, and buttress the political, economic, and social power bases of the ethnic minority groups.

ETHNIC PLURALISM

Ethnic pluralism is the belief that ethnicity and ethnic-group culture, and the subsequent cultural and ethnic diversity manifest in large groups of different peoples, are realities in American society.[23] Emphasizing ethnic-group differences and similarities, the theory does not focus on the racial or genetic basis of human groups as did the melting pot and racial separation theories. Rather, the theory posits that people have a right to an ethnic-group culture as well as the right to choose their cultural affiliation. According to this theory, ethnic minorities are to be included in American society as contributing and legitimate ethnic group peoples and, as such, are worthy of the dignity and respect accorded any citizen. Emphasis is also placed on the interdependence of ethnic groups—ethnic groups need each other, as they all can benefit from the creative vitality and uniqueness each obtains. Thus, ethnic pluralism does not advocate racial or ethnic separation (the racial separation theory), nor does it advocate eradication of non-white ethnic-group cultures (the melting pot theories). Rather, ethnic pluralism reaffirms the unity-within-diversity notion of the cultural pluralism theory.

Novak, in *The Rise of the Unmeltable Ethnics*,[24] develops the thesis that white ethnics have not been melted into a homogeneous single group. Rather, white ethnics as well as minority ethnics have retained much of their ethnicity. In 1975–76, the National Council for the Social Studies appointed a task force to develop rationale and curriculum guidelines for multiethnic education. The task force of multiethnic education specialists, in conjunction with an advisory board of educators throughout the United States, provided an affirmation of ethnic pluralism:

> In the United States, ethnic diversity has remained visible despite the assimilation process that takes place in any society made up of many different ethnic groups. Although ethnic affiliations are weak for many Americans, a large number still demonstrate at least some attachments to their ethnic cultures and to the symbols of their ancestral traditions. The values and behavior of many Americans are heavily influenced by their ethnicity. Ethnic identification may also be increased by many because of their racial characteristics, language, or culture.[25]

THE PROCESSES OF ASSIMILATION:
ENCULTURATION AND ACCULTURATION

The above enumeration of communal theories is not intended to be all-inclusive. Other theories, such as Warner's class/caste,[26] Myrdal's moral dilemma,[27] or various leftist paradigms,[28] are helpful explanations of some aspects of communal living. The communal theories are given other names: sometimes they are referred to as "assimilation" theories which serve to explain how the host society, Anglo U.S. society in this context, has received and absorbed immigration groups or ethnic minority groups. I have used the term "communal theories" rather than the term "assimilation" because of its wide-ranging definitions and negative connotations. A common definition—that "assimilation" means total abrogation of one's culture and adoption of Anglo-American culture—defines the term as a weapon for cultural imperialism or the means for a total take-over of one group by another. This has as a reference the policies and practices of European colonial powers.

Between 1492 and 1900, European countries wishing to expand their mineral and food resources conducted "discovery" expeditions to locate land on the American, Asian, and African continents for purposes of exploitation. To exploit the mineral and agricultural resources and transport them to the mother country, indigenous groups were also exploited. The Europeans developed policies and practices which enabled them to control and use the indigenous groups as a labor source. In return, the Europeans gave the indigenous groups the "benefits" of European civilization; that is, Europeans felt they had a responsibility to "civilize" indigenous groups. This ethnocentric attitude of the superiority of European civilization became known as the "white man's burden." Another policy was to send groups of people who would establish a colony and home base for the mother country. The first Europeans on the North American continent—the English, French, and Spanish—combined use of all three practices. Militia, Christian missionaries, and pilgrims were sent to colonize the continent. Later, the U.S. government colonized in the western hemisphere—in Puerto Rico, the Hawaiian Islands, and the Philippines. The colonizing country would send its militia, its Christian missionaries, and sometimes its own citizens. By force and by education (the indigenous groups were taught Christianity and the language of the mother country), the colonizers imposed their cultures on the indigenous groups, subjugating them to a lower class/caste status, and, by degrees, encapsulating their cultures. The indigenous groups confronted three dubious options: (1) to be "assimilated" and subordinated by the colonizer, (2) to be expelled from one's home, family, and group, or (3) to be killed for not choosing assimilation or expulsion.[29]

Another common view of assimilation is that to be a loyal American, one must adopt the English language, the American culture, and forget one's own language and culture. Such assimilation is seen as patriotically correct. This attitude is based on the nationalistic and nativistic beliefs that prevailed in the United States between the middle nineteenth and early twentieth centuries. In the process of developing a national identity, U.S. citizens tended to view certain religious, cultural, and national groups as threats to the so-called American nation. The American nation was perceived as an English-speaking, white, Protestant country.[30] At different times, and in varying degrees, anti-foreigner movements, protests, and riots were waged against Jews, Catholics, Chinese Americans, black Americans, and other nonwhite or non-Protestant groups. Some Protestant sects, such as the Latter-Day Saints (Mormons), were viewed as foreigners, a threat to the national identity, and forced to migrate to the West from their eastern settlements. Even the term "American" to describe a U.S. citizen, which was derived from explorer Amerigo Vespucci's first name, was viewed as the exclusive domain of white, Protestant U.S. citizens. Other peoples in Canada, Mexico, Central and South America were not considered Americans.[31]

Anthropologists and sociologists tend to use the term *assimilation* as a generic concept. People are assimilated into a group through enculturation (or socialization) and acculturation.[32] The process by which one learns one's own culture is called *enculturation* (or *socialization*); enculturation describes how a person is taught the customs, norms, and acceptable behaviors of the group.[33] Sociologists use the term "socialization" to describe how a person learns the culture one inherits at birth. Thus, socialization also describes how a person is taught the customs, norms, and acceptable behavior of one's own group. *Acculturation* refers to the learning of a new or different culture.[34] I will explain the difference between the two terms by describing the experiences of two different groups of teenagers: first-generation Mexican teenagers and historically ethnic minority Mexican American teenagers. I chose these two groups because of my personal knowledge about them. The process described is applicable to any other cultural or ethnic group.

Teenagers who were born in Mexico, reared in the Mexican culture and language, and then migrate to the United States must undergo the process of acculturation in order to assimilate or fit into the new society. In Mexico, the teenagers learned and fully internalized most of the values, beliefs, and attitudes of their respective groups. Their families held a status position and a role within Mexican society. Now the teenagers must learn a new culture. They must assimilate into the new society by learning its language, its values, beliefs, and attitudes; they must develop a status position and a role within the host or new society. But they cannot simply forget their former Mexican culture. It is ingrained in them, constituting their self-identities, their feelings, and, if you will, their humanity. The teenagers must develop a bicultural identity, one that allows them to live in the society and one that allows them to retain their former culture. There are problems inherent in developing a bicultural identity. They must reconcile values and beliefs that differ and may seem mutually exclusive. What roles should males and females play? What if acceptable female roles in the new society conflict with those in Mexico? How should one treat one's mother, father, and teachers? Through trial and error, by experimenting with different roles and modes of behavior, the teenagers will eventually develop some balance between the two cultures with which they are comfortable. They will also develop the adaptive technique of switching cultures depending upon the immediate setting and circumstances.

The degree to which the new culture's values, beliefs, and behaviors are internalized depends upon the individual teenager and his or her feelings, needs, and experiences in the new culture. Maintaining a comfortable balance between the two cultures is a process that will continue into adulthood. How teenagers react to the bicultural experience depends upon the understanding and sensitivity of people from the new society. In some regions of the country, where prejudices and biases against Mexican peoples are high, they will be compelled to deal with rejection, resentment, and intolerance; participation in school activities, dating non-Mexicans, and other adolescent activities will be tinged by the negativism the teenagers experience. Some will reject their Mexicanisms, allow friends and teachers to call them by an English name (Dick rather than Ricardo), deny any knowledge of the Mexican language, and perhaps call themselves Spanish Americans or Americans. Others will reject the new society, insist on speaking Mexican Spanish, and date and associate only with other Mexican people. Others will attempt to reconcile the two forces, seeking friends and associates among all groups, using Mexican Spanish or English depending upon circumstances. These teenagers will experience rejection and alienation also. If they are lucky and find a sympathetic teacher— something that doesn't always occur—and can find sympathetic non-Mexican peers, and if their parents are lucky enough to get and hold good jobs, these teenagers will come to terms with group prejudices and biases. It must be understood that the problem is in attempting to develop a bicultural identity in a hostile human environment. The problem, and therefore the solution, lies within the human environment.

Teenagers born in the United States and reared in Mexican American culture and language must undergo the process of socialization or enculturation to assimilate or fit into American society. How should parents socialize their children? First, take the question of language. Parents may feel that English is the de facto official language of the United States. To survive, their youngsters must learn English well, and so these parents will go to any length to teach their children English. They may not speak Spanish to their children, while still speaking Spanish to grandparents, relatives, and friends; they may even discourage the use of Spanish. Other parents may feel that Spanish is their mother tongue, and no matter what, the youngsters will use Spanish. Understand that learning a language requires learning a culture. As teenagers, these Mexican American teenagers have experienced schooling in a middle-class, white attitude. They have learned from their families the appropriate beliefs, values, and behaviors for school survival. The teenagers also have learned how to handle their grandparents. They've learned that respect for others, especially for the elderly, is part and parcel of being Mexican American. The parents may be removed far enough from their ancestral ties that they may not consider themselves Mexican American. They may regret loss of their roots and encourage their children to learn Spanish and study Mexican culture. Or, they may encourage their children to do as they have done, anglicize and look to the day they're considered equals in their communities.

School attendance may or may not be difficult for these teenagers. Depending upon the language and cultural environment at home, they may find the school environment—its curriculum, activities, and teachers—either very alien or in many ways very similar to their home environment. In neighborhoods where the concentration of Mexican Americans is high, or where there are anti-Mexican American prejudices and biases, teenagers more than likely will have difficulty with school attendance. Because schooling is still largely based on white, middle-class cultural values, and because schools tend to reflect the prevailing ethos and mores of their communities, these teenagers may develop a high degree of ambivalence when faced with the conflict between their own culture values and those of the school. Such ambivalence, often caused by the monastic view of teaching and learning, may lead to withdrawal from the alien school setting.

Whose culture is right? How do I grow up Mexican American in an Anglo school and a Mexican American home? Do I have to choose between the two cultures? Why can't I have both? If these teenagers are lucky, sympathetic teachers will help them answer the questions; if they are not so lucky, they will encounter nonsympathetic or unsympathetic teachers who are defensive about the questions because of ethnic biases, or who feel that everyone should assimilate into the "mainstream" culture. Some teenagers will seek refuge in peer groups, associating primarily with other Mexican Americans. Others will attempt to strike some balance of Anglo and Mexican American associates. All of these teenagers are attempting to develop a self-identity that is compatible with their home and school teachings. At best, the school environment may be somewhat similar to some of their home environments; at worst, the school environment may be hostile to their home environments. Learning where they fit in, and learning the appropriate values and behaviors to live in the environment of the home and school, these teenagers develop switching mechanisms, and to some extent develop a bicultural identity.

As you can see, generalizations about both the Mexican and the Mexican American teenagers are suspect. Both are developing bicultural identities, but the nature of their ancestral ties, their experiences as youngsters, and their home and language environments differ. The Mexican teenagers are learning a new culture and are attempting to get into a new culture from the outside. The Mexican American teenagers are not learning a new culture; rather, they are learning about two cultures and attempting to reconcile them in light of the home and school environments. Enculturation and acculturation, in this context, are similar processes with the differences between them lying in the individual perspectives and life situations of the teenagers.

SEGREGATION AND DESEGREGATION IN EDUCATION

To make sense of the complexity of theories pertaining to communal living, we will consider segregation, desegregation, and integration as they apply to education in the United States. Speaking broadly, legal as well as social segregation of ethnic minorities was a reality until 1954 when the U.S. Supreme Court declared segregation unconstitutional. From 1776 to 1954, for 178 years, contact between whites and minorities was minimal in secondary institutions. Yet, in primary institutions such as in families and homes, contact between blacks and whites was much greater. While whites and blacks or Native Americans were in contact with each other in primary institutions, secondary institutions such as the public schools were segregated. Public school curricula and teacher preparation programs were based on the values, beliefs, and material culture of the white majority groups. Inclusion of ethnic minority values, beliefs, and cultures was minimal.

Now our society is in the infant stages of desegregation. Desegregation requires open access to all public agencies and all the opportunities guaranteed to U.S. citizens. By slow and painful degrees, contact between whites and minorities is increasing. Sometimes the only way to insure contact is by making it mandatory. Thus, children are bussed to schools to insure contact between white and minority students. We are also in the infant stages of "curricular desegregation"[35]

—that is, we are beginning to include the cultures of ethnic minorities in curricula and teacher preparation programs. To insure that curricular contact occurs, the National Council for the Accreditation of Teacher Education (NCATE), the organization that accredits teacher education programs throughout the United States, has mandated a "multicultural education standard" for all NCATE teacher preparation programs in the United States:

> Multicultural education is preparation for the social, political, and economic realities that individuals experience in culturally diverse and complex human encounters. These realities have both national and international dimensions. This preparation provides a process by which an individual develops competencies for perceiving, believing, evaluating, and behaving in differential cultural settings. Thus, multicultural education is viewed as an intervention and as an on-going assessment process to help institutions and individuals become more responsive to the human condition, individual cultural integrity, and cultural pluralism in society.
>
> Multicultural education could include but not be limited to experiences which: (1) promote analytical and evaluative abilities to confront issues such as participatory democracy, racism and sexism, and the parity of power; (2) develop skills for values clarification including the study of the manifest and latent transmission of values; (3) examine the dynamics of diverse cultures and the implication for developing professional education strategies; and (4) develop appropriate professional education strategies.
>
> Standard: The institution gives evidence of planning to provide for multicultural education in its advanced curricula—in the content for the specialty, the humanistic and behavioral studies, the theory relevant to the specialty, with direct and simulated experiences. . . .[36]

Now every NCATE teacher training program in the United States must have multicultural courses, labs, seminars, and experiences available to students. If no multicultural courses or experiences are required, the program could lose its accreditation: a college could not recommend teaching certificates for its students. In short, one's teaching degree would not be certifiable in some states, and without a certified teaching degree, one cannot teach in a public school.

When desegregation is completed in the United States, integration will commence. Societal integration of whites and minorities requires more than equal access and opportunities, and more than physical contact between whites and minorities; it requires that whites and minorities be equally valued and accepted as fellow human beings. Ultimately, integration requires the eradication of racism and implementation of the brother- and sisterhood of all U.S. citizens. Integration of curricula and teacher education programs requires more than just courses or modules on minorities. Integration requires that the curricula of teacher education programs be permeated by multicultural values, beliefs, and experiences. This stage will be possible only after curricula are desegregated. As a teacher, you will be faced with the challenge to desegregate all of the teaching and learning that occurs in your classroom. As a teacher, you will be challenged to change your focus from the Ptolemaic to the Copernican perspective on the universe of teaching and learning.

COMMUNAL THEORIES AND TEACHING IN A PLURALISTIC SOCIETY

What relationship exists between the communal theories and teaching and learning in a pluralistic society? The relationship between the theories and teaching is that students are products of one or more of the communal theories. As such, they develop social identities which influence the way they perceive their teachers, peers, and the subject matter taught to them. Consider that we live in a free society. We have freedom of and from religion, free speech, and many other freedoms, so long as we behave within the constraints of the U.S. Constitution. These are not absolute freedoms; they are relative freedoms which must be exercised responsibly. We agree: I may choose the food I eat, the friends I make, the woman I marry, the place I live, the church I attend; I may also choose not to marry, not to eat certain food, not to live in certain neighborhoods, and not to attend church. Still, these choices are not absolute, independently determined choices. They are conditioned choices, conditioned by the factors which have influenced me most, primarily social class, ethnic group, geographic location, and perhaps, the religious affiliation of my parents and family. Where I grew up, the social class status I inherited and the societal role given me by my racial or ethnic-group membership shaped and conditioned my perspectives, attitudes, and beliefs. These factors did not set for life my potential for making free choices. They merely shaped my attitudes and life circumstances so that certain choices were not available. The point is that one lives in a certain neighborhood, marries certain types of people, associates with certain kinds of people and organizations because communal life theories have affected the general group structure within which one lives. Within the structure, one can make certain changes, or one can choose to leave the structure in an attempt to change one's circumstances. I may change my social class through education, for example. I may change neighborhoods—if I can get the money—by moving to a more affluent neighborhood. But, if I am visibly a member of an ethnic minority group, a black American for example, I cannot change how some people perceive my black skin negatively even though I may be a doctor or university president. The history of one's life circumstances has an impact upon the way one goes about the business of living with other people.

COMMUNAL THEORIES AND LIVING
IN A PLURALISTIC SOCIETY

How have the theories affected living in the United States? Clearly, we live in a pluralistic society. We have a heritage of three vigorous Judeo-Christian religions; Protestant, Catholic, and Jewish. Currently, eastern religions are vigorous. We have a heritage of white and minority ethnic-group cultures, and there is a revitalization of ethnic-group cultures. While plurality is a reality in American life, certain aspects of this plurality affect communal living and need to be examined more closely.

We live in an ethnically stratified society. Herberg's study and the Glazer-Moynihan study both describe American society as religiously and ethnically stratified. Religious ties are strong, and while interdenominational marriages occur among Protestants, interreligious marriages between Protestants, Catholics, and Jews are minimal. The infrequency of interreligious marriages has a direct bearing on the nature of the family, the primary institution in most societies. Since the religion of one's family generally makes a strong impact on one's values, attitudes, and associates, the low rate of intermarriage serves to strengthen and perpetuate a group's traditional values. Ethnic ties are strong and act much like religious ties. Both Herberg's and Glazer-Moynihan's studies describe minimal interracial marriages: while ethnic minority groups hold membership in the Protestant, Catholic, or Jewish faiths, few interracial marriages occur within each religion.

Further, the history of ethnic minority racial segregation, removal, and relocation has served to bolster ethnic and racial stratification. We should not forget that American society was legally segregated by race for 178 years of its 200 years of existence. History has a way of percolating the past into the present. Given 178 years of ethnic minority segregation from whites, it is not surprising to see white ethnic and ethnic minorities acting out the scenarios of the past. White flight from the cities to avoid contact with ethnic minorities is no doubt based on fears and prejudices which were developed and embedded in white ethnic cultures for nine-tenths of the nation's existence. It is also not surprising that ethnic minorities view with jaundiced eyes liberal pleas for desegregation. The experience ethnic minorities have had with desegregation has been one-sided: ethnic minorities have been asked to blend into the dominant white group cultures at the price of losing their own.

Our communities are ethnically stratified. The "little Polands" and "little Italys" are not ethnic enclaves of the past. While most of the residents of these enclaves have moved uptown or across town where others of their generation reside, some still exist. Neighborhoods still by and large coalesce on the basis of white ethnic and ethnic minority affiliations. Herein lies the challenge for teachers, because in American society—as in all societies—people's lives are interdependent. Although this communal fact is obscured by our emphasis on the ethos of self-reliance and rugged individualism, the reality is that all of our lives are dependent upon others, something we realize when we experience personal or social catastrophe. When a loved one dies in our family, we are amazed and pleased when various members of our local community or distant relatives or friends offer assistance and condolences.

Inasmuch as people are interdependent in a society, the kind of group interdependence allowed depends largely on the communal theories people effectuate in their daily lives. For example, throughout the United States, growers (i.e., corporate farmers) of agricultural produce acknowledge their dependence upon migrant laborers to pick and clear the harvest. The migrants are allowed to live on the farms where they are temporarily employed and are expected to leave the farm as soon as their work is completed. While on the farm, they are not allowed to mingle with the farmer's family. Dating and courtship between the farmer's teenagers and the migrants' teenagers are taboo. Consequently, interdependence between farmers and migrants is solely economic. Social, marital, or political interdependence is not allowed to occur. Both farmers and migrants, in their unconscious acceptance of economic interdependence, are operating on communal theories that have percolated from the past into the present. Of course, because the migrants are powerless, they are not in a position to choose which communal theory they wish to live with. The growers, because they control production and are thereby powerful, are in a position to impose an Anglo-conformity communal theory.

U.S. society is a cluster of varying human and legal communities held together by a core political value system vaguely labelled the American creed. More than a governmental system, the creed is purportedly a way of life based on Judeo-Christian morals and ethics— the Mosaic Code and the Golden Rule—as well as generic humanistic beliefs such as "All men are created equal with certain inalienable rights." To determine a social identity, to answer the basic questions of "who am I?" and "what is my role in society?" one is given broad but extremely vague guidelines by the creed. Instead, one must turn to more specific value and belief systems like those rooted in the home, school, and community. Then one must somehow reconcile the more specific value or belief system with the broadly based beliefs of the creed. In American society, U.S. citizens have an American nationality, a more specific group affiliation (religious, cultural, ethnic, economic), a localized self-image, and a specific occupational identity. To further complicate this game of musical chairs known as acquisition of a social identity, the communal theories, because they pervade American society, set the game's tenor.

Given only the broad ideals of the American creed, people have devised their own belief systems to guide their day-to-day societal interactions. The American creed has been used as a negative gauge, a rationalization to explain away the insidious impact of racism and elitism. A poor, illiterate, and unskilled person is in dire straits because of a character flaw, according to the American creed. The fact that this individual was born into a group which was historically restricted from the opportunities of a good job and a good education is irrelevant. In the American creed, the individual is responsible for his or her condition, regardless of the social and economic restrictions experienced by the individual's group.

The theories of communal living provide a *modus operandi*, or operational principles by which one's self-interest can best be enhanced. In the tradition of American pragmatism and individualism, if the theory one embraces enhances one's survival, then the theory is good. Of course, the attitude that what is good for me is good for the society is an attitude, in the long view, that is defeatist for the individual and the society. In my view, people have used the communal theories to conduct their daily lives. The American creed, rather than serving as a way to gauge and perhaps change communal behavior, has become a lofty ideal vaguely absorbed at Fourth of July picnics and other patriotic occasions. Rugged individualism is no longer a viable ethos. The time has come when people in the U.S. must look to collective or communal living as a more viable ethos. We have reached a point in U.S. society where we must acknowledge and nurture an interdependence of fates among all U.S. citizens. Rugged individualism may have been viable for Anglo pioneers; it is not viable for U.S. pluralistic social living.

Notes

1. Henry B. Parkes. *The American Experience*. New York: Random House, 1955.
2. W. Lloyd Warner. *American Life: Dream and Reality*. Chicago: University of Chicago Press, 1962.
3. Milton Gordon. *Assimilation in American Life*. New York: Oxford University Press, 1964.
4. Isaac B. Berkson. *Theories of Americanization*. New York: Arno Press, 1969.

5. James Banks. *Teaching Strategies for Ethnic Studies*. New York: Allyn & Bacon, 1975.

6. Alexis de Tocqueville. *Democracy in America*. New York: Harper & Row, 1966, pp. 291–312.

7. Jean de Crevecoeur. "Letters from an American Farmer," in Oscar Handlin's, *Immigration as a Factor in American History*. Englewood Cliffs, N.J.: Prentice-Hall, pp. 148–149.

8. Mark Krug. *The Melting of the Ethnics*. Bloomington, Ind.: Phi Delta Kappa Foundation, 1975, pp. 11–16.

9. Henry Fairchild. *The Melting Pot Mistake*. Boston: Little, Brown, 1962; see also, Elwood Cubberley. *Changing Conceptions of Education*. New York: Riverside Educational Mimeographs, 1909.

10. Henry J. Turner. *The Frontier in American History*. New York: Holt, Rinehart and Winston, 1920, pp. 22–24.

11. Berkson. *Americanization*, p. 98.

12. Horace Kallen. *Cultural Pluralism and the American Ideal*. Philadelphia: University of Pennsylvania Press, 1956.

13. Will Herberg. *Protestant, Catholic, Jew*. Garden City, N.Y.: Doubleday (Anchor Books), 1960.

14. Nathan Glazer and Patrick Moynihan. *Beyond the Melting Pot*. Cambridge, Mass.: Harvard University Press, 1963.

15. Pierre L. van den Berghe. *Race and Racism, A Comparative Perspective*. New York: Wiley, 1967, pp. 77–79. (van den Berghe argues that almost all U.S. presidents until Kennedy espoused racist positions regarding blacks and other ethnic minority groups.)

16. Thomas Jefferson. "Notes on the State of Virginia," in Gilbert Osofsky, *The Burden of Race: A Documentary History of Negro-White Relations in America*. New York: Harper & Row, 1967, pp. 49–58.

17. John A. Garraty. *The American Nation*. New York: Harper & Row, 1966, pp. 256–266.

18. Osofsky. *Burden of Race*, p. 74.

19. "Abraham Lincoln's Address on Colonization," in Osofsky, *Burden of Race*, pp. 122–123.

20. Garraty. *American Nation*, p. 768; see also Roger Daniels, *Concentration Camps USA: Japanese Americans and World War II*. New York: Holt, Rinehart and Winston, 1971.

21. Gunnar Myrdal. *An American Dilemma*. New York: Harper & Row, 1944.

22. See especially U.S. Civil Rights Act, 1964.

23. Talcott Parsons. "Some Theoretical Considerations on the Nature and Trends of Change of Ethnicity," in Nathan Glazer and Daniel Moynihan, eds., *Ethnicity: Theory and Experience*. Cambridge: Harvard University Press, 1975, pp. 63–65.

24. Michael Novak. *The Rise of the Unmeltable Ethnics*. New York: Macmillan, 1971.

25. National Council for the Social Studies. *Curriculum Guidelines for Multiethnic Education*. Arlington, Va.: NCSS, 1976, p. 9. Reprinted with permission of the National Council for the Social Studies.

26. W. Lloyd Warner. *Social Class in America*. Chicago: Science Research Associates, 1949.
27. Myrdal. *American Dilemma*.
28. Saul D. Alinsky. *Reveille for Radicals*. New York: Random House, 1946.
29. Bernard J. Siegel. "Conceptual Approaches to Models for the Analysis of the Educative Process in American Communities," in George Spindler, *Education and Cultural Process*. New York: Holt, Rinehart and Winston, 1974, p. 43.
30. Oscar Handlin. *Immigration as a Factor in American History*. Englewood Cliffs, N.J.: Prentice-Hall, 1959, pp. 167–199.
31. Handlin. *Immigration Factor*, pp. 5–10.
32. Handlin. *Immigration Factor*, pp. 5–10.
33. Carol R. Ember and Melvin Ember. *Cultural Anthropology*. Englewood Cliffs, N.J.: Prentice-Hall, 1973, pp. 17–33.
34. Ember and Ember. *Anthropology*, pp. 385–389.
35. The term is Dr. James Boyer's and is elaborated in James Boyer and Joe Boyer, *Curriculum and Instruction Beyond Desegregation*. Manhattan, Kan.: Ag Press, 1975.
36. National Council for Accreditation of Teacher Education. *Standards for Accreditation of Teacher Education*. Washington, D.C.: NCATE, 1979, p. 13. Reprinted with permission of the National Council for Accreditation of Teacher Education.

Chapter 4
Schools and
Their Communities

In communities throughout the U.S., people go about the business of making a living unaware of the communal theories upon which they operate. Most people who conform to the laissez faire, individualistic U.S. social system are more absorbed by pursuing their self-interests than by any type of community interest. Consequently, they do not consciously act out the communal theories discussed in the preceding chapter. In other words, most people do not consciously think of a communal theory, then, on the basis of its assumptions, design their daily living practices. Instead, most people will unconsciously adhere to and practice their unique renditions of the Anglo-conformity melting pot, the ethnic and racial synthesis melting pots, or the cultural plural ism theories as they conduct daily affairs. Within any community, if enough like-minded people express their communal theories, and if they form an informal consensus of what the communal theory should be, then the school's programs and educators' attitudes will to some degree reflect the prevailing communal theory. The school will reflect a general consensus about what makes a good community. Because every school district lies within a local human and geographic community, the school is affected by much of what occurs within its region, the country, and the world. Consequently, what actually happens in a classroom on any given day in a U.S. public school is to some degree influenced by events in the many loosely interconnected communities that impinge upon the school, its teachers, and curriculum. Students thus acquire some of their culture through the school, as its teachers—through their cultural sieves—transmit and interpret the events of the outside communities for the students.

In the United States, public schools are a community affair. The schools are made up of children from the community adjacent to the school and, with minor exceptions, public schools reflect their human communities. As commonsensical as these words may sound, their significance should not be ignored. Because schools are community affairs, they represent and reflect the prevailing community values and beliefs in their locales, just as children will reflect the values and beliefs of their parents. Therefore, what is taught and what is learned in any classroom is tremendously influenced by the community's values and beliefs. Teaching in a New York City ghetto neighborhood, for example, and teaching in a rural Wyoming school district are vastly different experiences because the schools' communities differ.

Just what is a "community"? Elsewhere in this text (see Chapter 9) a distinction is made between a "human" and a "civil" community. Here it is sufficient to define a community as a group of people living under the same government in the same locale. In a small, rural school district the school's community is easy to define. But in large urban cities— Houston, Los Angeles, Kansas City, Boston, to name a few—the school's community is not so easily defined. Due to school desegregation and busing pressures as well as more traditional changes and shifts in populations, urban communities tend to change continuously. Nevertheless, schools still serve human communities.

THE BASIC STRUCTURE OF THE PUBLIC SCHOOL

The basic governing structure of a public school is its district. A school district is a geographic construct; within the district are facilities for schools, maintenance and storage, a board of education, and central administration. Some districts have acreage for agricultural activities such as tree farms, livestock, and dairy barns, or for vocational training facilities such as auto mechanics and machine shops. Some districts have postgraduation vocational training programs; most districts coordinate their pregraduation programs with local vocational and technical institutes or community colleges. The district's land boundaries are usually the same as its town or city of residence. Some districts are organized by counties, especially those located in remote, rural areas. Generally, the county districts operate elementary and perhaps junior high schools; busing transportation for high school attendance in nearby towns and cities is provided for rural students. In some districts, the certified personnel in the schools—teachers, counselors, administrators—are the highest paid workers in the town or city. The educators are consulted for various reasons other than strictly school matters. Assisting with income tax forms, reading and interpreting legal documents, and sundry other services are provided by the educators at no cost to the people in the district. In other districts, the certified personnel are members of the genteel poor classes teaching students who have travelled more and further than they, and who often have better automobiles than they do. In some urban districts, the educators—usually middle class—commute from the suburbs to teach in the inner city.

American school districts are variegated: in some respects, they differ, and in other respects, they are quite similar. Every school district has a broad community base, drawing students whose parents engage in various occupations, such as professionals, white-collar workers, blue-collar workers, and mechanics. In smaller towns and rural areas, the district and the community are often one and the same, and school activities such as Friday night basketball games, graduation ceremonies, or school plays are community-wide activities. *In the broadest sense of the word, a school's "community" consists of varied social groups who interact with each other, developing cooperative and interdependent networks of relationships. The net result of these relationships is the functional operation of the school. In other words, people work together (cooperation) because they need each other's skills and talents (interdependence) to make a living. This cooperative, interdependent venture also helps provide the community's children a school* (through taxation, school bonds, mill levies). Community interdependence and cooperation dispute the myth that our society is essentially competitive. We really live in a cooperative society as far as schooling is concerned.

Within a school district, which is a geographic rather than a demographic construct, several communities may coexist. In fact, most urban school districts are stratified, with coexisting ethnic and socioeconomic subcommunities. In most urban districts the subcommunities are readily visible because of neighborhood patterns. The very rich and the very poor live in the oldest parts of the city. The very rich often occupy the older homes, the so-called heritage area of the city. The very poor often live in the oldest industrial areas which are close to their jobs. White ethnic groups usually live in city areas traditionally relegated to them. While segregation ordinances are prohibited, ethnic minorities are often compelled by economic and social pressure to stay in the neighborhoods relegated to them. Often when ethnic minorities attempt to move from their neighborhoods to traditionally white neighborhoods, whites move to the city's rim or suburbs —the "white flight" phenomenon—thereby perpetuating segregated neighborhoods.

Within most communities there exists what sociologists call a power elite. The power elite are the people within a community who control its basic economic activities. These people consist of bankers, lawyers, business executives, corporation officials, landowners and others (large ranch and farm owners in some communities) who influence how people make a living. The power elite is not an official or formal group. Instead, it consists of powerful individuals who legally control different parts of the community's economic system. Their decisions on issues involving, for example, who gets a loan or who buys a certain house in a certain neighborhood affect the community's economic and social relations. The key point is that all school districts are in some way accountable to the power elite and the various subgroups in their districts. *Large and small districts alike—and the schooling therein—are community affairs.*

TRADITIONAL PURPOSES OF THE PUBLIC SCHOOLS

The fundamental reason for our public schools is to provide students skills, knowledge, and attitudes to enable them to live and work in a democratic society. Deciding on appropriate skills, knowledge, and attitudes is the responsibility of the people in the school's community. This tradition of local control over the school has been diluted over the years, but as an ideal condition, the notion of local control is deeply embedded in the general American democratic value system. Because of this, the educational philosopher John Dewey believed that the public school as a social institution was the quintessence of American democratic institutions.[1] Members of the school's local community elect individuals to serve as their representatives on the school board. The school board, as a lay board (theoretically any member of the local community can be elected to the school board), determines the school's policy. The policy includes statements about appropriate survival skills, knowledge, and attitudes, based on the values of the individual board members and the community at large.

Teachers who are thought to be compatible with the school district's policy and its underlying values are hired to implement the policy. The essential decisions about what should be taught are made by school board members. They are not made by teachers, college professors, administrators, or any other persons. Teaching in a public school is not as simple as this may sound. The school board may represent the wishes and concerns of certain powerful community groups only, or it may acquiesce to the superintendent, allowing the superintendent to determine policy. The board may not be unified in its views about what should be taught, or who should teach. School board members are elected because of the value system they represent. Some communities are content with a strong superintendent, one who has become a tradition of sorts, and elect a school board to give him or her free play with the school system. Urban communities may elect school board members who represent "antibusing" positions, or "back-to-the-basics" positions, or other popular views. Many communities don't really think much about who is elected for the board. The school has fulfilled its traditional functions over the years, and as such, the community expects it to continue to do so.

THE SCHOOL'S COMMUNITIES

School boards and the schools they oversee do not exist in a vacuum. Federal, state, and community laws influence the day-to-day operations of a school. The value systems of people in the local, state, regional, national, and international communities influence what is taught in the school. The school and its teachers must respond to legal, political, economic, religious, and social forces that exist outside the local community while simultaneously responding to the values and aspirations of the local community. To understand the value dynamic of teaching in the public schools, consider how the school exists in the context of at least five communities: the local, the state, the regional, the national, and the international community. Each community is not homogeneous. Indeed, each to some degree is pluralistic, but each community in some manner influences what is taught in school. Each community, and subgroup of a community, operates on the assumption that its values are the fundamental, critical values that will enhance the student's survival. The questions of whose view is correct, when it is correct, and for whom it is correct are not easy to answer, but teachers, as implementers of educational policy, must respond to and work with these competing value systems (see Figure 4.1).

Each community has either political power or political influence which is used to affect teaching and learning. The local community has the most direct influence and power to determine school policy. The local community elects members of the school board, and, theoretically, any citizen of the local community can be elected. However, in reality extreme members of a community, especially those who are leftist or Marxist, are not likely to be elected. The local community can also choose to raise or lower the taxes used to operate its school

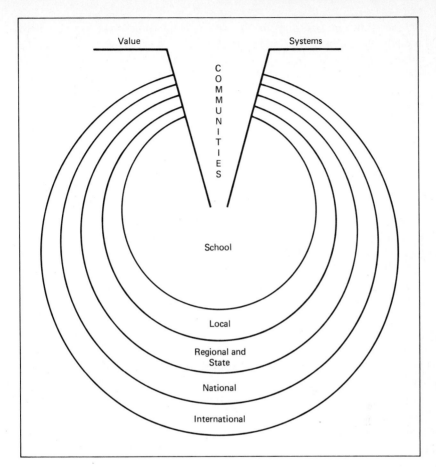

Figure 4.1   School and Its Communities

system. The powers to elect board members and to raise or lower school support taxes give the local community considerable power over the school district. Yet school board members are considered to be state officials who are responsible to the state government. Usually, the school board officials are responsible to the state's department of education, which in turn is responsible to the governor's office. The state has legal power and sociocultural influences over the local school. Each school district must be in compliance with its state regulations and laws.

STATE AS A COMMUNITY

Public school education is considered a state function, and the state is ultimately responsible for providing a free public education for all of the children residing in the state. Education must be provided equally throughout the state: that is, equal access to a free public education must be provided. "Free" education means the state must use the revenue that is raised through taxation of individuals, industry, and business to pay the education costs. Tuition charges and other types of charges to attend school are prohibited. While the expense to send children to school should be kept at a minimum, because of weaknesses and loopholes in most state educational finance systems, parents are asked to help defray costs by paying for certain items, such as the cost of hot lunches, fees for rental of musical instruments, or materials to be used in a wood-working shop or home economics class. Also, because some communities can afford to pay the taxes for better school facilities, most states have unequal school facilities. Within some school districts, it is apparent that the more affluent neighborhoods have the new buildings, more equipment, more paraprofessionals, and other resources when compared to the schools in less affluent neighborhoods.

THE NATIONAL COMMUNITY

School districts are locally controlled and responsible both to their local constituents and their state laws and regulations. Public schooling is viewed as the legal responsibility of the state. Likewise, educational practices in each state must be in compliance with the U.S. Constitution and other federal laws and regulations. School districts are thus required to provide all students with equal educational opportunities in nonsegregated schools; this is a federally mandated educational policy.

Equal opportunity to attend nonsegregated schools means that states are prohibited from operating racially segregated schools and classrooms. In 1954, the U.S. Supreme Court in *Brown* v. *Topeka Board of Education*[2] prohibited school districts from deliberately segregating schools on the basis of race. Prior to the 1954 *Brown* decision, ethnic minority students were formally or informally segregated from white students. (Formal, or de jure, segregation was mandated by state law; informal, or de facto, segregation was caused by neighborhood residential patterns and dominant antiintegration attitudes.) The segregated schools were justified on the legal grounds of an older Supreme Court decision, *Plessy* v. *Ferguson*, which allowed states to maintain segregated facilities, including schools, so long as they were "separate but equal."

In *Brown* the Supreme Court found enough tangible evidence, as well as psychological and educational testimony, to support the argument that segregated, separated schools were inherently unequal. The facts of *Brown* were that black segregated schools received a disproportionately small share of financial resources from the states, and the segregated black schools were older and more hazardous. The facts were seen as evidence that black schools were separate but not equal. The quality and the nature of the teaching and learning that occurred in the schools were not assessed. Rather, the facts of the *Brown* case emphasized the material inequality of black schools. The public mythology that the quality of teaching and learning was poor in the black schools prevailed, although we still have no concrete data or evidence to support the myth. In fact, one might easily believe that the teachers, in order to teach in the ill-equipped and under-financed schools, were dedicated and committed to their students.

Provisions under the U.S. Civil Rights Act of 1964[3] require school districts to comply with the school desegregation orders that emerged from the *Brown* case. The U.S. Office of Civil Rights has the authority to investigate charges of school discrimination and other forms of unequal educational treatment. If a school district is found in noncompliance with the various equal opportunity regulations, it faces loss of its federal financial aid. Once found in noncompliance, the district is mandated to devise a plan which would alleviate the civil rights violations. Then it must demonstrate to officials of the Office of Civil Rights that it has made a good faith effort to initiate the plan and thereby alleviate the educational inequities.

School districts have available to them resources for general and technical assistance in alleviating educational inequities. The Civil Rights Act of 1964 provides appropriations for General Assistance Centers to be established in every federal region in the country. Further, each state can be funded to operate a Technical Assistance Center within its state education agency. Also, school districts can be funded jointly with universities to establish in-service desegregation institutes for their teachers and staff. However, state and local agencies do not always take advantage of these resources.

Equal educational opportunity must be provided for students who (1) may not speak English, (2) may have limited English-speaking abilities, and (3) may live in homes where a language other than English is the dominant mode of communication. Authority to require school districts to alleviate inequities based on a student's language background came from the *Lau* v. *Nichols*[4] decision. The *Lau* v. *Nichols* suit was a class action on behalf of Chinese-speaking students who attended the San Francisco schools. In the lawsuit, the students presented facts that revealed that Chinese students were expelled from school more often, dropped out of school more often, and were low achievers more often than non-Chinese students. This was seen as evidence that the school district's English-only policy placed Chinese-speaking students at a disadvantage. The school district defended its English-only policy, arguing that Chinese American students were provided an equal opportunity to a free public education because they were provided the same textbooks, in the same language (English), and were taught by equally qualified English-speaking teachers. The Supreme Court ruled in favor of the students. The court's decision was based on the notion that the same program for all students in the same language was no guarantee of an equal opportunity to learn, especially when the students didn't speak or understand English. Consequently, the court ruled that schools must provide special language programs for students who don't understand or speak English. Schools usually adopt English as a second language or transitional bilingual programs to meet the *Lau* requirement. (See the bilingual model in Chapter 8 for a description of these programs.) Technical or general assistance, similar to that provided for general school desegregation, is available to school districts.

"Equal opportunity" to a free public education also means that schools must provide equal, nonsegregated facilities and educational experiences for physically and mentally handicapped students, for female as well as male students, and, of course, for all students regardless of religious or political backgrounds. In other words, handicapped students can no longer be segregated all day in "special" education classes. Under Public Law 94–142, Education for All Handicapped Children,[5] handicapped children must either be mainstreamed in regular classes or, in special classes, provided with an individualized educational program geared to their specific needs. Female students can no longer be excluded from participation in school athletic teams, or from school subjects formerly considered for male students only, such as industrial arts and auto mechanic classes. Further, schools must make an effort to eliminate segregated subjects once considered to be the domain of female students, such as home economics, typing, and clerical skills classes. Technical and general assistance is available to school districts to help alleviate discrimination against handicapped as well as female students. (See Title IX, Education Amendment Acts, 1973.)

For Native Americans, who were granted U.S. citizenship as late as 1924, the Indian Education Act of 1972[6] provides federal assistance for equal opportunities in schools and universities. The act, commonly regarded as Title IV, has five parts: part A provides school districts funds to meet the special needs of Native Americans in their classrooms; part B provides funds to Indian tribes as well as state and local educational agencies to improve educational opportunities for Native Americans; part C provides funds for adult education to Indian tribes and local and state agencies; part D provides a federal office, the

Office of Indian Education within the U.S. Office of Education; part E provides funds to universities to train persons to serve Native American children. The significance of the Indian Education Act is that Indian tribes can receive direct assistance from the U.S. government without the bureaucratic interference of the Bureau of Indian Affairs. Further, the act affirms that Native American youth and adults are to be accorded educational opportunities on equal grounds with other groups.

The bottom line to equal educational opportunity is that school boards, administrators, and teachers must be committed to providing equal educational opportunities. While the equal opportunity laws mandate, they cannot insure that students will be provided equal opportunities. *Adults in charge of schooling are the people who can insure that equal opportunity happens. Laws, in and of themselves, cannot guarantee equal educational opportunity, but committed people can.*

REGIONAL AND INTERNATIONAL COMMUNITIES

The *regional community* has no legal or political power over schools, per se. What the regional community has are the values, customs, and attitudes which have evolved in different geographic regions of the United States. For example, schools in the southwestern United States are influenced by the pervasive cultural forces of the Anglo, Mexican American, and Native American peoples in that region. In the South, schools are influenced by the pervasive cultural forces of various peoples: the "hill" people, the French and Cajun peoples, blacks, Native Americans, and at one time the Spanish. What is important to understand is that the school exists within the context of a regional community and is influenced by the region's cultural and social forces. The state school system and its districts are ultimately responsible to and governed by the Constitution, Supreme Court decisions, the laws enacted by Congress, and the regulations promulgated by various federal cabinet offices which are administrative branches of the president's office, particularly the Department of Education.

The *international community* does not have political or legal authority over public schools either. However, political, economic, and social forces and circumstances have an impact on the public schools.[7] For example, after the U.S. government's involvement in the Vietnam war ceased, thousands of Vietnamese refugees emigrated to the United States. Within months, schools throughout the United States were enrolling Vietnamese children. Most of them spoke no English; all of them had a distinctively different cultural background than their new teachers and classmates. Schools had to redesign language and cultural programs and arrange for Vietnamese teacher aides, translators, and curriculum materials.

The effects of other forces in the international community may be much more indirect but just as pervasive. Take, for example, the economic and political pressures on the United States from so-called third-world, oil-rich countries. Their actions have changed the way business, labor, industry, and educational leaders perceive them, and have made us all aware of the critical interdependence of nations throughout the world. Certainly, these changes have been reflected in the classroom. Table 4.1 summarizes the complexities of the relationship between the school and its communities.

STUDYING THE LOCAL SCHOOL COMMUNITY

"Good grief," you might exclaim, "I just want to teach kids how to read, or spell, or how to shoot a basket, or think like a mathematician, or. . . . Now you're telling me that I have to be a politician who tries to please everyone, and at the same time never pleases anyone." The political realities of teaching in the public schools require that you understand the political dynamics of the school and its communities so that you can adroitly manage your classroom experiences rather than be managed by political and social forces. You should be realistic about the local community, sensitive to its prevailing *ethos* and *mores*,

Table 4.1 RELATIONSHIPS BETWEEN SCHOOL AND COMMUNITIES

COMMUNITY	AUTHORITY	INFLUENCES
Local	Elects school boards, determines educational policies through school board, raises and lowers local taxes for school revenue.	Local religious, ethnic, economic, political groups express concerns and apply pressure to influence policies and practices.
State	Education is legal function of the state. State constitution, laws, State Department of Education regulations basis of educational policy.	State religious, ethnic, economic, political groups exert pressure to influence educational policy, laws, and regulations at the state level.
National	U.S. Constitution and federal laws, Supreme Court decisions pertaining to students' civil rights.	National religious, ethnic, economic, political groups exert pressure to influence policy at the federal level.
International	No legal authority, but considerable influence and impact on the U.S. through economic, political, military events.	

and above all, knowledgeable about its socioeconomic base. You should study the local community as though you were an anthropologist trying to understand a different culture.

When studying a cultural group, anthropologists use an observation technique called participation-observation.[8] Simply put, the technique is to participate fully in the cultural group experience while attempting, at times, to observe discrete behaviors and attitudes within the cultural group. In the setting of teaching and learning, use of the technique is explained in the following scenario:

You have been hired to teach in the Cottonwood School District. You move to Cottonwood, rent an apartment, find your school, and quickly are swept into the swing of events: teaching classes, meeting colleagues, attending school events and professional meetings. Halfway through the year, you decide to stick it out another year if rehired. You've established home base, but now you've got to build your career on your teaching effectiveness, which relies on your knowledge of your specialty as well as your knowledge of the community. If you're deficient in your specialty, during the summer you can travel, take college courses, or read to alleviate deficiencies. Now how to study the community:

1. Begin with a blank slate. Try to erase all the gossip and grapevine folk wisdom you've heard about the community.

2. Join some nonschool related community group, such as a civic club, a church group, or a community action group.

3. Become involved in the group's activities and develop friends within the group. Listen to them as they share concerns and interests. Then share your concerns about becoming an effective teacher in the community. Listen to their advice. Their comments will reveal their value systems as well as their perceptions regarding the prevailing ethos and mores, the powerful business and social cliques—the so-called power structure—of the community.

4. Weigh and consider their perceptions with your feelings, values, and perceptions. Remember that you should not judge their perceptions; you should instead consider their reference so as to understand why they feel the way they do.

5. Survey the community. Get in your car and ride around it. Contrary to public myth, most communities are stratified according to some broad categories, such as social class, professional and vocational class, religious, racial, or ethnic-group membership. Ride around the community. Visit stores and industries in the community and try to get a feel for the daily dips and curves of the community. Visit cemeteries and read the tombstones. Americans, especially those who can afford the costs, are particular about where they bury their dead. Others have no choice because they are poor, or because many cemetery owners discriminate against ethnic minorities. Thus, in the Southwest, clear lines are sometimes drawn to mark the cemeteries in which Mexican Americans are buried. The same is the case in

other parts of the country, such as the South, where black and white cemeteries are still segregated according to race. Don't be reluctant to visit with local business, labor, and religious leaders. Get their opinions about the purpose of teaching and learning. Why are they paying taxes for schools, ask them?

6. Visit with as many parents as you can. Get to know your students' homes and parental backgrounds. Walk to the homes, or if your students are bussed to school, take a bus to visit parents. Get a feel for the students' lives outside school. Maintain your respect for the parents and students, and maintain your self-respect. Remember that regardless of cultural, social class, or ethnic-group affiliation, the parents have in common with you concern for the welfare and education of their children. If they sense in you a genuine commitment to the teaching of their children, they will respond in kind by working with you to enhance their children's education.

7. Once having accomplished all of the above, you should have a good feel for the community if as a participant-observer you have kept an open mind about the community's people and cultural groups, if you have become genuinely involved in some community group's activities, and if you have become acquainted with your students' parents and home environments. Also, keep in mind that people, communities, and groups change. Therefore, for as long as you teach in the community, you must continue the participation-observation role.

I share this scenario with you so that you may avoid the pitfall of becoming an alienated teacher in the community. Even though you may be a first rate scholar, ignorance about the local community can spell failure for a new teacher. Here I will digress to tell my war story about the time I attempted to teach an important lesson, but out of ignorance of the community, nearly failed and nearly lost my job.

In a southwestern United States small town, I took a job as an American literature teacher. I soon realized that my students could not appreciate contemporary American literature because they believed that social class and ethnic minority discrimination did not exist in the community, in spite of the facts that the poor people lived on the east side of the tracks, and Mexican Americans and Native American adult males could only frequent certain stores and churches. I decided to sensitize my students to the anguish of poverty and racism through American literature. Consequently, I developed a unit on great American writers who had addressed the themes of poverty and racism. First, we read John Steinbeck's *The Grapes of Wrath*. No sooner than the second chapter, the school board demanded a meeting with me, my principal, and the superintendent. I attended the emergency meeting where a report was read about how my students' parents objected to *The Grapes of Wrath*. Why had I chosen *that* novel? When I explained my goals and objectives, the school board members praised my efforts to counter elitist and racist attitudes in the community. They also reminded me that fifty percent of the community were Oklahoma people who had lived in the Dust Bowl of Oklahoma, who had lost their land, and who had migrated west in hope of a better life. *The Grapes of Wrath* was so close to the truth that it hurt too much. Parents demanded my resignation, altruistic goals or not! I decided to visit the disgruntled parents, teach other novels (such as *The Adventures of Huckleberry Finn*, which is much more controversial since it deals with white racism, violence, and poverty), and learn better the community. I kept my job and achieved my goals. End of a nonfairy tale.

Moral: as a teacher you are hired to teach skills, knowledge, and attitudes considered by some community members as essential to the survival of their children. Because your students are not your children, you must consider the values, beliefs, and attitudes of parents when making decisions about teaching and learning. Consequently, you must be true to yourself and true to parents. You must have the courage of your convictions, and you must never allow yourself to be in a position where you only carry out orders. I am asking you to be a real professional, a person who acts on well-articulated assumptions, specific educational goals and objectives, and applies them in such a manner that students benefit from their implementation. I do not mean to paint a grim picture of incompatible forces. But teaching and learning activities, after all, are assertions of values. In fact, you will teach what you value, and for better or worse, your students soon sense what you value. How you resolve value influences of the school's communities which conflict with your values is an ongoing process, a process which should always receive your most serious consideration.

Hold your judgments about the community and the schools in abeyance. Discuss with experienced teachers and administrators your observations, but again, listen to these voices of experience with professional objectivity. Some teachers and administrators have ethnocentric biases about minority students and will share them with you, thereby creating a skewed picture of your teaching-learning situation. Some experienced teachers and administrators have commitments to excellence and can provide you with very helpful hints, resources, and ideas for dealing with minority students *and* the school's community forces.

SCHOOLS AS A COMMUNITY AFFAIR

This chapter's recurring theme is that schools are a community affair. Like all human affairs, some fare better than others. Some teachers and administrators are very responsive to their communities; this is often the case in white, suburban school districts, where educators maintain constant communication with parents, informing them of school meetings and events. Parent-teacher organizations, such as the PTA (Parent-Teachers Association), although often controlled by the teachers or administrators, actively involve parents in school activities like fund raising for new playground equipment. In other schools, teachers and administrators are aloof from their communities, and condescending toward parents and other community members. These educators view themselves as several notches on the social totem pole above the squalid clients they are supposed to serve. In particular, this second category of school people is most evident in urban lower-class or ethnic minority schools. When asked about their posture, these educators will assert that school and community relationships are a two-way street which the parents do not use. Parents, according to these educators, rarely attend meetings or teacher-parent conferences. When asked what the educators have done to improve the "two-way street" so as to pave the way for better relations, the gist of their answers is usually that they've done little or nothing. Instead, by their aloofness, these educators have antagonized or alienated their parent clients. In some rural districts, educators who are aloof from their communities may soon find themselves unemployed. In these communities, parents and community members place high stakes in the school and its activities. A Friday night basketball game is a major recreational event, and the school play is a primary cultural arts activity in their eyes. These parents expect cooperation from the educators. In other rural areas, the educators run the schools with an iron fist and parents and community members acquiesce. In the final analysis, schools exist because some community of people, through tradition or accident, are compelled under law to send their children to some kind of school.

Of course, there are a few small communities, such as the Amish people, who send their children to school for only part of their education, kindergarten through eighth grade. The Amish then educate their children in their socioreligious way of life. At times in the state of Utah, polygamist communities have chosen to provide schooling for their youth rather than sending them to some of the local district's schools. These nonconforming communities must comply with local and state regulations by providing or allowing some education of their children because education is an important interest of the state. Even though these nonconforming communities may isolate their youth, they cannot completely shut out the impact of the state, national, and international communities.

This chapter has analyzed the relationship that exists between the school and the loosely interconnected communities that influence teaching and learning within the classroom. Students learn their culture through their homes and families, and they learn their culture through the general communal living beliefs and habits within their respective communities. They acquire additional cultural orientations through the schools and their teachers. The teachers and the schools serve as conduits that interpret the events of all the communities that have an impact on the school. Teachers are in the position of cultural ambassadors interpreting and explaining the outside world to their students. The teacher must support or counter local or regional biases which may or may not be congruent with his or her own biases or beliefs. Speaking out against local mores and beliefs has cost a few teachers their jobs, but in the final analysis, teachers should keep the courage of their convictions, especially when they pertain to ethnic and racial biases that militate against healthy student growth and development.

Notes

1. John Dewey. *Democracy and Education.* New York: Macmillan, 1916; see also, Richard Pratte. *Ideology and Education.* New York: McKay, 1977.
2. *Brown* v. *Board of Education.* 345 U.S. 972, 1954.
3. U.S. Civil Rights Act, 1964.
4. *Lau* v. *Nichols.* 414 U.S. 563, 1973.
5. Education for All Handicapped Children Act—1975. 20 USC 1401, 1975.
6. The Indian Education Act of 1972, P.L. 92–318.
7. Richard Remy. *International Learning and International Education in a Global Age.* Washington, D.C.: National Council for the Social Studies, 1975.
8. Severyn T. Bruyn. "The Methodology of Participant Observation," in Joan I. Roberts and Sherrie K. Akinsanya, *Educational Patterns and Cultural Configurations.* New York: McKay, 1976, pp. 247–263; see also, Gerry Rosenfeld. "Shut Those Fat Lips." *A Study of Slum School Failure.* New York: Holt, Rinehart and Winston, 1971; see also, James P. Spradley and David W. McCurdy. *The Cultural Experience: Ethnography in Complex Society.* Chicago: Science Research Associates, 1972.

Chapter 5
Ethnocentrism, Racism, Stereotyping

If students acquire their culture in their homes, communities, and schools, where do they acquire ethnic and racial biases and prejudices? Do their parents and teachers unconsciously transmit ethnic and racial biases? Prejudice against ethnic and racial minority peoples is a persistent problem in the United States, and it affects teaching and learning in public schools in both subtle and obvious ways. Some of the obvious ways are beyond this book's scope. However, a visit to a typical urban school district reveals obvious forms of institutional discrimination. Many schools located in poor neighborhoods serve mostly ethnic minorities. Note that these schools are physically dilapidated and poorly equipped when compared to schools in more affluent neighborhoods. More subtle ways that students acquire ethnic and racial biases are through the attitudes of their parents as well as the prevailing attitudes expressed in their communities and schools. Most teachers do not consciously teach prejudice. Rather, they may fail to counter the biases that penetrate their classroom walls, because these biases are endemic to U.S. communal living.

This chapter describes the sociocultural forces of ethnocentrism, racism, and stereotyping common to American life but not understood or discussed in standard teacher education programs. The intent is to clarify the processes of the sociocultural forces so that teachers can better deal with these pernicious and very real social forces. Understanding these forces can also provide teachers a way to approach cultural relativism and the notion that cultures can be different without being either better or worse.

ETHNOCENTRISM AND CULTURAL RELATIVISM

The *raison d'être* of cultural relativism in the classroom is to allow students to benefit equally from the schooling experience irrespective of their ethnic, racial, or cultural backgrounds. It is now axiomatic that ethnic minority students do not benefit equally from public schooling when their academic success rates are compared to those of white, middle-class students; this can be attributed in part to the strong white, middle-class bias of most U.S. public schools. Thus, we find that cultural relativism alone is not enough. Its effects can be neutralized by extreme forms of ethnocentrism—racism, prejudice, stereotyping, discrimination—that occur outside the classroom, especially if they are allowed to slip into the classroom through unconscious attitudes and beliefs of teachers, other educators, and students. To proactively counter these extreme forms of ethnocentrism, educators need to understand not only the nature but also the types of ethnocentrisms that can be dealt with in the public school classroom. Unlike Don Quixote, teachers need to be selective about the social windmills they take on to insure that the encounter is successful and benefits their students and communities.

Extreme ethnocentrisms are unpleasant realities. They take their toll in the daily conflicts of intergroup, interethnic relations of American society. "Racism," "prejudice," "stereotyping," "discrimination" are loaded with negative connotations; in ostensibly polite company, these negative social phenomena are not discussed, but this only serves to intensify their tenacity. Therefore, it is critical that we discuss the terms from as objective as possible a point of view. Admittedly, objectivity is not easy. I will define the terms broadly and then discuss each as pertinent to ethnic and racial relations in American communal life.

ETHNOCENTRISM, CULTURAL PRIDE, CHAUVINISM, AND DEGRADATION

The universal attitude of pride in one's own ethnic or cultural group is known as *ethnocentrism*.[1] Ethnocentrism serves the function of providing a group with solidarity and unity. An ethnic or cultural group is solidified by a pervading sense of peoplehood, as in the phrase "We, the People," of the Constitution. The sense of peoplehood is felt with differing degrees of intensity by its members. As such, ethnocentrism is a dynamic social force that can be cohesive or corrosive in a society. When ethnocentrism causes bigotry and intolerance, or whenever ethnocentrism causes alienation and social dejection, it is corrosive; whenever it causes group and individual self-esteem, it is cohesive. Thus, ethnocentrism appears within a society in at least three variegated forms: cultural pride, cultural degradation, and cultural chauvinism.

Cultural pride is a positive form of ethnocentrism. In this context, cultural pride refers to self-respect or self-esteem for one's ethnic or cultural heritage. It is necessary for positive group identity and is essential to ethnic group solidarity. It is also helpful in the development of positive self-identity for individual group members. When group members are allowed to grow in the awareness that their group has a rich heritage reaching back over centuries of cultural development, they can experience a sense of roots in the past and continuity in the present. By taking pride in their group's heritage, the members can develop self-esteem, and they can continue acting within their group's tradition to contribute to the overall society.

Ethnic groups in the United States have been allowed to develop cultural pride so long as the groups have also espoused beliefs in the core national ethos, such as "freedom and justice for all." Knowledgeable of the dual responsibility to country and to ethnic group, ethnic groups have achieved highly commendable wartime records as demonstrated by the World War II crack fighting units of Japanese Americans or the fact that more Mexican Americans have been awarded Congressional Medals of Honor than any other group. Because of strong Americanization forces, prejudices, and discrimination, some ethnic groups have experienced *cultural degradation*. These groups have been made to feel that their cultures are inadequate, backward, or inferior. Consequently, cultural degradation is a corrosive form of ethnocentrism. When an ethnic group experiences cultural degradation, some of its members may respond by developing attitudes of low self-esteem and self-rejection. Other members may respond by developing hostile attitudes and intolerance toward other ethnic groups.

An extreme form of ethnocentrism, *cultural chauvinism*, is an attitude that another group's ways are not only different but also are perceived as being wrong and inferior to one's own group culture. This type of group pride is similar to the Ancient Greek notion of pride, or hubris, which denoted arrogance. Ethnic-group pride is a form of ethnocentrism and can be contrasted to cultural chauvinism.

Cultural chauvinism presumes that one's in-group culture and people are superior to others, and typically, the out-group peoples are perceived as "barbaric," or "uncivilized," devoid of the in-group's redeeming values and ways. Any ethnic or cultural group is capable of chauvinistic beliefs and behaviors but it does not follow that all ethnic or cultural groups are necessarily chauvinistic. When Brown Chicano Power advocates asserted that "brown is beautiful" they did not necessarily imply that white was ugly, nor did they assert that brown skin was superior to white. It follows that ethnics and members of cultural groups can have ethnic group pride without being chauvinistic. Clearly, ethnic biases and prejudices usually spring from chauvinism rather than ethnic-group pride which stresses positive group identity. Ethnic pride here refers to self-respect or self-esteem as well as respect for one's ethnic or cultural group affiliation. Ethnic-group pride, while a mild form of ethnocentrism, is necessary for positive group identity and is essential to cultural and ethnic group revitalization. Cultural chauvinism, a corrosive form of ethnocentrism, is not necessary for group survival and not essential for cultural and ethnic-group revitalization.

The distinction between group pride as a cohesive form of ethnocentrism and cultural chauvinism and degradation as corrosive forms of ethnocentrism is made to respond to the often heard accusation that ethnic groups are currently indulging in "nationalism" and "reverse prejudice." It's true; many white ethnic groups and minority groups are currently attempting to revitalize their group cultures, and in the attempt are rekindling pride in their cultures. These revitalization efforts would not now be necessary if the impact and potency of the Americanization policies that existed in the first half of this century had not so thoroughly stifled their ethnic-group languages and cultures. In actuality, ethnic revitalization is perceived by many ethnics as a necessary, human reaction to the excessive cultural chauvinism and degradation precipitated by nativistic U.S. policies and laws during the early twentieth century.

There will be critics who will say that ethnic-group pride is doublespeak for ethnic-group chauvinism. My only reply to these critics is that if they had ever experienced great feelings of inferiority because of their ethnicity, or if they had ever felt the humiliation and economic loss of racial and ethnic discrimination, they, too, would be advocates of their self-esteem. If these critics have never felt ethnic and racial discrimination, they perhaps can never understand these words. If they have felt ethnic and racial discrimination, they cannot help but admit that these words do not adequately express the rage, humiliation, and indignation caused by cultural chauvinism and degradation.

RACISM: THE MORAL DILEMMA

Most of us are aware of racism, prejudice, and stereotyping in our communities and in ourselves. Some of us are more aware than others. All of us have difficulty discussing racism and prejudice without being defensive, cautious, angry, or timid. Fear, anxiety, and timidity block communication and hinder understanding; we need to set aside these human reactions so we may begin to understand the causes and results of racism, prejudice, stereotyping, and discrimination, particularly as they affect teaching and learning in a pluralistic society.

Katz, in a thorough study of racism in American life,[2] concluded that racism exists because of a serious cleavage between white American beliefs and actions; while some white Americans believe in equality and human rights, they act upon racist assumptions about people of color or racial minorities. According to Katz, the moral cleavage between beliefs and actions is rooted in American social, political, and economic history. In short, white racism is endemic to the American experience:

> The reality is: racism exists. It has been a part of the American way of life since the first Whites landed on the continent. Although the United States prides itself on its ideologies about human rights and particularly on its philosophies of freedom and equality, the bleak reality is that, both historically and presently, this country is based on and operates under a doctrine of White racism.[3]

A myriad of studies support the Katz thesis. On a national scope, the Myrdal study,[4] the United States Commission on Mental Health Report,[5] and the Kerner Presidential Commission Report[6] all support the thesis.

How could racism evolve in a society based on Judeo-Christian precepts of brotherhood and equality? In *Race and Racism, A Comparative Perspective*,[7] van den Berghe developed the thesis that current racism in the United States exists because of a complex dynamic of group conflict which evolved over a long period of our history. Basically, racism has served an economic function for white groups and individuals who have benefitted from the exploitation of and discrimination against racial minority peoples. While some white Americans have professed a belief in equal opportunities irrespective of race, ethnic, or social class affiliation, they have not practiced these beliefs when their economic interests were advanced through racial and ethnic-group discrimination. The moral dilemma of racism in American life is that Americans have espoused ethical values of human equality, while at times practicing unethical beliefs of racial and cultural superiority, thereby contradicting the widely professed values of human equality.

Racism—as does ethnocentrism—serves the function of providing an in-group defense against other out-groups by building racial group allegiances and unity. The important difference between ethnocentrism and racism is that racism can serve the function of maintaining a rigid caste-like system between a powerful, dominant, in-group race and other subordinate, powerless racial outgroups. In the antebellum South a racial caste-like social system evolved as a means for southern plantation owners to dominate blacks. A myth of white racial superiority and black racial inferiority evolved to rationalize white dominance. Again, racism served an economic function in that it provided white southerners beliefs that supported an economic system based on the free slave labor of blacks.

At one time, the terms "racism" and "prejudice" were used interchangeably. In this context, "racism" is the attitude that one's racial group is inherently superior to another. "Prejudice" is a negative judgment about an ethnic or racial group formed beforehand without knowledge, analysis, or evaluation of the facts about the group. While one can have positive prejudices, I am using the term "prejudice" as it is used in general American vernacular—as a negative, predisposed bias. A "stereotype" is an oversimplified, often negative conception about a member or members of a particular ethnic or racial group. "Discrimination" consists of direct or indirect act of exclusion, distinction, differentiation, or preference on account of racial or ethnic-group membership. Clearly, discrimination is an act, and, as such, it is definable in explicit terms. Racism, prejudice, and stereotype are attitudes which are manifest in discriminatory acts.

"Racism" is the attitude that one racial group is inherently superior to another.[8] Racist attitudes are extreme ethnocentrisms that reflect the prevailing norms of a racial in-group toward a racial out-group. When racist attitudes are carried out into behaviors, they result in expressions of ridicule and hate, in acts of exclusion and discrimination, and in genocide against the alleged inferior out-group. An example of biological racism carried to the degree of mass genocide is the Aryan race theory Adolph Hitler described in his autobiography *Mein Kampf*.[9] The theory, and its ideology of Aryan racial superiority, provided German Nazi officials a rationale for exterminating European Jews who were blamed (scapegoat theory) for the economic problems of Europe during the decades between 1920 and 1940.[10] German Nazi officials conducted propaganda campaigns (expressions of ridicule and hate), practiced private and official discrimination against Jews regarding property ownership and employment opportunities (acts of discrimination), and exterminated more than 6 million Jews in the Nazi concentration camps (mass genocide). Ironically, Jews are not a racial group, per se; Jews can be described more accurately as an international religious-ethnic group with a membership consisting of most known human races living on all of the major continents of the earth. While Jewish Americans were allowed to enter military services in the U.S. Armed Forces to fight against the Nazis, many of them were concurrently prohibited entrance to some American colleges and universities.[11] Thus, in the decades between 1920 and 1940 antisemitism was not exclusive to German society; it was practiced in the form of exclusion and discrimination in American society by educated U.S. citizens against American Jews.

Racism is past history, one might argue. In particular, biological racism—the attitude that one's race is genetically superior to others—has been discredited internationally, especially in the scientific community. Even the Ku Klux Klan, the epitome of biological racists, changed its focus from biological racism to white, Protestant chauvinism during the 1920s and 1930s so that Jews and Catholics (irrespective of race) along with blacks bore the brunt of their hatred. Clearly, biological racism is not a creditable scientific theory or a viable political ideology. It is past history. Further, one might argue that desegregation of the armed forces and public schools, the Civil Rights Act, increased numbers of interracial marriages, all these and many other examples tend to refute the existence of racism in contemporary U.S. society. It's true: antidiscrimination laws exist; some degree of interracial marriages and school and military desegregation exist. Most official racism has been banned by federal laws and U.S. Supreme Court decisions. But, poorly enforced and meekly supported as they are, these laws and court decisions cannot in themselves change racist attitudes. What remain are racist attitudes and beliefs which have their roots in both the folkways and official racism of U.S. society. Racist attitudes and beliefs persist in contemporary society because, as with traditions and folkways, they are deeply ingrained in the minds and consciences of many Americans. Racist attitudes perish slowly.

INDIVIDUAL AND COLLECTIVE RACISM

The preceding discussion on racism focused on the collective racism of white Americans. However, just because white racism was and is a real group social force in American life does not mean that all white Americans are racists in belief or behavior. Rather, it's important to consider that while collective racism can exist in a society, not all members of the society will be racists, as author Lillian Smith so lucidly described in her novel, *Killers of the Dream*,[12] which is about living as a white, nonracist southerner in the South. Conversely, individual racism can exist in the absence of formal, collective racism.

Consequently, it's possible that some nonsouthern, white Americans may believe and behave as white racists even though their region of the country never formalized a system of collective racism like that in the antebellum South.

CAUSES OF INDIVIDUAL RACISM

The causes of individual racism are many. There are any number of reasons why a person may harbor racial prejudices against a person of another racial group. Social scientists have isolated various human experiences which provoke racism and prejudice.[13] However, in the final analysis, racism and prejudice should be attributed to multiple causes, since they are as complex as the humans who harbor them. Theories pertaining to single causes for racism and prejudice range considerably, with varying anthropological, sociological, psychological, and historical emphases. I have categorized these theories into eight types rather than list the total number from various academic perspectives:

1. Ignorance Theory
2. Unpleasant Experience Theory
3. Negative Trait Theory
4. Scapegoat Theory
5. Pathological Personality Theory
6. Anti-Minority Liberation Theory
7. Ethnic Purity Theory
8. Internal Colony Theory

Table 5.1 describes the theories.

Theoretically, if a racist's symptoms could be isolated to manifestation of any one of the causes, a change strategy could be prescribed. Like any problem that exists, the person who owns the problem must first admit the problem, and then determine to resolve or in some way counter it. Because racist and prejudicial attitudes and behaviors are contrary to Judeo-Christian morality, it is apparently easier on the conscience to suppress rather than to admit that one harbors racist attitudes and actions; many prejudiced people will simply not acknowledge their racial and ethnic prejudices. Rather than admit existence of them, these persons will deny them, saying such things as, "I don't have *that* problem," or "I discriminate against everyone equally." This avoidance tactic, what I call the "no problem problem," simply delays resolution of the racist and prejudicial attitudes and behaviors.

Table 5.1 THEORIES OF RACISM

THEORIES ON RACISM AND PREJUDICE	ETIOLOGIES OF THEORIES
Ignorance	Racism and prejudicial attitudes and actions are caused by ignorance; a person just doesn't know the hated group and is acting on limited or biased data pertaining to the hated group.
Unpleasant Experience	A prejudiced or racist person has had unpleasant experiences with the hated persons or groups, generalizes the unpleasant experience as characteristic of the whole group: e.g., an Anglo boy gets beat up in a fight with a Mexican American boy; the Anglo boy then dislikes all Mexican American boys because they are all "mean."
Negative Trait	The prejudiced person imputes traits considered obnoxious by his or her group as characteristic of the hated groups. A stereotype exists for most ethnic groups: e.g., "the tight Scotsman, the rich Jew, the sneaky Mexican, the Italian latin lover."
Scapegoat	The racist person's prejudices are symbolic of the person's own fears, hopes, aspirations: e.g., the unsuccessful businessman blames the Jews in the community for his lack of success. Subconsciously the racist may fear that he is the cause of his failure, but rather than accept the blame, he transfers it to the hated cultural or racial group.
Pathological Personality	This places extreme racists and extremely prejudicial persons into a pathological category. According to the theory, persons with delusions of grandeur and paranoid and sadistic tendencies may hold prejudices against some hated group. The racist here has an extreme personality disorder and may be found among leaders of hate groups. This type of racist, while very dangerous, is not as common as the less extreme type.
Anti-Minority Liberation	In times of change, economic depressions, and other social crises when competition for land and basic resources is intensified, racism and prejudice against minority groups increase, thwarting the liberation of minority group members, according to this theory. A social dynamics theory, it describes the social

climate during periods of crisis: e.g., during World War II, Japanese Americans were dispossessed of their property, their constitutional and civil rights, and relocated from their west coast homes to concentration camps in the interior United States. According to the theory, disfranchisement and relocation of Japanese Americans thwarted their opportunities to establish and stabilize their group. Indeed, relocation did have the effect of dividing and weakening the group's development as a United States ethnic group.

Ethnic Purity	Under this theory, the racist avoids and prevents contact with some feared group to insure the racial or ethnic "purity" of the in-group. Those prejudiced persons who take "white flight" to segregated neighborhoods to avoid contact with minorities are examples of attempts to protect the "purity" of a certain in-group.
Internal Colony	Racism is a functional myth within certain geographic sectors of the United States: the Southwest, the urban ghetto, and the Indian reservations are in fact virtually colonized countries or groups. The colonized are people of color who are suppressed by myths of the racial superiority of the colonizer and the inferiority of the colonized. Racism serves to sustain the myth and thereby sustain the internal colonies' color/caste system. With colonialism, a colonizer invades a certain geographic area, subdues the indigenous population (the colonized), and then exploits the natural and human resources. With internal colonization, the colonizer both literally and figuratively invades a certain region, subdues the indigenous population (the colonized), and then commences to exploit. The internal colonial explanation for racism is a relative newcomer in the social sciences. Black intellectuals spawned the internal colonial thesis in the early 1960s to serve as the metaphor that describes the black experience in urban America.[14] Later, Blauner[15] demonstrated how the process of European colonization was similar in all essential ways to the process experienced by blacks in the urban ghettos. Among authors who have applied the rationale are Acuña in *Occupied America*,[16] Deloria in *Custer Died for Your Sins*,[17] and Malcolm X in *The Autobiography of Malcolm X*.[18]

NOTE: References for all footnotes within Table 5.1 are included with all references in *Notes* section at the end of Chapter 5.

If the cause of racial prejudice could be isolated, then a prescription to counter the cause might be possible. Table 5.2 presents the causal theories, briefly describes them, and provides change strategies to counter the origins. As you will quickly note, only five of the causes can be countered by teaching-learning approaches because of their nature. All of them require fundamental changes in the economic and political structure of our society.

These types of racism can be countered in the public school setting: Ignorance, Unpleasant Experience, Negative Trait, Scapegoat, and Ethnic Purity. The types of racism that cannot be countered in the public school setting are: Anti-Minority Liberation, Pathological Personality, and Internal Colony. They require strategies beyond the means of the classroom: the Anti-Minority Liberation and Internal Colony types require fundamental changes in the economic and political structures of the country, changes which can be made only by those who hold political and economic power. The Pathological Personality type requires competent psychiatric care and is beyond the limits of the classroom.

PSYCHOLOGICAL DESCRIPTIONS OF RACISM

Generic psychological descriptions for racist and prejudicial attitudes and actions are not so difficult to identify. Research studies report that a racist personality exhibits tendencies toward dogmatism and authoritarianism. The racist personality structure is rigid, manifesting categorical thinking and/or insecure feelings with people who are racially or culturally different.[19] Racist attitudes and feelings revolve around the axis of fear of cultural differences; in other words, cultural differences, and the people who exhibit them, pose a felt threat to the racist. To alleviate the fear and remove the insecurities caused by contact with racially and culturally different people, the prejudiced person will tend to avoid and exclude the "different" people from his or her social circles, neighborhoods, and schools. This kind of avoidance pattern, when practiced by enough members of a group, leads to social and neighborhood exclusion and segregation of racial outgroups.[20] Isolated and segregated away from the out-group, the ingroup members substitute misconceptions, myths, and stereotypes about the feared group for the more authentic traits that contact might actuate.

Racism can be analyzed as an intergroup reality that functions on a continuum between covert and overt degrees of action and behavior (see Figure 5.1). At the continuum's base, covert racism is an emotional experience, a feeling of distaste, discomfort, or anxiety toward a member or members of a racial group. This feeling, however acquired, re-

Table 5.2 CHANGE STRATEGIES AGAINST RACISM

THEORY	CAUSE OF RACISM	CHANGE STRATEGY
Ignorance	Ethnic/racial illiteracy; poor understanding of culturally different peoples.	New data; new knowledge about culturally different peoples. (Ethnic Studies Model)
Unpleasant Experience	Bad experience with cultural/racial groups.	Positive experiences with cultural/racial groups, preferably on a one-to-one basis. (Intergroup Relations Strategy)
Negative Trait	Same as Ignorance, but stress on stereotypes about cultural/racial groups.	Same as for Ignorance, but stress frontal attack on stereotypes. Do not replace stereotypes with "positive" stereotypes; rather, study racial/cultural groups from the groups' perspective. (Ethnic Studies Model/Intergroup Relations Strategy)
Scapegoat	Racism and prejudice with a purpose. Racism represents something more basic, such as desire to maintain class/caste system in which minority groups remain second-class citizens. Frustrations ostensibly caused by racial/cultural group; thus, racist hostile toward members of the group.	Reason with students about how democracy cannot function with tyranny of the majority, which is self-defeating, or with a second-class citizenship class/caste system. Appeal to universal human rights. (Human Rights Strategy)
Anti-Minority Liberation	Economic and political change provokes fears and insecurities in racist, who benefits from the status quo. Thus, racist attempts to block progress of cultural/racial group.	An economic and political problem which requires political and economic solutions, such as fundamental changes in government and financial system.
Pathological Personality	Racism a pathological syndrome of deeply repressed fears, anxieties, and other emotional disorders.	Competent psychoanalysis or therapy.
Ethnic Purity	Extreme form of ethnocentrism which uses racist attitudes and actions to prevent contact with certain racial/cultural groups.	Planned and controlled contact with the hated group. Unplanned, arbitrary contact can do more harm than good. (Intergroup Relations Strategy)
Internal Colony	Racism is a functional myth to sustain a color/caste colonial system within the United States.	Fundamental economic and political rearrangements to dismantle the internal colonial structure.

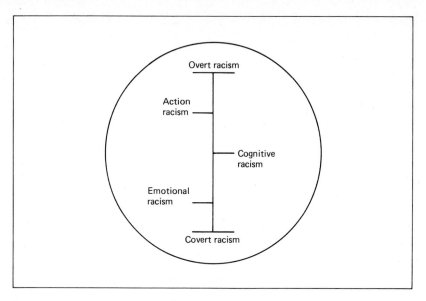

Figure 5.1   Degrees of Overt and Covert Racism

mains a feeling which is suppressed, hidden, and avoided; covertly racist attitudes are deep structure feelings suppressed almost entirely out of consciousness. At the continuum's zenith, overt racism consists of actions—such as avoidance, discourtesy, exclusion, exploitation, and violence—directed against members of a racial or ethnic out-group. The civil rights movement of the 1960s was a movement against overt racism. Minority groups, with assistance from white groups and individuals, launched an all-out attack against discrimination in public housing, public schools, and public health and social welfare programs. Demands were met: laws were enacted which in effect prohibited overt racism in public institutions.

At the continuum's middle range is cognitive racism. Cognitive racism consists of characteristics of both emotional and action (behavioral) racism. In the middle range, a person may feel (emotional) prejudices against an ethnic or racial group, and may also act out those feelings. For example, one sees emotional racism when parents object to the marriage of their ethnic majority daughter to an ethnic minority male. These parents, who are opposed to overt racism and who support principles of equal opportunities, will oppose the marriage on grounds other than race or ethnicity. Citing ostensible religious or social class differences, the parents express concern for the future stability of the marriage. The bottom line of their opposition is "they are not ready for such a radical move." In other words, the parents still harbor fears and prejudices about the social and genetic hazards of interracial marriage.

The covert-overt continuum provides a way of conceptualizing racism as a matter of degrees rather than absolutes. Thus, a racist can be a "little" prejudiced, "somewhat" prejudiced, or "very" prejudiced. What are the differences between a person who is an emotional racist, a cognitive racist, and an action racist? The differences are matters of degree. The extremes are easy to explain. If you are a member of a hate group, a group that advocates and conducts acts of violence against members of ethnic or racial out-groups, as do members of the Ku Klux Klan, then your racism is overt. If you are a member of a love group, for example, a Christian church which condemns ethnic and racial prejudice but maintains ethnic and racial segregation in the decision-making process of the church, you are a supporter of emotional racism. Consider the fact that many Christian denominations segregate ethnic and racial minorities. Rather than integrating them into the church structure, ethnic minority groups are "allowed" to have their "Second Baptist Church" or "La Iglesia de los Baptistas." These are the benevolent racists, who for all intents and purposes do not mean to be exclusionary, but their action or inaction is what allows such segregated churches to exist.

The cognitive racist is not so easy to identify. This is the person who has been taught through early socialization that certain ethnic and racial out-groups are inferior. This person would insist that the evidence supports such a notion. Yet this person is bothered by the fact that some minorities are superior—for example, Albert Einstein and Henry Kissinger as Jews. The cognitive racist tries to rationalize these individuals as exceptions to the rule of their race. Thus, Martin Luther King, Jr., was an exception to the rule that black Americans are inferior, or former U.S. Representative Carl Albert of the state of Oklahoma (part white and part Native American) was an exception to the rule that Native Americans are racially inferior.

Looking at racist thinking and behavior from the vantage point of a continuum extending from overt to covert degrees of reality provides another way of understanding racism in American life. Understand that racist attitudes and behaviors are learned; they are not inborn or genetically transmitted. Racism is learned.[21] A child is born without racism. Dependent on parents for sustenance, the child assumes and adopts the parents' attitudes and values, attitudes and values which represent the parents' group norms. At an early age, the child exhibits preferences for associating with members of the majority or the in-group.[22] By age 4, white children may show a preference for being white and a dislike of blacks.[23] The people who are viewed by the child as the out-group are determined by the dominant racism of the child's society (blacks in the South; Mexican Americans in the Southwest; Native Americans in whatever regions they live in; Asian Americans in the West) or region, even though the child has no contact with the perceived out-group. Before the age of 12 or 13, the child is usually not aware of his or her racism, but as the child progresses into the teens, awareness of racism increases. A preteenage child usually cannot give reasons for racist attitudes, but during the teens, children usually recite traditional in-group reasons for their racism.[24]

A greatly misunderstood method for changing racist attitudes and improving intergroup relations is the so-called contact thesis.[25] Early proponents of this thesis felt that racist attitudes could be diminished by more contact between the in- and out-groups. The rationale was that racist attitudes evolve through limited or no contact between groups, thereby creating a social space in which racist attitudes can grow. However, reduction of racist attitudes and feelings requires more than contact.[26] In other words, mere contact alone will not significantly reduce racist attitudes; in fact, more contact may serve to perpetuate or increase racist attitudes. For example, merely busing black and white students to the same schools so that they will come in contact will not necessarily change the students' attitudes toward each other. Mere contact alone may exacerbate the prevalent group hostilities. What is done with the contact—how school officials and teachers create a school climate conducive to equal-status student contact— will determine the contact's efficacy. The contact thesis fails to consider that the nature and degree of contact between groups, in a historical and contemporary context, have an impact on the groups' perceptions and attitudes. It is naive to believe that unplanned or uncontrolled contact between minority and majority group students will make a positive difference in their interpersonal relationships. In fact, this type of contact may do more damage than no contact at all. Since the history of racial minorities and whites in our society has consistently placed minorities in a subordinate role and status, there is no reason to believe that mere in-school contact will change the attitudes and beliefs of white or minority students.

TEACHERS AND ETHNIC AND RACIAL DISCRIMINATION

Do teachers unconsciously transmit ethnic or racial biases? And, do teachers discriminate against ethnic and racial minority students? Answers to these questions are "yes," "no," and "sometimes." Traditionally, classroom teachers have been expected to represent a high degree of moral and ethical standards. At one time, teachers were forbidden to smoke, court in public, swear, or use obscene language. In other words, teachers were expected to be the epitome of respectability. Now it is clear that these expectations were unrealistic, and teachers (especially those in urban areas) have much more ethical and moral latitude. In fact, few if any teacher certification requirements address the question of teachers' morality. The same is the case with teachers' attitudes regarding race or ethnicity. An avowed racist and an avowed nonracist could with almost equal ease achieve certification in most states, because the questions of a person's racial attitudes and ethnocentrisms are simply not raised in the process of teacher certification.

At times, teachers do transmit unconscious ethnic and racial biases. These biases may represent ethnic group pride (mild ethnocentrism), or they may represent cultural chauvinism (extreme ethnocentrism). At times, teachers do discriminate against minority students. These acts of discrimination may be based on notions of biological racism— for example, treating racial minority students as though they are incapable of learning because of the genetic inferiority of their racial group. Or, the discrimination may be based on notions of cultural chauvinism—for example, treating ethnic minority students as though they are incapable of learning because they have "no culture" or a "deficient culture." Few teachers operate from notions of biological racism. Some probably operate from notions of cultural chauvinism.

How can bias and discrimination be discerned in teachers? We have seen that ethnocentrism, racism, and prejudice are attitudes. These attitudes, when translated into behavior, are manifested in expressions of ridicule and hate, and in acts of exclusion, violence, and genocide. When teachers discriminate against ethnic and minority students, they may use expressions of ridicule, such as telling ethnic jokes in class or making ethnic slurs ("Quit acting like a bunch of wild Indians!"). They may discriminate with acts of exclusion: for example, neglecting to include minority students in important classroom activities requiring leadership. Or they may discriminate by holding low academic expectations for minority students. A teacher may have racist or ethnocentric attitudes and yet not discriminate; conversely, a teacher may not have racist or ethnocentric attitudes and yet discriminate. The question here is how can one detect teacher discrimination?

TOWARD A TYPOLOGY OF TEACHER DISCRIMINATION

Sociologist Robert Merton developed a typology of ethnic prejudice and discrimination. The typology describes four types of ethnic and racial discriminators:

1. Unprejudiced nondiscriminator—"all-weather" liberal
2. Unprejudiced discriminator—"fair-weather" liberal
3. Prejudiced nondiscriminator—"fair-weather" illiberal
4. Prejudiced discriminator—"all-weather" illiberal[27]

The first type believes in the American creed of equality and opportunity and doesn't discriminate against people of color. The second types believes in the creed, but doesn't always practice it. He or she will practice the creed when made aware of and made to feel guilty about the dissonant behavior. The third type doesn't believe in the American creed and doesn't believe it applies to people of color, but will practice it if forced to by social pressure or the law. The last type is an avowed racist who doesn't believe in the creed and doesn't practice it.

Applying the Merton typology to teachers, one might type teachers into four categories:

1. The prominority nondiscriminating teacher
2. The prominority discriminating teacher
3. The antiminority nondiscriminating teacher
4. The antiminority discriminating teacher

A type 1 teacher serves as a spokesperson for minority students, and has high expectations of them, inspiring them to excell. A type 2 teacher quietly supports and encourages minority students, although he or she may not have high expectations of them. This kind of teacher can be made to feel a need for a change in attitudes and can be trained to become a type 1 teacher.

A type 3 teacher doesn't believe in the American creed of equal opportunity, but as a responsible professional, will instruct any student who enrolls in the class; this type will more than likely remain distant, even remote, from the minority students. If teaching in a school community highly supportive of minority students, such a teacher will be under pressure to be more nurturing. The reverse is also true; in an antiminority school community, the teacher may be rewarded in various ways for discrimination. Collegial pressure by type 1 teachers and administrators on type 3 teachers could change their attitudes to type 2 attitudes, at least. In a school where most of the teachers are type 3, administrative leadership would have to apply pressure to change their attitudes. The problem is compounded when the majority of teachers and administrators are type 3, all presumably hired by type 3 school board members or the superintendent. In this case, nothing can really be done to change attitudes. A type 1 or 2 teacher's choices would be either to leave the school, to "buck the system" continually, hoping to change it, or to accept the prevailing ethos and make minor changes in student attitudes in the classroom.

The type 4 teacher is an extreme case of personality rigidity. The type 4 teacher doesn't believe in equal opportunity and overtly or covertly discriminates against minority students. Only in a very non-discriminatory school community, where social pressure would not reward and might even punish type 4 behavior, would a type 4 teacher be nondiscriminatory.

Although individual people are not types, we can use the four types discussed above to assess where one stands in relation to ethnic and racial minority students. Yet the problem with attempts to assess teacher discrimination is that racism and cultural chauvinism are attitudes which can be transmitted to students without deliberate acts of discrimination. Amorphous human factors, such as tone of voice, innuendo, and other transluscent acts can nevertheless transmit ethnic and racial bias. Cultural and ethnic group stereotyping speaks to this point.

CULTURAL AND ETHNIC STEREOTYPING

There is much truth in the adage, "birds of a feather flock together." Or, the group one is in, the company one keeps, and the social circles one circulates in, all can teach racism and prejudice. It is not surprising to find college-educated white Americans who have stereotypic notions about black Americans—stereotypes taught them by their respective groups. Having had little contact with black Americans in the public schools or in colleges. and having only their group's folk wisdom knowledge about blacks, these college-trained individuals know very little about the largest minority group in the country. Neither is it surprising to meet college-trained minority people who have a variety of stereotypes about white Americans, especially since stereotyping is the result of limited and distorted information about some out-group. We now turn our attention to the concept of stereotyping.

What motivates stereotyping? Economic gain? Social gain? Domination over a particular group? Or simply human insensitivity to others? All of these, perhaps? Cultural and racial stereotypes stem from at least two of the causation theories, the negative traits and ethnic purity theories. Members of an ethnic or racial in-group will impute negative traits to some out-group. By imputing these negative traits to the out-group, members of the in-group have a reason to avoid contact with out-group members. Avoidance in turn assures the preservation of the "purity" of the in-group. Understand that in normal human interaction *social typing* is necessary.[28] Social typing is what people do in the course of daily events: that is, we make assumptions about the way certain types of people should act, and then we act on those assumptions, treating the person according to our assumptions, and thereby providing that person a role in our relationship. For example, we assume that a lawyer will be meticulous and thorough about our legal problems. We expect a lawyer to ask all types of minute questions so as to become thoroughly informed about our legal problems. We expect the lawyer to tell us whether we really have a case, or whether, in the lawyer's opinion, the law would support our case. We also type people by stigmatizing them on the basis of physical characteristics such as deformities, weight, and height; we are all familiar with such stigmatizations as the "jolly fat person," or the "agile midget."

A racial or cultural stereotype is a kind of social type.[29] A stereotype is an in-group's oversimplified conception of members of an out-group. The conception is devoid of traits valued by the in-group and is loaded with traits devalued by the in-group. Consider a stereotype about Mexican Americans in the southwestern United States. There exists a southwestern Anglo conception about Mexican Americans: an image of a Mexican slumped against a cactus plant, a tequila bottle in one hand, taking a siesta. This image is supposed to reflect Mexican American cultural values: they are lazy, sleep in the middle of the day (they lack industry!), and get drunk on tequila. Notice that the stereotype is devoid of the Anglo values of the work ethic and sobriety; rather, the image is loaded with traits devalued by the Anglo group such as drunkenness and laziness. In other words, in-group members develop exaggerated perceptions about some out-group largely because the in-group has little data or contact with the out-group or because the stereotype serves to support the material or economic interests of the in-group. Depicting Mexican Americans as lazy serves to vindicate the low wages Anglo farmers pay Mexican American migrant workers. High wages would only be paid to hard workers! Then the in-group commences to treat members of the out-group on the basis of the stereotype. By assigning the out-group a stereotypic social role, the in-group can treat out-group members in such a manner that many out-group members come to believe they actually have the assigned stereotypic traits. Thus, a self-fulfilling prophecy is effectuated.[30] A person who is treated as inferior by enough people will eventually believe he or she is inferior. Once the beliefs of inferiority take hold, such a person will act inferior in relation to others, and other people will reciprocate by treating the person as inferior. Such people perceive themselves, and are perceived by others, as inferior. For example, students who are treated by teachers as though they were not very smart will eventually believe they are not very smart. And eventually, they won't be very smart, according to standardized tests.

THE SELF-FULFILLING PROPHECY

Students respond to the expectations of their teachers. When teachers convey to students expectations based on stereotypes, the results can be potent. Rosenthal and Jacobson's well-known studies on the effects of teachers' expectations of students' academic performance illustrates the point. In their book, *Pygmalion in the Classroom*, Rosenthal and Jacobson tell of their experiments with an academic potential stereotype.[31] A group of youngsters, academically at various ranges of skills and knowledge, were identified as late bloomers. Their teachers were told that these students were tested with new types of intelligence tests, and that these tests revealed the youngsters to be exceptionally bright. Overtly, the teachers did not treat the "late bloomers" differently. However, through such subtleties as facial expressions, tone of voice, and a general ambiance of acceptance conveyed to the late bloomers, the teachers conveyed to the students that they were exceptionally bright. By the end of the experiment, the youngsters were exceptionally bright, according to standardized tests. The point is that the teachers treated the youngsters on the basis of a stereotype, and the youngsters reciprocated by assuming that role; the rest became a self-fulfilling prophecy.

The self-fulfilling prophecy is an important social phenomenon for teachers to understand. Simply put, the self-fulfilling prophecy for teachers means that if teachers define a student's capabilities as real, then they are real in their consequences.[32] For example, if teachers define the students' capabilities as below average, expecting them to be and treating them as though they were below average, then over a period of time, they will be below average. Of course, the opposite is true. If teachers expect excellence of their students and treat them as though they *were* excellent, then after a period of time they would be excellent. Unfortunately, teachers expect less of minority students, and thus minority students produce less. Research studies show the self-fulfilling prophecy to be an all-too-true phenomenon.

What happens to ethnic minority students when teachers treat them on the basis of stereotypes? And, *do* teachers treat minority students on the basis of stereotypes? The U.S. Commission on Civil Rights conducted a study[33] analyzing the verbal and nonverbal interaction of teachers and students in the public schools of Texas, New Mexico, Arizona, and California. The study investigated the kind and amount of verbal and nonverbal interaction which actually occurred between teachers and Anglo and Mexican American students. The study reported:

> Mexican American pupils . . . received considerably less of some of the most educationally beneficial forms of teacher behavior than did Anglos in the same classroom.[34]

In the 429 classrooms that were observed, the study verified that teachers spoke less often and less favorably to Mexican American students than to Anglo students. Anglo students were praised more and challenged intellectually more often than were Mexican Americans. But, the teachers verbally scolded or disciplined the Mexican American students more often than Anglos. Thus, in both quality and quantity of verbal and nonverbal interaction, teachers tended to favor Anglo over Mexican American students. The teachers in this study unconsciously assumed that Mexican American students were more unruly and required more discipline. Also, the teachers assumed that the Mexican American students were less bright than the Anglo students. Thus, the Anglo students were asked the more difficult questions and were praised more for their responses than were the Mexican American students. If these teachers continue to act on their stereotypes about the Mexican American students in their classes, the students will internalize the stereotype as role expectations to which they must conform. Eventually, standard instruments and deportment reports will reveal that these Mexican American students are less bright and more unruly than their Anglo counterparts. It's important to understand that in the southwestern United States there is a stereotype about Mexican Americans which attributes to them violent characteristics, the characteristics of the *bandito*. Also, the stereotype attributes to them a low level of intelligence and a poor command of English. The teachers in this study were simply transferring the stereotype to their Mexican American students, assuming they would be more unruly and less bright than their Anglo counterparts. They treated the students according to their expectations, and the self-fulfilling prophecy held true.

These teachers were not bigots bent on suppressing minority students. Rather, they were type 2 teachers, unprejudiced discriminators who meant no harm to their students. The teachers were both from the Anglo and Mexican American groups, and yet they all treated the Mexican American students inequitably. But because they were unaware of the impact of group ethnocentrism, racism, prejudice, and the consequent stereotyping that occurs in most communities, they operated on folk wisdom and stereotypic data they had acquired in the southwestern communities. We must also remember that teachers can harbor stereotypes about a variety of other kinds of students: the "spoiled WASP," the "jiving black," the "dumb Pollack," the "smart Oriental," the "defiant Indian," or the "greaser." ("Greaser" has many connotations; it's applied to Mexican American students in the Southwest and in the Midwest to poor white students, such as "the Fonz" of the popular TV program, *Happy Days*.) One only has to visit enough teacher lounges to hear comments like "those kind of kids," or "you can't expect much from their kind" to understand how easily teachers fall into the trap of stereotyping and labelling their students.

One last point about stereotypes. They change as the nature of intergroup relations changes. Consider the way stereotypes about Native Americans have changed. I analyzed 15 different American history books which had been written between 1890 and 1930. These books were written with college students in mind. Original accounts in the history books describing events prior to the westward expansion of the colonists referred to the Native Americans as "Noble Savages." The Iroquois nation was used as the model. The Native Americans were considered innocent, courageous, and honest, but because they chose to live in the forests and chose not to adopt the Christian religion, they were considered savages. During the period of westward expansion, when Anglo pioneers were bisecting the continent and when Native Americans were being removed or crowded further and further west, the original accounts of Native Americans described them as "savages." Because of the intense conflict between the Native Americans and the government, they were described as having lost their nobility. No longer innocent and good, the Native Americans were portrayed as uncivilized warriors. The Sioux tribes were used as the model. After the intense conflict ceased, especially after the last Native American battle for survival, the Battle of Wounded Knee, the accounts of Native Americans referred to a "conquered savage." The Cherokee tribes were used as the model. The accounts portrayed the Native Americans as an almost extinct group who had reached the end of the trail. Because they were now subdued, and because some had taken up the ways of the pioneers, the stereotype portrayed them as conquered, defeated, and almost civilized. But, because many of the tribes chose to retain their religion rather than abandon it for Christianity, they were considered somewhat savage, or without Christian souls.

Now all three stereotypes exist in various regions of the country, depending on the nature of the relationship between the Native Americans and the peoples of the communities in the respective regions. During the conflict at the site of the Battle of Wounded Knee in 1972 in South Dakota, people in South Dakota were quoted as believing that "Indians had a heritage of savagery and violence," and that their current upheaval was proof of that heritage. When I lived in

Oklahoma, non-Indian people would tell me that they were proud of the Indian blood in their family and commence to claim that their grandfather was married to a Cherokee princess, and they were the progeny of a conquered but noble savage. I have even read reports published by the Bureau of Indian Affairs which cite teachers as reporting the reason for the high failure rate of Native American students is that the students, and their Native American tribe, had lost their spunk. The teachers felt that the Native American students failed because they were the progeny of a conquered people.

THE IMPACT OF ETHNOCENTRISMS ON SCHOOLING

What impact do racism, prejudice, stereotyping, and discrimination have on schools, teachers, and students? How can the impact best be understood? What follows is an analysis of public school policies and teacher and staff practices that operate from ethnocentric assumptions. The analysis is based largely on my experiences as a classroom teacher as well as on observations and study of public schooling accrued while I conducted pre- and in-service training of teachers and other school personnel.

Almost daily, many students in American public schools experience assaults on their ethnicity. Quietly, they succumb to these assaults, conceal their beliefs, and suppress their feelings. They learn to cope, to tune in or tune out as the occasion demands. The ethnic conflict students experience in schools is fundamentally one of *misunderstanding* by teachers. Some teachers do not understand that racism and ethnocentrism are endemic in American society and influence teaching and learning. Much of the cultural conflict is not so much a case of the "teacher bent on suppressing minorities," as it is a case of teachers who have not been prepared to teach ethnically different students. By and large, public schooling is a white, middle-class affair. This is neither good nor bad, but in my view, it is a reality important to understand. Teachers and other school personnel go about the business of schooling, unconsciously transmitting white, middle-class values, attitudes, and beliefs. Some educators still view the teaching-learning universe from a Ptolemaic, monistic perspective. Educators are not to be faulted for establishing an educational system based on the values of white, middle-class culture. Under the circumstances, they have done a commendable job. While some educators have unconsciously transmitted the cultural values and beliefs of the white middle class, they have also transmitted the culture's attendant ethnic biases, prejudices, and stereotypes. At best, if they have not deliberately transmitted ethnic biases, prejudices, and stereotypes, they have done little to counter the racist phenomena which pervade American society and which become evident when school policies, programs, and practices are analyzed and evaluated.

School policy is stated in guidelines that enumerate the school rules but do not state the assumptions upon which the rules are based. For example, a midwestern urban high school's grading policy reads in part: "teachers should compensate in their instruction and grading for the cultural deficiencies of the school's disadvantaged students." This policy is based on potentially divisive assumptions: (1) that minority students aren't capable of the same high standards as majority group students; (2) that minority students should be treated preferentially since they have deficiencies; and (3) that minority students are culturally deficient rather than just different. These assumptions encourage preferential treatment of one group of students to the detriment of another, and they can cause both groups to realize less than their full potential. Students' reactions might be: "Why work harder? The blacks get Bs and they don't do as much as we." Or, "No use to work harder anyway, the teacher doesn't think we (blacks) are very smart." Care must be taken with school policies to insure all students equal educational benefits. Policies that discriminate against students or that hinder or block equal educational benefits are unlawful and educationally inexcusable.

Common everyday teaching practices can also impede equal educational benefit. Transmission of culture is essential to teaching. The teacher transmits culture through attitudes, beliefs, perceptions, language styles, and other personal attributes. Much of the transmission is unconscious. Many times teachers and other school personnel reveal their ethnic biases through routine practices. Native American students from Bureau of Indian Affairs boarding schools have told me of practices they perceived as racist. According to one account, whenever a Comanche student was heard speaking in the Comanche dialect, the teacher (or any other staff member) would hit the student to "beat the Comanche" out of him. Other Native American students have told of having their hair cut by a school principal or of being forced to wear shoes on certain Native American religious days in violation of tribal traditions.

The school does not exist in a vacuum. As an integral part of the neighborhood, the local community, and the state, the school's climate will reflect the ethos and various mores of its communities. Teachers and staff may serve as conduits through which the social climate is transmitted to the students in the school. Consequently, analysis of practices should focus on both the intergroup relations and overall climate fostered in the school, and the roles and responsibilities delegated to the students in the school.

Subtle prejudicial practices may be discerned in the roles and responsibilities delegated to students. Which students traditionally receive most of the social rewards of the school? Do the minority students receive their fair share of the social rewards? Are they cheerleaders? Are they on the debate team? Who is involved in school plays? Which students are traditionally assigned to leadership duties in the school? Do members of the minority student groups escort school guests and visitors? Are members of the majority group always placed in charge of minority students? Subtle manifestations of ethnic conflict can be discerned in the school's intergroup relations. When a fight occurs, is a sincere attempt made to determine whether the fight was caused by interpersonal or intergroup conflict? If the cause of the fight seems to be based on intergroup conflict, what is done to resolve the conflict and improve the emotional climate and interaction between the groups in conflict?

Tracking and ability grouping practices have a negative influence on the school's intergroup relations because these practices tend to isolate students along cultural, racial, or economic lines, and thereby perpetuate in-school segregation and unequal educational benefits. Ability grouping has the effect of segregating minority students within the school and dooming them to failure. Once placed in a low track, rarely do they advance to a higher track. These students are deprived of the academic experiences and skills that would prepare them for college entrance and a consequent professional career. Also, tracking and ability grouping deprive majority students of positive relationships with minority students. Indeed, majority students develop a false sense of academic superiority. Tracking reinforces the feeling of superiority and teaches the myth that the majority group is superior to the minority groups. Under these circumstances, what kind of positive attitudes toward minorities can the students learn? The negative consequences of tracking and ability grouping—stereotyped attitudes toward minorities and predetermined academic failure for minority students—far outweigh whatever administrative expediencies tracking and ability grouping practices provide. Both tracking and ability grouping should be abandoned and replaced by heterogeneous grouping or individualized instruction. Last, counselors and teachers have tended to advise minority students to pursue nonacademic, nonprofessional advanced training which has led to a paucity of minority professionals and academicians. Counseling minority students to enter certain programs based on a single-interest inventory instrument, a culturally biased achievement test, or on stereotypic career aspirations and expectations will tend to relegate those students to vocational programs. These types of counseling practices, compounded by tracking and ability grouping, are clearly discriminatory, and are damaging to majority and minority students alike.

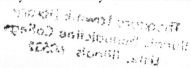

Here a personal experience is used to illustrate how biases in practices can occur. A teacher invited me to visit his seventh-grade classroom which purportedly accommodated both fast and slow learners. Some students sat in small groups in the center of the room where they were to help each other. Other students sat alone, away from the groups, and facing the walls. According to the teacher, these students were slow learners, easily distracted, and needed the discipline imposed by their seating arrangement. They were not to talk or share information. All of the students facing the walls were black; the students in the small groups were white. Though the teacher denied he segregated students according to their race, this permanent seating arrangement had the effect of racial segregation. The teacher felt that the "black kids are bussed in from a poor neighborhood that has bad schools, so it takes them a while to catch up." Why couldn't the faster students help the slower students? Were the blacks really slower? Or were they labeled "slow learners" because of culturally biased test scores? These questions were not satisfactorily answered by the teacher who, incidentally, has never invited me back to his classroom. Nevertheless, the teacher's practice of isolating students according to race conveyed to the students notions of white superiority and black inferiority, a classic instance of nonverbal racism.

The above comments on teacher practices are equally applicable to the nonteaching staff, whose pervasive effect upon school climate should not be ignored. For example, the attitude that a cafeteria worker takes toward certain ethnic foods will be communicated to the students. If the cafeteria worker abhors bagels, for example, then the abhorrence will be conveyed to both the Jewish and non-Jewish students. When I taught school in Wisconsin I knew of a janitor who watched Polish students carefully when they went to a restroom because according to him, "Pollacks are known for their dirt," and they allegedly threatened the sanitary conditions of the restrooms. I could never figure out how the janitor could tell the difference between a Polish and a non-Polish student! Nevertheless, the janitor taught students stereotypes about Polish teenagers, and in doing so, negatively influenced all students' educational development.

The opening question of this chapter was: "if students acquire their culture in their homes, in their communities, and in their schools, where do they acquire ethnic and racial biases?" Ethnic and racial biases are acquired through the conventional wisdom and traditional beliefs that still exist and pervade the home, the schools, and U.S. communities. In other words, ethnocentrism and racism and their manifestations, ethnic and racial stereotypes, are endemic to the American social class/caste scene. (While they have changed in their emphasis, they have not changed in their effect.) Young people will acquire these misconceptions and biases unless they are countered by information and experiences that teach about people of color. Part II of the text presents models and strategies for the encounter.

Notes

1. E. James Davis. *Minority-Dominant Relations.* Arlington Heights, Ill.: AHM Publishers, 1978, p. 49.
2. Judy H. Katz. *White Awareness.* Norman, Okl.: University of Oklahoma Press, 1978.
3. Katz. *White Awareness,* p. 4.
4. Gunnar Mydral. *An American Dilemma.* New York: Harper & Row, 1944.
5. U.S. Commission on Mental Health. *Joint Commission on Mental Health.* Washington, D.C.: U.S. Government Printing Office, 1965.
6. Kerner Commission. *National Advisory Commission on Civil Rights.* New York: Bantam, 1968.
7. Pierre L. van den Berghe. *Race and Racism, A Comparative Perspective.* New York: Wiley, 1967, pp. 21–26.
8. R. Daniels and H. H. Kitano. *American Racism: Exploration of the Nature of Prejudice.* Englewood Cliffs, N.J.: Prentice-Hall, 1970, p. 2; see also, Kurt Lewin. *Resolving Social Conflict.* New York: Harper & Row, 1948, p. 85.
9. Adolf Hitler. *Mein Kampf.* Boston: Houghton Mifflin, 1943, p. 654.
10. William Shirer. *The Rise and Fall of the Third Reich.* New York: Simon & Schuster, 1960, pp. 231–234; see also, Nora Levin. *The Holocaust: The Destruction of European Jewry, 1933–45.* New York: Schocken Books, 1968, pp. 3–24.
11. President's Commission on Higher Education. *Higher Education for American Democracy.* New York: Harper & Row, 1948, vol. 2.
12. Lillian Smith. *Killers of the Dream.* New York: Norton, 1961.
13. Lloyd Allen Cook. *Intergroup Relations in Teacher Education.* Washington, D.C.: American Council on Education, 1951, pp. 26–31; see also, Gordon Allport, *The Nature of Prejudice.* Garden City, N.Y.: Doubleday, 1958.
14. Kenneth B. Clark. *Dark Ghetto.* New York: Harper & Row, 1965; see also, Stokeley Carmichael and Charles V. Hamilton. *Black Power: The Politics of Liberation in America.* New York: Random House (Vintage Books), 1967.
15. Robert Blauner. *Racial Oppression in America.* New York: Harper & Row, 1972; see also, James A. Geschwender. *Racial Stratification in America.* Dubuque, Iowa: Brown, 1978.
16. Rodolfo Acuña. *Occupied America: The Chicano's Struggle Toward Liberation.* San Francisco: Harper & Row (Canfield Press), 1972.
17. Vine Deloria, Jr. *Custer Died for Your Sins: An Indian Manifesto.* New York: Macmillan, 1970.
18. Malcolm X. *The Autobiography of Malcolm X.* New York: Grove Press, 1964.

19. T. W. Adorno. *The Authoritarian Personality*. New York: Harper & Row, 1950.
20. Andrew Greeley. *Why Can't They Be Like Us?* New York: Dutton, 1971, p. 156.
21. Gordon W. Allport and Bernard M. Kramer. "Some Roots of Prejudice," *Journal of Social Psychology*, 1946, 22: 6.
22. M. E. Goodman. *Race Awareness in Young Children*. New York: Collier, 1964.
23. J. Morland. "Racial Acceptance and Preference of Nursery School Children in a Southern City." *Merrill-Palmer Quarterly* (August 1962): 372–380.
24. George Henderson. *To Live in Freedom*. Norman: University of Oklahoma Press, 1972, pp. 101–119.
25. Paul F. Secord and Carl W. Backman. *Social Psychology*. New York: McGraw-Hill, 1964, p. 433.
26. Secord and Backman. *Social Psychology*, p. 435.
27. Robert Merton. "Discrimination and the American Creed," in R. M. MacIver, ed., *Discrimination and National Welfare*. New York: Harper & Row, 1949, pp. 99–126.
28. Peter Berger and Thomas Luckmann. *The Social Construction of Reality*. New York: Doubleday, 1967, pp. 32–34.
29. Roger D. Abrahams. "Stereotyping and Beyond," in Abrahams and Rudolph C. Troike, *Language and Cultural Diversity in American Education*. Englewood Cliffs, N.J.: Prentice-Hall, 1972, pp. 22–23.
30. Charles P. Loomis. *Social Systems: The Study of Sociology*. Cambridge, Mass.: Schenkman, 1976, pp. 90–93.
31. Robert Rosenthal and Lenore Jacobson. *Pygmalion in the Classroom*. New York: Holt, Rinehart, and Winston, 1968, pp. 5–9.
32. Robert K. Merton. *Social Theory and Social Structure*. New York: Free Press, 1957, pp. 421–438.
33. U.S. Commission on Civil Rights. *Teachers and Students*. Washington, D.C.: U.S. Government Printing Office, 1973.
34. U.S. Commission on Civil Rights. *Teachers and Students*, pp. 17–18.

Part II
MODELS
AND STRATEGIES

Part II describes two instructional models, ethnic studies and bilingual education, and two instructional strategies, human rights and intergroup relations, that can be used to provide equal educational opportunities for all students. The models are described as instructional modes by which pluralistic teaching and learning experiences can be implemented. The *ethnic studies model* is generic and can be utilized in most classrooms irrespective of ethnic or racial complexion and irrespective of subject matter. As such, ethnic studies is described as a permeation model that can be utilized to permeate the classroom and the school with multiethnic experiences. The *bilingual education*

model is described as a mode for reaching and teaching students who do not speak the language dominant in the host society. Specific types of bilingual education programs described are those based on the sociopolitical policies of different nations: vernacularization, internationalization, assimilation, and pluralization. Then three forms of bilingual education in the United States are described: transitional, maintenance, and restoration. Pertinent educational issues are addressed, especially thorny issues that revolve around bidialectalism, bilingualism, and bilingual literacy. Because bilingual education is a linguistic and cultural intervention model, stress is placed on coupling it with the ethnic studies model.

The instructional strategies are classroom management approaches. "Management" in this context does not refer to coercive discipline techniques; rather, the instructional strategies are approaches focused on teaching genuine democratic living. The *human rights strategy* is a decision-sharing strategy by which teachers and students participate in decisions that affect their classrooms' climate and tenor. Teaching styles—the laissez faire, democratic, and autocratic styles—are described as they pertain to human rights classroom management. Nonverbal communication is highlighted to stress the importance of setting a positive, pluralistic classroom climate. Then basic principles and an organizational scheme for implementing human rights strategies are described. While the human rights strategy is a classroom governance strategy, the *intergroup relations strategy* is a social group intervention strategy. It is an approach to improving the relationships between students who are racially, ethnically, or culturally different. The strategy is based on the equal-status contact theory and can also be used to improve relationships between male and female students or between handicapped and nonhandicapped mainstreaming students. A distinction is made between intergroup relations and interpersonal communications as strategies. Both approaches stress improved communications, the first stressing improved intergroup communications among students, and the second stressing improved teacher-student communications. The human rights and intergroup relations strategies are introduced as means to democratize teaching and learning. They are predicated on fundamental ethics of rule by law rather than rule by power or fiat. As such, they are described as basic strategies applicable to most classrooms.

Chapter 6
Introduction to
Instructional Models and
Strategies

The individual models and strategies will be described in separate chapters beginning with the ethnic studies model, but before describing them, we need to define pertinent instructional terminology and explain the nature and function of instructional models and strategies.

A variety of terms exist to describe types of cultural instruction. "Transcultural education," "intercultural education," "cross-cultural education," are examples. There is confusion about the meanings of "multicultural education," "bilingual education," and other cultural approaches. *Multiethnic instruction counters racism, ethnic bias, and ethnic stereotypes in classroom experiences, in curricular materials and contents, and in teacher behaviors.* The focus is on improving classroom climate as well as academic content to nurture nonbiased instruction. *Multicultural instruction counters elitism, racism, and sexism.* The multicultural approach is a broad encounter with the effects of poverty, prejudice, and sexism. The importance of treating elitism and sexism in classroom teaching and learning cannot be overstated. To avoid the pitfalls of terms that come into fashion and then are soon obsolete, the models and strategies described in this text go beyond rhetoric; they are intended to assist classroom teachers in their encounters with racism, ethnic bias, and stereotyping in their classrooms, their curricula, and their own behavior. However, the models and strategies are pliable enough for use in countering sexism, elitism, handicapism, and other misconceptions that people have about certain groups of people. They are modes that can be used to focus on the pluralistic nature of American society. They are rational, structured approaches to teaching about ethnicity in American life as well as to promoting better understanding and honest relations between ethnic majority and ethnic minority students. Table 6.1 outlines four types of models and strategies to be discussed.

The models and strategies have emerged as a result of the collective activities of educators, concerned citizens, public school teachers, parents, and hosts of other people who believe that communal living can be vastly improved through education. By now, these activities are recognized as the forces or impulses to democratize public schooling,

Table 6.1 MULTIETHNIC INSTRUCTIONAL MODELS AND STRATEGIES, CLASSIFIED BY TYPE AND GOALS

MODELS AND STRATEGIES	TYPE	GOALS
Ethnic Studies: James Banks, University of Washington	Academic inquiry, generalizations, and assessment of group experience.	Primarily for development of ethnic literacy or for building cognitive understanding about ethnic groups.
Bilingual-Bicultural Instruction: Joshua Fishman, Yeshiva University	Linguistic and cultural intervention.	Designed to interface instruction for linguistically and culturally different learners in the United States.
Human Rights: Glen Snider, University of Oklahoma	Ethical classroom management and interaction.	Designed to foster use of democratic procedures to assure equal educational treatment for all students.
Intergroup Relations: Hilda Taba (Deceased)	Social interaction and interpersonal relationships.	Designed to promote favorable contact and interpersonal relationships between ethnic minority and ethnic majority students.

a force deeply embedded in the democratic cultural praxis of American society. The intellectual basis for democratizing public schooling was established during the early decades of this century by educational scholars such as John Dewey, George Counts, Boyd Bode, C. H. Judd, and others.[1] Democratizing schools is by no means an easy task. Traditionally, public schools and their curricula have not been designed to focus specifically on democratic living. Rather, they have been designed to focus on teaching the fundamentals of academic disciplines, as the current "back-to-the-basics" social mood indicates. Teachers and other public school professionals have been trained in the pedagogy of the academic disciplines, particularly those who work in the secondary levels, although elementary level teachers have also been taught the methodology of discrete disciplines. Thus, teachers have tended to view their primary function as "history" teachers or "language arts" teachers, that is, as transmitters of the basics of some academic discipline, to whom the social and emotional development of students is only a secondary function.[2]

Those who wish to democratize schooling, teaching, and learning confront a difficult situation: focusing on democratic living is at best a secondary function of teachers. At worst, the secondary function is shared with other focuses, such as the student's intellectual and emotional development. The problem is that all the functions are intertwined. For example, the student's moral development is dependent upon cognitive development, which in turn is dependent upon biological and social maturation. Given the complexity of human development, teachers bet on a sure winner by opting to focus first on the basic skills of academic disciplines, and second on the social and emotional development of students.

I believe that teaching democratic living is fundamental to classroom learning and can be taught and learned concurrently with other academic studies. My belief is supported by the *Cardinal Principles of Elementary Education* published by the U.S. Bureau of Education in 1918. It listed civic education as one of seven concurrent cardinal principles:

> [Civic Education] . . . should develop in the individual those qualities whereby he will act well his part as a member of neighborhood, town or city, state, and nation and give him a basis for understanding international problems.[3]

Professor Richard Gross has proposed a revitalization of the cardinal principles and emphasized that schools should model the principles rather than merely espouse them. For example, he called for institution of "civic interest and participation" principle, with schools acting as centers for the community's participatory democratic activities.[4]

The instructional models and strategies are premised on the notion that teachers need conceptual frameworks to use as a basis for preparing students to live in a democratic, pluralistic society. As such, the models and strategies can be utilized concurrently with other teaching and learning activities. In essense, the models and strategies provide a means by which a teacher can develop a multidimensional focus while teaching, rather than a unidimensional focus. For example, while students are being taught how to read they can also be taught how to share interpretations of what they read. With the ethnic studies model, the literature the students read would reflect multiethnic themes, people, and situations. With the intergroup relations strategy, ethnic minority and ethnic majority students would be encouraged to share interpretations of what they read. By developing a multidimensional focus, teachers can infuse or integrate the multiethnic models and strategies with their goals for other teaching and learning activities.

The models and strategies suffer from the perceptions of some educators that they are coded words for "minority education" or "disadvantaged education"; they are intended to be inclusive rather than exclusive, providing conceptual frameworks applicable to all public school classrooms and all students. While they are discrete, they are by no means mutually exclusive. The ethnic studies model and the intergroup relations strategy basically establish the major goals of pluralistic instruction: (1) to foster better understandings of ethnic groups, and (2) to foster better interpersonal contact between ethnic minority and ethnic majority group members. The human rights strategy and bilingual-bicultural model are variants of the first models and strategies, bringing ethical and linguistic dimensions to teaching and learning.

The models and strategies are generic and therefore can be utilized by any classroom teacher while teaching in any established area of studies. For example, secondary teachers such as physical education teachers, science teachers, industrial arts, and home economics teachers all can utilize the models and strategies within their specialties, just as elementary teachers can utilize them during any of their daily activities in music, art, language arts, science, mathematics, social studies and physical education. The multiethnic instructional models and strategies have these characteristics in common:

1. They provide means by which equal educational opportunities can be provided for all students.
2. They spring from a sociocultural basis, particularly from notions about culture and ethnicity.
3. They are inclusive of all students from all ethnic groups.

Each model or strategy has a discrete function. Still, there is no reason why all of them couldn't be utilized in a synthesis approach. In other words, different aspects of each model or strategy could be incorporated into a reconstituted model. A teacher may want to improve interpersonal relations and increase the students' knowledge about certain ethnic groups. By combining the intergroup relations strategy with the ethnic studies model, students could work together on projects which focus on ethnic-group history or culture. Or, a teacher may want to foster the students' right to their home language or dialect using aspects of the bilingual model and human rights strategy combined.

One word of caution pertaining to the models. Each model or strategy operates from its major assumption regarding the nature of learning. For example, the intergroup relations strategy operates on the assumption that favorable attitudes can be formed through sustained interpersonal contact; the ethnic studies model's assumption is that favorable attitudes can be formed through increased knowledge about ethnic groups. A body of research on attitude change through interpersonal contact and increased knowledge reports that favorable attitudes toward ethnic-group individuals can be fostered through both increased interpersonal contact and increased knowledge.[5] Each model or strategy can be utilized discretely, but for greater impact on attitude formation and change, it is advisable that more than one of them be utilized simultaneously. In particular, the bilingual instruction model would yield minimal impact on attitude formation and change if used without the bicultural model, which is a variant of the ethnic studies model. Thus, the models and strategies can be used for their combined effect—to build cultural/ethnic understanding, respect, and, then, harmony. The baseline would be the ethnic studies and bilingual education models; ethnic studies would provide new knowledge about how ethnic groups perceive themselves, and bilingual education would provide a linguistic and culturally compatible school experience for non-English-speaking students. At the intermediate level, the intergroup relations strategy would provide contact between different ethnic and cultural groups. The contact, when buttressed by the new knowledge gained from the ethnic studies model, would assist students to understand others who differ culturally or ethnically. At the third level, the human rights strategy would provide students a sense of community and interdependence. When buttressed by the knowledge of ethnic studies and the contact of intergroup relations, the human rights strategy could lead to a change in behavior—that is, behavior that would show that students respect cultural and ethnic differences. The format is simple: new knowledge, new contacts, and new behaviors. We are now ready to examine in detail the models and strategies.

Notes

1. John Dewey. *How We Think.* Boston: Heath, 1910; see also, George Counts. *Dare the School Build a New Social Order?* New York: John Day, 1932; Boyd Bode. *Modern Educational Theories.* New York: Macmillan, 1927; C. H. Judd. *Education and Social Progress.* New York: Harcourt Brace Jovanovich, 1934.
2. Bruce Joyce and Marsha Weil. *Models of Teaching.* Englewood Cliffs, N.J.: Prentice-Hall, 1972, pp. 32–33.
3. *Cardinal Principles of Secondary Education: A Report of the Commission on the Reorganization of Secondary Education.* Washington, D.C.: U.S. Government Printing Office, 1918, No. 35.
4. Richard Gross. "Seven New Cardinal Principles." *Kappan.* (December 1978): 5.
5. Arnold Rose. *Studies in the Reduction of Prejudice.* Chicago: American Council on Race Relations, 1948, pp. 17–20; see also, Lloyd Allen Cook. *Intergroup Relations in Teacher Education.* Washington, D.C.: American Council on Education, 1951, pp. 85–87; E. Hartley and R. Hartley. *Fundamentals of Social Psychology.* New York: Alfred Knopf, 1961, pp. 726–739; see also, Gwen Baker. "Multicultural Training for Student Teachers," *Journal of Teacher Education.* (March 1973): 306–308; see also, G. L. Redman. "A Model for Human Relations Inservice Training," *Journal of Teacher Education.* (May–June 1977): 34–38.

Chapter 7
The Ethnic Studies Model

The practice of teaching about ethnic groups in some kind of class-room arrangement is not new. Such teaching existed in the New England colonies, primarily to preserve German Lutheranism and the German language and culture[1]; in the latter decades of the eighteenth century, Japanese and Chinese ethnic group schools were established in Hawaii and in California[2]; almost simultaneously on the east coast, especially in New York City, Jewish schools were established. The Japanese, Chinese, and Jewish schools were attempts to maintain the group's religion, language, and culture. They were supplemental to the public schools so that students attended them after public school hours, in the evenings, or on weekends. These schools provided more than religious instruction; they taught the group's culture and language along with its religion, with the goal of maintaining the group's language and culture.[3]

ORIGINS OF THE ETHNIC STUDIES MODEL

Teaching about ethnic groups was primarily within the sphere of church-related education until the twentieth century when Julius

Drachsler[4] and other scholars proposed intercultural studies for the public schools. The idea of the intercultural studies approach was to teach all students about the cultures of the new European immigrants and thereby foster better cultural understanding among students. Cultural pluralism was the philosophic base of intercultural education. By teaching about the new immigrant cultures and nurturing respect and understanding for the immigrants' languages, customs, and traditions, intercultural education eased the otherwise harsh melting pot assimilation process experienced by the immigrant students. It also taught nonimmigrant students to understand the cultures of immigrant students. Ethnic-group community social agencies, such as Jane Addams's Hull House in Chicago, used intercultural education with adults and younger immigrants.[5] However, intercultural education emerged as a reaction to existing Americanization programs which emphasized American English and history and deemphasized and frowned upon foreign languages and cultures. Intercultural education was perceived as a buffer program for new immigrants rather than as a means of promoting cultural awareness and understanding among all students. Thus, with minor exceptions, intercultural education was phased out of public education as the European immigrant groups were Americanized into their respective communities.

In the middle 1960s minority groups were compelled to pressure public schools, colleges, and universities to implement ethnic studies courses and programs as a means to desegregate the school and university monocultural programs. At first, these ethnic studies programs and courses were simply a way to give ethnic minority groups instruction in their languages and cultures within the educational system. Later, as the programs and courses developed, their goals expanded to include fostering cultural understanding and respect for these languages and cultures. Rather than experience the fate of intercultural education, the ethnic studies programs and courses made an appeal to all students, thereby eliminating the "buffer" or "desegregation only" conception of ethnic studies and replacing it with the goal of cultural and ethnic understanding as the *raison d'être* of the courses and programs. Now some public schools, colleges, and universities have ethnic studies programs: some programs focus on specific ethnic groups (e.g., Italian American, Black Studies); others include several ethnic groups, using "Ethnic Studies" as an umbrella (e.g., Ethnic Studies: Chicano Studies and Native American Studies).

Ethnic studies courses and programs were bolstered when Congress passed the Ethnic Heritage Act which provides a national policy on ethnic studies as well as federal funds to develop training and curriculum materials pertaining to ethnic-group cultures. Programs funded under Title IX can (1) develop for use in elementary or secondary schools or institutions of higher education curriculum materials relating to the history, geography, society, economy, literature, art, music, drama, language, and general culture of the group or groups with which the program is concerned, and the contributions of that ethnic group or groups to the American heritage; (2) disseminate curriculum materials to permit their use in elementary and secondary schools or institutions of higher education throughout the nation; (3) provide training for persons using, or preparing to use, multiethnic curriculum materials; (4) cooperate with persons and organizations with a special interest in the ethnic group or groups with which the program is concerned to assist them in promoting, encouraging, developing, or producing programs or other activities which relate to the history, culture, or traditions of that ethnic group or groups.[6]

The American Association of Colleges for Teacher Education (AACTE) has endorsed the policy, "no one model American," to support ethnic studies:

> Multicultural education is education which values cultural pluralism. Multicultural education rejects the view that schools should seek to melt away cultural differences or the view that schools should merely tolerate cultural pluralism. To endorse cultural pluralism is to endorse the principle that there is no one model American. To endorse cultural pluralism is to understand and appreciate the differences that exist among the nation's citizens. It is to see these differences as a positive force in the continuing development of a society which professes a wholesome respect for the intrinsic worth of every individual.[7]

Further, AACTE, working jointly with the National Council for Accreditation of Teacher Education (NCATE), has formulated multicultural education standards. The new standards require practically every college or school of education in the United States to provide multiethnic courses or experiences for teacher education students in order to maintain NCATE accreditation (see Chapter 3). AACTE produced an analysis and annotated bibliography, *Multicultural Education and Ethnic Studies*.[8] The document succinctly summarized the philosophic history of multiethnic education and then provided a well-annotated bibliography on multiethnic books and materials. A more recent publication, *Pluralism and the American Teacher*,[9] provides theoretical bases and case studies for multiethnic education. AACTE has also identified model multicultural teacher education programs.

Other professional organizations have developed policies supportive of ethnic studies. The National Council of Teachers of English (NCTE) published its policy on the student's right to speak a dialect. Basically, the policy, "The Student's Right to a Dialect," endorses linguistic pluralism by encouraging English and language arts teachers to respect the student's ethnic, social, or racial dialect. Also, NCTE publishes multiethnic articles and periodicals and fosters publication of multiethnic literature. To broaden its scope as well as to eliminate implications of language ethnocentrism, NCTE changed the title of its elementary education journal, *Elementary English,* to *Language Arts.* Along this line, the International Reading Association publishes multi-ethnic articles and monographs. The Association of Supervision for Curriculum Development (ASCD) periodically publishes articles on multiethnic education. Phi Delta Kappa has published three fastbacks (nos. 84, 87, and 107), and a book, *The Melting of the Ethnics: Education of the Immigrants,*[10] on multiethnic concerns. The National Council for the Social Studies (NCSS) developed and disseminated *Curriculum Guidelines for Multiethnic Education*[11]: the guidelines for implementation of multiethnic education in public schools. The first guideline, and its subguidelines, set the guide's tone:

1.0 Does ethnic pluralism permeate the total school environment?
1.1 Is ethnic content incorporated into all aspects of the curriculum, preschool through grade 12 and beyond?
1.2 Do instructional materials treat ethnic differences and groups honestly, realistically, and sensitively?
1.3 Do school libraries and resources centers have a variety of materials on the histories, experiences, and cultures of many different ethnic groups?
1.4 Do school assemblies, decorations, speakers, holidays, and heroes reflect ethnic group differences?
1.5 Are extracurricular activities multiracial and multiethnic?

Other public professional and private organizations and agencies have endorsed educational policies supportive of ethnic studies. It appears that from the mid-1960s through the latter 1970s the ethnic studies movement took hold primarily because of its broad emphasis upon cultural awareness and understanding and its relevance to all students who live and work in American society; it speaks directly to the diversity in American life. Further, ethnic studies provides ethnic groups access to public school and higher education curricula and thereby provides experiences and courses that enrich the otherwise monocultural education programs.

ETHNIC STUDIES MODEL

• *Goal:* To foster increased knowledge about ethnic groups.

• *Operational assumption:* Increased knowledge about an ethnic group can foster positive attitudes toward that ethnic group.

• *Conceptual structure:* To study an ethnic group, it should be approached as

1. a group that is organic and in the process of changing and growing;
2. a group that is organized by a generic system of values and beliefs;
3. a group that is internally diverse;
4. a group that is similar to and different from other groups.

CRITICAL FACTORS FOR UTILIZATION

Using the ethnic studies model requires knowledge about the difference between teaching an experience and teaching about an experience. When Louis Armstrong was asked, "What is jazz?" he quipped, "If you don't know, I can't tell you." The same answer applies when the question is asked, "What's it like to be a Japanese American or a Seminole American, (or any other ethnic)?" The answer is not flippant; an ethnic experience per se cannot be taught. Teachers can teach about ethnic experiences, but they cannot teach what it feels like to be a member of an ethnic group. Membership in an ethnic group and participation in any or all of its social, cultural, political, or economic activities is a human experience unique to each person within the group. Teachers can teach only data and generalizations that describe the nature of an ethnic group. These data and generalizations can provide a view of an ethnic group's perspectives, an understanding of how and why the group has evolved, an awareness of its past experiences and present conditions, and sensitivity for its hopes, aspirations, and plights. To understand ethnic-group phenomena, a group must be viewed from within and from outside; or, to understand the nature of an ethnic-group experience, students should study how members of the group perceive themselves as well as how nongroup members perceive them. Key questions here are: How does the group define itself? What means does the group use to define itself? The insider perceptions are provided by the group's self-defined history, music, literature, language, and art forms. The outsider perceptions are provided by other groups who interact, or who have interacted, with the ethnic group under study.

When studying a group's self-perceptions, generalizations provide a frame of reference within which the group experience can be understood. The generalizations should not be considered "truths" or "verities"; rather they provide a benchmark for use in becoming better informed about the group. The generalizations should not be construed as the characteristics of individual group members, lest they promote stereotypes. Consider the generalization that racial minority groups have been oppressed by laws and social customs. There are sufficient data to support the generalization; still, not all racial minority persons have personally experienced oppression; nor do all racial minority persons feel oppressed. An individual's reaction depends upon unique experiences, life situation, and circumstances. An individual reaction at variance with the generalization does not invalidate the generalization; rather, the reaction indicates the multidimensionality of the ethnic experience.

Generalizations about ethnic groups should emphasize the dynamic nature of ethnic-group development. Ethnic-group specialists[12] have stressed the organic nature of group development, in particular how ethnic groups tend to maintain degrees of ongoing activism even though the groups are not visible in the press and mass media. All too often, ethnic groups are portrayed as sleeping dinosaurs who erupt into frenetic activism for short periods of time and then recede into antiquated sleep. The implication is that ethnic groups, like dinosaurs, are unchangeable and unadaptable organisms. In fact, if ethnic groups were like dinosaurs, they too would experience extinction. The dynamics that sustain the organic development of ethnic groups can be described as the human forces of change and conservation. As an ethnic group grows and develops, it must contend with the human impulse to conserve past practices, customs, and folkways and the impulse to change behaviors to adapt to current pressures of the physical and human environment. A balance between the two forces must be maintained continuously; conservation of too much of the past leads to decadence, or cultural lag. Too much or too rapid change causes disorientation, a sense of rootlessness, or what Toffler calls "future shock." To survive and to flourish, ethnic groups confront two forces, conserving and adapting behaviors, beliefs, and folkways in a continuous process of growth and development, a balancing act that produces stress and strives to minimize it. Figure 7.1 illustrates the dynamics of ethnic-group development.

THE MODEL'S OPERATIONAL PRINCIPLES

Teachers should approach teaching and learning about ethnic groups as a legitimate topic worthy of serious thought. Ethnic biases, stereotypes, and racist attitudes are learned in various ways in and out of the classroom. They can be countered by a serious study of ethnic groups, especially if imaginative and creative methods are used. Antiquated approaches such as rote memorization of dates of popular ethnic heroes are inappropriate. Rather, multimedia techniques and multi-instructional patterns (peer tutoring, field trips, simulations, etc.) are now recognized means by which teaching and learning can be both

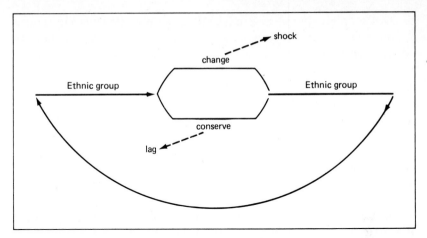

Figure 7.1 Dynamics of Ethnic-Group Development

serious and interesting. A serious study of U.S. ethnic groups would include but not be confined to the four principles which follow.

1. *Ethnic groups have unique experiences with the broader American society.* This principle focuses on the unique experiences ethnic groups have with the broader American society. For example, Native Americans, black Americans, and Irish Americans joined the broader American society under different circumstances. Irish Americans emigrated to the United States, accommodated to the Anglo-conformity melting pot, and progressed into the middle and upper classes. Black Americans were forced to migrate to the United States and then were enslaved for almost 175 years. After emancipation, they were segregated for 90 more years, and then progressed from enslaved status to lower-, middle-, and upper-middle-class status. Native Americans migrated to the North American continent long before Europeans arrived. The European colonizers declared them separate nations, making and then breaking treaties with each nation. Native Americans were eventually declared U.S. citizens (1924) but retained separate nation status. Forced from their homelands, they were placed on reservations; some were taken from the reservations, while others were kept there. Social status for Native Americans is tribally defined and should not be compared to the black and Irish American notions of social class status. Irish Americans encountered hostility toward their religion, Roman Catholicism. Blacks encountered slavery, and later, racial segregation and discrimination; Native Americans encountered dislocation, relocation, and separate nation status. Each group, in the attempt to participate in American life, encountered different experiences that influenced and formed its unique relationship with the broader society.

Each group should be studied as a unique ethnic group, not as though its early experiences were the same as or similar to those of other groups. The tendency is to lump ethnic groups together, assuming that each has undergone the same assimilation experience. Thus we have the myth that just as the Irish (or any other immigrant group) have been assimilated after starting at the bottom, so will Puerto Ricans (or some other ethnic minority group) be assimilated after starting at the bottom. For these purposes, Puerto Ricans are not foreign immigrants; they are U.S. citizens who merely choose to move from the island of Puerto Rico to the continental United States.

2. *Ethnic groups have definable demographic characteristics.* Ethnic-group peoples tend to live in certain areas, speak certain languages or dialects, and maintain their ancestral ties. Examples are: Japanese Americans tend to reside in the western United States and in Hawaii, although the U.S. government relocated them to various areas of the West and Midwest during World War II; Cuban Americans tend to maintain their Spanish language and culture while blending into the social scene. In particular, Cuban Americans, like other Spanish-speaking groups, have developed a bilingual capability in Spanish and English which is surpassed by few other groups. Greek Americans tend to maintain their ancestral ties with their mother country, Greece, and its traditions.

3. *Ethnic groups have elements of group homogeneity as well as heterogeneity; that is, intragroup differences and similarities exist.* The principle's best example is the Native American group. Native Americans are a tribal group, and in order of intimacy and interdependence, loyalty is first to the family, then to the clan, and then to the tribe. Within tribal groups there are variations. Among the Apaches (tribe) there are at least three distinctly different subtribal groups, each having different customs and traditions. Within each of the three subtribal groups, there are of course many families and clans to which individuals are primarily loyal. Thus, ethnic groups exhibit internal diversity in terms of traditions, customs, languages. For instance, at least 46 distinct languages are known to exist among Native Americans. Still, ethnic groups exhibit common values and beliefs. Generally speaking, Native Americans believe that people are a part of nature and must learn to adapt their ways to nature. An abiding respect for the ecology of the land, sea, and rivers is clearly a value held in common among Native Americans. Again, not every Native American holds these beliefs and values; nevertheless, as a group, Native Americans hold in common these values and beliefs.

4. *Ethnic groups have world views which can be understood through their literature, folklore, music, and other humanistic art forms.*

A group's world view can be understood by a study of its humanistic expressions. For example, as I have read the fiction and poetry of black writers, as I have listened to the music and folklore of black musicians and folklorists, I have been struck by the underlying message: a deeply felt assertion and affirmation of life and a genuine belief in the message of Christ that hope and love will prevail in the end. At first, the spirit of the Negro spirituals, the poetry of Langston Hughes, or the fiction of James Baldwin seem to be cries of despair. But as I listen and read more carefully, a profound sense of hope and compassion for other humans emerges. A group's world view can be understood by its humanistic expressions, but one should read a group's literature and study the group's humanistic tradition broadly and deeply. The adage "a little learning is a dangerous thing" holds true. A superficial study of a group's humanistic tradition can create stereotypes and misconceptions, doing it and the students little justice. In a very real way, the group's humanistic tradition should be approached with sensitivity to prevent reinforcing prevailing stereotypes and biases about the group.

TEACHING STRATEGIES

Since the model is so amenable to the teaching of social studies and language arts, I will suggest strategies outside these disciplines. The following are intended as suggestions which may lead to broader and deeper studies about ethnic groups:

Science

Students can research famous scientists, such as black inventors and medical doctors.

Students can study contributions Native Americans have made to pharmaceutical medicines.

Students can research various versions of the creation and evolution of the earth and the universe.

Students can study the similarities and differences of biologically different people. (A rigorous study of the concept of race, I feel, would serve to dispel most myths about racial superiority.)

Math

Students can study various ethnic groups' concepts of time and space.

Students can study how ethnic groups historically have calculated seasons and time of year. (A simple study of different calendars would go far in expanding the students' understanding of how different cultures measure time, e.g., Chinese or Aztec calendars.)

Home Economics

Students can study differing ethnic-group family patterns: nuclear, extended, single-parent families.

Students can study the differing foods, hairstyles, clothing styles (traditional) of various ethnic groups;

Students can study the viability of diverse ethnic group diets.

Physical Education

Students can study and learn the differing organized games of ethnic groups.

Students can study and learn the differing dances of ethnic groups.

More general teaching strategies follow. These suggestions were made in my Phi Delta Kappa fastback, *Fostering a Pluralistic Society Through Multi-Ethnic Education,* and are adapted here:

1. Students can study and discuss their ethnic heritage.
2. Ethnic minority group parents can be invited to school to visit and talk with students.
3. Students can study the contributions that all ethnic groups have made to the community.
4. Students can conduct surveys of their own ethnic group's geographic distribution and develop charts to record the information.
5. Students can make a multiethnic map of U.S. society using pictures from old magazines.
6. Any special ability of ethnic minority students, such as bilingualism, may be used to build their sense of belonging to the class. Sharing folktales, ethnic games, or songs are examples.
7. Field trips to other schools with diverse student populations can be planned so that students of different ethnic backgrounds can have one-to-one cultural exchanges.
8. A multiethnic reading table or reading shelf can be maintained by the teacher and students. It might contain ethnic magazines, newspapers, and books (e.g., *Ebony, Jr., La Luz, Wee Wish Tree*).
9. Students and teachers may work with PTA groups to conduct activities, such as a multiethnic song fest, that are cultural exchanges designed to improve community group relations.
10. A multiethnic student welcoming committee can be organized to greet all new students, teachers, and school personnel.
11. Role playing can be used to help students learn to take the role of out-groups as well as in-groups.

12. A multiethnic bulletin board should be maintained by the students displaying reports, pictures, and other items about persons from various ethnic groups.
13. A science teacher might demonstrate the similarities of racial groups by studying blood samples of blacks, Asians, etc.
14. Teachers in all subject areas can make an effort to incorporate a study of ethnic groups as they relate to the curriculum; e.g., Chinese math discoveries, black scientists and American inventions.
15. Schoolwide activities, such as Chicano dramas, blues festivals, and dances should be planned and conducted to offer students positive multiethnic experiences.

Teaching and learning about different ethnic groups is essential if students are to live and work in a society based on ethnic pluralism. Clearly, knowledge about different ethnic groups can lead to a better understanding of the groups.

USING THE ETHNIC STUDIES MODEL

The model is a conceptual frame of reference that can be used to teach or study any type of human group. Thus, it could be used to teach or study about the role of women in U.S. society, the role of certain cultural groups, such as pioneers, cowboys, trappers or traders, or the role of ethnic groups such as Irish Americans or Chinese Americans. Further, the model can be used on all grade levels and in any sociocultural setting. Clearly, the model has use in urban and rural areas where ethnic minority students are highly concentrated. But it is equally useful in suburban and other ethnically homogeneous communities.

Notes*

1. Joshua Fishman. *Language Loyalty in the United States*. The Hague: Mouton, 1966; see also, Garcia. *Learning in Two Languages*. Bloomington, Ind.: Phi Delta Kappa Education Foundation, 1976.
2. John E. Reinecke. *Language and Dialect in Hawaii*. Honolulu: University of Hawaii Press, 1969, pp. 119–132; see also, Arnold Leibowitz. *Educational Policy and Political Acceptance*. Washington, D.C.: Center for Applied Linguistics, 1971, pp. 6–44.

*Portions of material throughout Chapter 7 have been adapted from the following fastbacks, written by the author: *Fostering a Pluralistic Society*, no. 107, and *Learning in Two Languages*, no. 84 (Bloomington, Ind.: Phi Delta Kappa). They appear with the kind permission of Phi Delta Kappa.

3. Fishman. *Language Loyalty.*
4. Julius Drachsler. *Democracy and Assimilation.* New York: Macmillan, 1920; see also, William Vickery and Stewart Cole. *Intercultural Education in American Schools.* New York: Harper & Row, 1943.
5. Mark Krug. *The Melting of the Ethnics.* Bloomington, Ind.: Phi Delta Kappa Foundation, 1975, pp. 63–77.
6. *Ethnic Heritage Act, 1973,* Title IX of the Elementary-Secondary Education Act, 1973.
7. American Association of Colleges for Teacher Education, "No One Model American," *Journal of Teacher Education.* (Winter 1973): 264–265. Reprinted with permission of the American Association of Colleges for Teacher Education.
8. AACTE. *Multicultural Education and Ethnic Studies in the United States.* Washington, D.C.: AACTE, February 1976.
9. Frank Klassen and Donna Gollnick, eds. *Pluralism and the American Teacher.* Washington, D.C.: AACTE, 1977.
10. Ricardo Garcia. *Learning in Two Languages,* #84, 1976; James Banks. *Multiethnic Education,* #87, 1977; Garcia, *Fostering a Pluralistic Society Through Multiethnic Education,* #107, 1978; see also, Krug, *Melting of the Ethnics.* Bloomington, Ind.: Phi Delta Kappa Education Foundation, 1976. (All texts cited here were published by Phi Delta Kappa.)
11. National Council for the Social Studies. *Curriculum Guidelines for Multiethnic Education.* Washington, D.C.: NCSS, 1976. Reprinted with the permission of The National Council for the Social Studies.
12. Thomas Arciniega. *Public Education's Response to the Mexican American Student.* El Paso, Texas: Innovative Resources, Inc., 1977, pp. 8–20; see also, James Banks. "Cultural Pluralism: Implications for Curriculum Reform," in AACTE, *Multicultural Education and Ethnic Studies in the United States,* pp. 15–17; see also, Carlos Cortes. "Teaching the Chicano Experience," in Banks, *Teaching Ethnic Studies,* pp. 149–180; see also, Barbara Sizemore. "Shattering the Melting Pot Myth," in Banks, *Teaching Ethnic Studies,* pp. 73–102.

Chapter 8
The Bilingual
Instructional Model

What amazes me most about bilingual instruction is the phenomenal ignorance that surrounds it. Here I do not refer to people who work with bilingual education or people who are bilingual. I refer to various educators, college professors, school superintendents and administrators, counselors, and classroom teachers who carry around bags full of superstitions, myths, and outright ignorance regarding bilingual education. Even linguists trained in the science of language seem to carry the bag. Doesn't it make good sense if students can't understand you because they do not share your language and culture that you would teach in a language and culture your students could understand? The question is not rhetorical. Bilingual instruction is based on a fundamental principle of communication: communication is optimal when speakers and receivers share the same languages and cultures. Optimal communication between teachers and students is the nexus of classroom instruction.

AN OVERVIEW OF RESEARCH ON BILINGUALISM

In 1972, I conducted an intensive search and analysis of studies focused on the language development of Mexican American bilingual children. Soon I expanded my research to include other bilingual children of the United States but found that the bulk of bilingual language development research had been conducted among Mexican Americans. Unfortunately, to my knowledge, substantial research on the language development of other bilingual groups was not available.

Until the early 1960s, the majority of the studies focused on Mexican American bilingualism tended to reflect prevailing societal attitudes of the times. Pre-1935 documents presumed that Mexican American bilingualism was symptomatic of cultural deprivation. Formulation of language legislation in the southwestern United States, as well as educational policies and practices, reflected these presumptions —the "No-Spanish" and "English-only" laws and public policies that prohibited Mexican Americans from using Spanish in public institutions, including the public school classroom. Language segregation and, in effect, cultural isolation alienated the Mexican American from public institutions, especially in the political and economic spheres.

Documents of the second period, 1935–1955, revealed that the language legislation and public policies remained, but the studies' presumptions shifted to Mexican American bilingualism as a linguistic deficiency. These studies described bilingualism as the cause of the "alingual" condition of these Americans. Since the Mexican American speaks a "hodge-podge" of Spanish and English, the reasoning ran, he does not speak an acceptable form of either language. Therefore, he is without a language, or "alingual." Sociological texts written during this time embraced the "alingual syndrome" of Mexican Americans and recommended special education programs to ameliorate the language retardation caused by the syndrome. Southwestern state legislators debated the wisdom of bilingual school programs and bilingual public documents and public meetings since, in theory, the Mexican American was without a language.

Documents of the third period, 1955–1968, shifted from presumptions of cultural deprivation and linguistic deficiencies to a more neutral and less ethnocentric presumption: Mexican American bilingualism as a purely linguistic phenomenon. Studies during this period were confined to linguistic or psychological descriptions, excluding cultural and socioeconomic factors critical to the acquisition and development of two languages simultaneously. Consequently, language legislation and educational policies and practices retained the presumptions of cultural deprivation and linguistic deficiency. For example, federal legislation, especially the War on Poverty programs, authorized millions of dollars for compensatory programs to remedy the language deficiencies of the Mexican American. Changes have occurred in the contemporary period, 1968 to the present, in language legislation, Supreme Court rulings, and public policy statements that signal divergent attitudes regarding Mexican American bilingualism. These public documents, as well as research projects, are confronting and, at times, disputing the presumptions of deprivation and deficiency. It is too early to discern whether this trend is a significant divergence or merely a momentary shift of public and scholarly attitudes.

Nevertheless, the research and documents of the first six decades of this century, in effect, rendered Mexican Americans and their bilingualism—which has a history of more than 200 years of linguistic and cultural development—speechless and cultureless. My knowledge of Mexican American culture and languages, as well as the well-established history of Mexican American colonization in the southwestern United States, led me to seriously doubt the validity of such presumptions. On careful examination of the research of each period, I noted that the pre-1935 studies were merely exploratory. Methodologies were poorly contrived, and basic definitions of terms, such as "bilingualism," were at best based on the researchers' opinions. Few of the studies exhibited a knowledge of Mexican American English and Spanish and the attendant bilingual culture of the group. Studies during the second period were better designed, but they also exhibited little knowledge of Mexican American languages and cultures. Additionally, they were outwardly ethnocentric, referring to Mexican American Spanish and/or English as "bastardized," "adulterated," or similar pejoratives. The studies lamented the Mexican American's lack of cultural upbringing, referring to this group as a cultural hybrid, neither Mexican nor American. Studies of the third period avoided the research pitfalls and ethnocentric biases of the first and second periods, but they ignored socioeconomic and cultural factors which speak directly to the immense language diversity among Mexican Americans. Studies in the fourth period have refuted the presumptions of deprivation and deficiency, and have expanded to consider socio- and psycholinguistic dimensions. As you can see, studies on the language development of Mexican American children are fraught with serious empirical problems. Linguists have either been utterly naive, chauvinistic, or at worst, linguistic functionaires whose research has reflected the ethos of regional politics and politicians.

WHAT IS BILINGUAL INSTRUCTION?

Wherever bilingual instruction is being utilized, it is doing more good than harm. Students are learning along with conventional school subjects two languages, and at best, two cultures. Unfortunately, myths, half-truths, and outright ignorance about bilingual instruction persist. Colleagues of mine, specialists on various aspects of teaching and learning, have opposed bilingual education because it "doesn't teach English"; others have advocated bilingual education as the "panacea for teaching linguistic minority kids." The "doesn't teach English" colleagues argue that bilingual programs teach only one language, the students' non-English native language, which serves to further ghettoize them by not teaching them English. These colleagues accuse bilingual education of being "unilingual" or "monolingual" education. The "panacea for minority kids" colleagues argue that bilingual programs are the ultimate answer for minority liberation. Bidialectal programs for poor white students and black students are advocated along with bilingual programs for linguistic minority students. The "panacea" colleagues accuse bilingual instruction of more than it can deliver. Probably these colleagues have read very little about bilingual instruction. Or, if they've read books on the subject, they have nevertheless not given bilingual instruction the careful, objective study it merits. Had they done so, they would think of bilingual instruction neither as unilingual instruction nor as a panacea for the educational woes of linguistic minority students.

Just what is bilingual instruction? Bilingual instruction is using the student's strongest language as a medium of instruction to teach all school subjects as well as the English language in the (United States) along with the student's culture.

Now that bilingual instruction has been defined, the remaining part of this chapter will attempt to demythologize bilingual instruction. A special emphasis will be placed on bilingual instruction in the United States, stressing that bilingualism is an asset rather than a liability or a disease, that American teachers should use the natural language capabilities of their students to enhance rather than detract from teaching and learning in the pluralistic society. To demythologize bilingual instruction, the following aspects will be addressed:

The international dimension of bilingual instruction.
A historical overview of bilingual instruction in the United States.
The basic issues about bilingual instruction.

After addressing the area, a bilingual-bicultural instructional model is proposed, and then an analysis of the two prevailing instructional methods is presented.

INTERNATIONAL DIMENSIONS OF
BILINGUAL INSTRUCTION

Language is central to nationalism and the development of national identity. A nation's official language(s) carries and conveys the nation's symbols: oaths of allegiance, national anthems, and slogans in the national language embody the nation's spirit. The language serves to facilitate communication among the citizenry as well as to act as the national unification agent. Some nations have names and languages which are synonymous; for example, Spain and Spanish, Germany and German. Other nations have no such correspondence between names and their official languages; for example, United States and English, Canada and French and English. All nations have one or more languages recognized as their official language(s). Some countries, such as France, have one official language which is regulated by a language academy. Other countries, such as Canada, have an official bilingual policy which allows for two languages to coexist as the official languages. Some countries, India and the Soviet Union for example, have one official language which is used nationally, but allow regional languages and dialects to be used and taught within their respective regions.

The United States has no legal (de jure) language policy; at one time, most states prohibited the use of all non-English languages in public documents and institutions. Because of current bilingual education legislation and the *Lau* v. *Nichols* decision, the English-only laws have been rescinded in most states. However, the United States has a de facto official language, American English, which is not regulated by governmental agencies. Rather, social customs and usages tend to regulate the language. Non-English languages are now allowed in public documents and institutions, but their use is limited by varying state laws. To a great extent the United States is still an English-centric language nation. Non-English languages, which have been spoken by U.S. citizens ever since the nation's inception (e.g., French, Spanish, German), are considered "foreign" languages. Even the languages which are indigenous to the United States, the languages of Native Americans, are perceived as "foreign" by the general population.

Because language is central to nationalism, the decision as to which language or languages should be used in a nation's school as the medium of instruction is a critical national decision. The language(s) taught to the nation's future citizens become the embodiment of the national spirit and an agent for national unification. Eighteenth-century powers, such as England, France, and Spain, recognized the importance of language to national unity and control, and so always imposed their languages on the peoples they desired to colonize. In the United

States during the late eighteenth and early nineteenth centuries, feelings about American English ran so high that all of the states enacted laws that prohibited the use of any non-English language in the public schools.

There is a linkage between a nation's language policy and the language(s) used by its school teachers as the medium of instruction. Consequently, forms of bilingual instruction vary as implementation agents for a nation's language policy. Because nations have differing language policies, they also have differing goals for whatever bilingual programs they endorse. These goals are set according to such factors as the nation's desired national identity, its desired relationship with other countries, and the desired status of its linguistic minority populations. On an international scale, there exist at least four distinctly different types of bilingual instructional programs: (1) vernacularization, (2) internationalization, (3) assimilation, and (4) pluralization. These types are distinct because they focus on differing needs, statuses, identities, and language standards desired by different nations (see Table 8.1).

• *Vernacularization.* This type of bilingual program restores the nation's vernacular. The intent is to restore an indigenous language and establish it as the national standard. The Republic of the Philippine Islands is an example. This country was colonized by the Spanish and U.S. governments, and each imposed its langauge on the nation and

Table 8.1 TYPES OF BILINGUAL INSTRUCTIONAL PROGRAMS

VERNACULAR- IZATION	INTERNATIONAL- IZATION	ASSIMILATION	PLURALIZATION
NATIONAL NEED			
Subnational legitimacy	Supernational legitimacy	Cultural assimilation	Cultural pluralism
NATIONAL STATUS			
Emergent oppressed	Potential oppressed	Superactive majority group	Linguistic minority
NATIONAL IDENTITY			
Self-recognition	Other recognition	Monolingual melting pot	Multilingual pluralism
NATIONAL LANGUAGE STANDARD			
New vernacular as standard	Borrowed elitism: adopted foreign national language standards	Status quo elitism: standard substandard language, languages and dialects	Egalitarian language standard: separate and equal language standards

prohibited the use of any other language in all public institutions. Now that the Philippine nation is free of Spanish and U.S. rule, it has declared that the vernacular language native to the Filipino, Tagalog, is the standard language of the nation. Henceforth, all public documents and institutions will use the new language. Under the vernacularization program, the national status of the once oppressed country is now emerging from foreign domination. The national identity desired by the emergent oppressed country is self-esteem and self-pride in the indigenous language(s) and culture of the country. The new vernacular is established as the nation's language standard. Yet, because the Spanish and English languages are known by the citizenry, bi- and trilingual programs using Tagalog, Spanish, and English can be established. Emphasis is upon building literacy in the indigenous language and culture as well as in another language.

• *Internationalism.* This type of bilingual program is multilingual. Schools teach in more than two languages. The intent is to create a multilanguage nation. Switzerland, where four languages are taught to students, is an example. The nation is landlocked and surrounded by European countries; to successfully interface with these countries, and to maintain legitimacy with them, the citizens need to speak their languages. Switzerland's national status is one of being potentially oppressed; if its citizens cannot speak the languages of surrounding countries, the country is in danger of economic, political, or military oppression by the other nations. The country thus desires to be recognized by other nations as an equal. It has multiple language standards in that the language standard of four other countries are adopted by the country.

• *Assimilation.* This is a cultural assimilation program. The intent is to assimilate foreign language speakers into the dominant linguistic and cultural group of the nation. Some bilingual programs in the United States are examples. These programs presume the status of a superactive majority group that wants to assimilate some linguistic minority group. The majority group perceives the nation as a monolingual melting pot which has one standard language; other languages, or dialects of the standard, are perceived as substandard languages or dialects. The student's "substandard" language or dialect is used as the medium of instruction to compensate for his or her limited English-speaking abilities. Use of the "substandard" language dialect is transitional. As soon as the student learns English well enough to receive instruction, then use of the student's language is discontinued and instruction is in English only.

• *Pluralization.* This type of program is a cultural pluralism program. The intent is to allow different language and cultural groups to coexist within a nation, as well as to equalize schooling by using the student's home language and culture as the base of instruction. Some U.S. bilingual programs are examples. In these programs, the non-English language group is perceived as a linguistic minority group that has a right to maintain its bilingual-bicultural status. Maintaining a group's language and culture is perceived as necessary to perpetuate the multilingual pluralism of American society. The nation's language standard is egalitarian—that is, each language has its respective standard. American English dialects or non-English languages are perceived as having separate and equal standards.

BILINGUAL INSTRUCTION IN THE UNITED STATES

In the United States, various forms of assimilation, pluralization, and vernacularization programs are used in the public schools. The programs are called respectively "maintenance," "transitional," and "language restoration" programs. Because of the complicated and diverse nature of these bilingual programs, this section will provide an overview. I hope to demythologize much that is currently believed about bilingual instruction. Much of the material in this section was originally reported in my book, *Learning in Two Languages,*[1] published by the Phi Delta Kappa Educational Foundation.

Before the Europeans colonized in the United States, many non-European languages were spoken by the original settlers of the American continent, the Native Americans. The European languages of the first colonists were Spanish, French, Dutch, and English. As early as the 1550s, essays, poetry, and documents were written by Spanish writers who settled in what is now the southwestern United States. The United States has a history of linguistic diversity, especially as the later immigrant languages were added to the languages spoken by the European colonizers and Native Americans. The nation also has a history of dual language instruction in its public and private schools. For purposes of discussion, I have divided the history of bilingual instruction into four time periods:

1550–1815: Bilingual instruction for religious reasons
1816–1887: Bilingual instruction for maintenance of native languages
1880–1960: Waning of bilingual instruction for religious and language maintenance
1960–1975: Resurgence of bilingual instruction for equalization/compensation in public schooling

During the first period, 1550 to 1815, bilingual instruction was first used in what is now the southwestern United States. In the later 1550s Jesuit and Franciscan missionaries utilized the tribal dialects to teach Christianity to southwestern Native Americans. In what is now New England, bilingual instruction was used by Protestant missionaries in Native American schools; indigenous dialects were used to introduce Native Americans to the "habits and art of civilization." Knowledge of the English language, Christian beliefs, and Anglo culture were considered "civilized." The Native American dialects were tolerated rather than respected. No attempt was made to develop literacy in the dialects. Also, in New England, bilingual instruction was utilized by the German Lutherans to teach the High German dialect. The Lutherans formed bilingual seminaries to teach both in the German and English languages. By 1880, more than 140 Lutheran bilingual schools were established. In 1815, a conference of the Evangelical Lutheran Teachers in Virginia issued a resolution calling for bilingual (German/English) instruction for Lutheran students. The resolution suggested that if teachers could not teach bilingually, then the local congregations were to procure a bilingual minister who would teach bilingually for three months each year in the Lutheran schools.

Before the second period, bilingual instruction was used for religious instruction in church-related schools, including the schools for Native Americans. Although the private schools continued to operate, the second period, 1816 to 1887, saw the rise of free public schools that used bilingual instruction. In 1834, a free school law passed in Pennsylvania allowed instruction in both German and English for students who did not speak English as a primary language. In 1839 the state of Ohio required German and English bilingual instruction for German American students in elementary schools. During the second period, eleven states and one territory enacted laws that allowed bilingual instruction in schools. These were: Pennsylvania (1834), Ohio (1839), Territory of New Mexico (now Arizona and New Mexico) (1850), Wisconsin (1855), Illinois (1857), Iowa (1861), Kentucky and Minnesota (1867), Indiana (1869), Oregon (1872), Colorado (1887), and Nebraska (1913). Throughout most of the second period, city school districts such as Cincinnati, Dayton, Indianapolis, and Baltimore maintained bilingual public schools. In the Territory of New Mexico, provisions were made for bilingual (Spanish and English) instruction; these provisions were rarely implemented in the few public schools established during the early years of the territory. Bilingual instruction waned for Native Americans after a congressional commission established boarding schools and assimilation policies for Native Americans; the bilingual schools were a threat to the government's expansionistic plans. The purpose of boarding schools was to remove Native American children from their homelands and to eradicate their languages and cultures, replacing them with English and Anglo culture in hopes that the children would not return to their homelands. Then, after several generations, land abandoned by the assimilating Native Americans would be available for Anglo pioneers. By 1871, the government took complete control of the schools, imposed an English-only rule, and eliminated the missionary bilingual schools. Even the schools operated by Native Americans—such as the Cherokee system of twenty-one schools and two academies—were eliminated by government takeover. The policy precipitated the decline of Native American literacy.

In the third period, 1887 to 1960, both religious and public bilingual instruction decreased. Yet this period saw the largest influx of non-English-speaking immigrants. Between 1887 and 1920, more than twenty distinguishable European languages (other than English) were spoken by U.S. citizens. During this period numerous Asian languages were brought into the country. In addition, the tribes of Native Americans spoke many distinguishable dialects. During this period of tremendous population growth, language legislation and laws were most restrictive. English-only statutes and policies were enforced in most states. These statutes prohibited the use of any language (except English) as a medium of instruction in the public schools. In some states, the statutes provided for revocation of a teacher's certification, if caught in the "criminal act" of using any language other than English to teach. Students who violated the English-only rules of their schools were subjected to physical punishment or paying small fines or detention in a study hall. As recently as the 1950s I knew teachers who "dared" to teach in Spanish in New Mexico. Given circumstances of geographic isolation, these teachers did not lose certification—but there was always that risk!

The diminishing of bilingual instruction and the sprouting of English-only statutes or laws can be attributed to the strong nativistic sentiments that pervaded the United States. During the period between 1880 and 1960, the country was engaged in two world wars, two police actions—Spanish-American War and Korean War—in addition to other military incursions. The use of any language other than English was viewed as un-American or unpatriotic. Non-English speakers were viewed with suspicion. Thus, non-English speakers tended to discontinue speaking their primary language and to discourage their children from learning it. Still, by 1959 more than 25 European languages were spoken by U.S. citizens. Some bilingual schools were established during the third period, notably those for Chinese, French, Greek, Jewish, and Japanese American students. The Chinese and Japanese American schools were criticized strongly prior to World War II. Most of the schools were disbanded during the war, and only a few survived after the war.

The fourth period, 1960 to 1979, experienced a resurgence of bilingual instruction. In 1966, Dade County schools felt the impact of more than 20,000 Cuban Spanish-speaking refugee students. Two model bilingual programs were established to accommodate the Spanish-speaking students. The Coral War elementary school was set up as a completely bilingual school. Other schools in Dade County provided Spanish language arts instruction at all grades for Spanish-speaking students. The projects used federal and local funds to finance the two model programs, and in a sense, the Dade County experiment was the first time the federal government was involved in the implementation of bilingual public schools.

In 1968, Public Law 90-247, the Bilingual Education Act, was enacted. The Bilingual Education Act, the seventh amendment to the Elementary and Secondary Education Act of 1965 (Title VII), declared that it was "to be the policy of the United States to provide financial assistance to local education agencies to develop and carry out new and imaginative elementary and secondary school programs designed to meet the special education needs . . . [of] children who come from environments where the dominant language is other than English." The act stipulated that it would be the policy of the U.S. government to assist financially in the development and implementation of bilingual education programs in the public schools in the United States and its trust territories.

In 1973, the act was changed to the Comprehensive Bilingual Education Amendment Act of 1973. The act was amended to extend, improve, and expand assistance for the training of bilingual teachers and bilingual teacher trainers. The act's policy recognized that (1) large number of children have limited English-speaking ability, (2) many of these children have a cultural heritage which differs from that of English-speaking people, and (3) a primary means by which a child learns is through using his or her language and cultural heritage. The act provided financial assistance for extending and improving existing bilingual-bicultural programs in the public schools, for improving resource and dissemination centers, and for developing and publishing bilingual-bicultural curriculum materials. Assistance was also provided for stipends and fellowships so teachers and teacher-educators could be trained in bilingual-bicultural methodology. According to the 1978 project summary report issued by the Office of Bilingual Education, Washington, D.C., bilingual education programs which received funding for the 1978–79 school year were located in public schools, colleges and universities, and resource and dissemination centers.

A major catalyst for bilingual instruction was the 1974 Supreme Court ruling in *Lau* v. *Nichols* that provisions for the same teachers, programs, and textbooks in the same language for all students in the San Francisco school district did not provide equal educational opportunity when the native language of a sizable portion of the student body was not English. In this case, the students were Chinese Americans, who showed low academic achievement and high attrition. Their primary language was Chinese. While the ruling did not mandate bilingual instruction for non-English-speaking or limited English-speaking students, it did stipulate that special educational programs were necessary if schools were to provide equal educational opportunity for such students. Moreover, school districts with more than 25 linguistic minority students must provide them a special language program in all academic areas. The U.S. Office of Civil Rights can freeze the federal funds of any school district which does not comply with the *Lau* decision. The *Lau* decision may have as much impact for linguistic minorities as did *Brown* v. *Topeka Board of Education* for black Americans. While *Lau* did not establish a bilingual policy for the United States, it made bilingual instruction lawful in the public schools. Moreover, linguistic minorities no longer leave their native language(s) at the schoolyard gates.

This brief overview of U.S. bilingual instruction is not all-inclusive. Sporadic attempts were made to establish bilingual schools for the many tribes of Native Americans. Jewish schools have been established in a bilingual mode. Many ethnic groups attempted to establish some form of bilingual school to preserve their native languages and cultures. Also, the U.S. Office of Civil Rights played an active role in the development of current bilingual programs. The overview reveals major shifts in the purposes of bilingual instruction: during the first period, bilingual instruction was used to propagate various Christian denominations; the second period and third period used bilingual instruction to maintain native languages and culture (with the exception of Native American programs). The last period, actually the contemporary period, uses bilingual instruction to provide equal educational benefits for linguistic minority students.

In retrospect, three American ethnic groups have fought gallantly for bilingual-bicultural instruction: Native Americans, German Americans, and Mexican Americans. Native Americans have confronted a history of concerted efforts by the U.S. government and its agents, the Bureau of Indian Affairs and Christian missionaries, to obliterate their languages and cultures.[2] In spite of those concerted efforts which began before the Declaration of Independence was signed, Native Americans have used the bilingual-bicultural method to build for themselves educational systems far superior to those developed by non-Native Americans. The best example is the educational system built by the Cherokee tribe. When the Oklahoma Cherokee Nation built an education system, they built it with a common school system, a normal school system, and a higher education system. By 1852, according to Weinberg,[3] the Oklahoma Cherokees had a better school system than either of the neighboring states of Arkansas or Missouri. The Cherokee system was a bilingual system; Cherokee language and culture were taught on the basis of the language syllabary developed by the Cherokee scholar, Sequoyah.

German Americans have confronted American anti-Germanic attitudes which go back to before World War I. Fishman, in his analysis of language loyalty in the United States,[4] reported that German Americans were the most literate bilingual ethnic group in the United States. They produced bilingual literature, radio programs and school curricula; yet, German Americans were not allowed to maintain their languages and cultures through the public schools. Some important exceptions to this generalization assisted the growth of bilingual-bicultural education, in particular the development of bilingual public schools in Ohio and Indiana.[5] In fact, German Americans fought vigorously for bilingual-bicultural instruction, but because the German nation has twice in this century been the political enemy of the U.S. government, the German American struggle for bilingual-bicultural instruction succumbed.

Mexican Americans have struggled for bilingual instruction for a long time. For example, the original constitution of the state of New Mexico stipulated that Spanish-speaking teachers were to be trained so as to teach the Spanish-speaking natives of New Mexico. The bilingual teaching stipulation was largely ignored in New Mexico. Further, in violation of the state constitution, the Spanish language was prohibited in all public institutions, including the public schools, in New Mexico. Other southwestern states also prohibited the use of any language other than English in their public schools. Yet, in remote areas of the Southwest, a few teachers utilized the bilingual-bicultural method. Thus, while Mexican American culture developed in the Southwest, its development was not supported by the educational system.

When the first bilingual education law was enacted in 1968, it included the Spanish-speaking Cuban and Mexican American students. It was through the political and personal efforts of Mexican Americans and their Anglo *compadres* that bilingual-bicultural education became what it is today: a largely unrecognized but nevertheless significant educational movement in the United States.

Keep in mind these three groups—Native Americans, German Americans, Mexican Americans—who have had to fight for their right to a language and a culture within the American scene. As of 1980, their struggle continues. One lesson they have learned is that no matter how desirable bilingual-bicultural instruction may be, its value is not easily recognized by others in American society.

BASIC ISSUES IN BILINGUAL INSTRUCTION

There are basic issues pertaining to bilingual instruction. These issues are raised here in question form and then answered. The intent is to clarify the issues and thereby render the bilingual instructional model more feasible.

What is bilingualism? The greatest degree of bilingualism is full literacy in two languages. "Full literacy" means that a bilingual person can speak, read, and write in two languages with the same proficiency as native speakers of the two languages. Of course, this is achieved by few bilinguals; most bilinguals can best be described in terms of degrees of literacy in two languages. Some bilinguals may be fully literate in one language, but may only understand a second language. Or, some bilinguals may speak two languages but may be fully literate only in one language. Some bilinguals may be fully literate in one language but may only read in a second language. Some bilinguals may be fully literate in two languages, but may only speak one language with the control of a native speaker. Figure 8.1 illustrates the varying degrees of bilingual literacy.

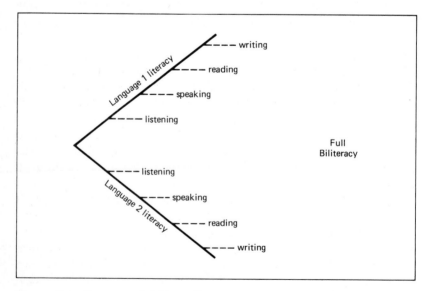

Figure 8.1 Degrees of Bilingualism

Does bilingualism enhance the reading and language achievement of the bilingual student? In studies of bilinguals who were instructed in their second language, which was weaker, adverse effects were shown in school progress and results. Macnamara's studies[6] in Ireland of bilinguals instructed in Gaelic instead of English showed a deterioration in school achievement. In the majority of Macnamara's studies on mathematics achievement, it was reported that bilinguals were slower than monolinguals in problem arithmetic (verbal reasoning) but not in mechanical arithmetic (computation). Macnamara attributed the differences in the findings to the differences in tasks. In tasks of mechanical arithmetic the subjects were required to carry out an operation with arithmetical symbols, but in tasks of problematic arithmetic the subjects were required to read and interpret prose statements. In a study on the effects of bilingualism on reading, Macnamara[7] found that articulation and oral communication in the weaker language were slower for the bilingual and that encoding of ideas and organizing of syntactic patterns possibly occurred with less rapidity in the weaker language. The general finding that, for the bilingual, reading in a weaker language takes longer than reading in the stronger was reported by studies in 1959 and 1960. Earlier studies reported like results. Welsh bilinguals instructed in their weaker language demonstrated progressive retardation in all areas of school achievement.[8] Such a retardation was also reported to occur over two years of primary teaching in the vernacular in Manila.[9]

Complete reliance upon the above findings would lend support to the assumption that bilingualism, per se, is detrimental to language development. Yet in studies where the bilingual's second language was not the weaker language, and where the bilingual could develop both languages fully, the bilingual's language development was not impaired. Having two languages seemed to have a positive effect on school achievement. Apparently, being bilingual facilitated the awareness that there are varying ways to say the same thing. Peal and Lambert[10] explored the effects of bilingualism on intellectual functioning and reported that when socioenvironmental variables are controlled bilinguals perform better than monolinguals on verbal and nonverbal intelligence tests. The investigators reported that the bilingual subjects had several advantages over their monolingual peers: (1) a language asset, (2) greater cognitive flexibility, and (3) a greater ability in concept formation than the monolingual. The investigators concluded that the bilinguals appeared to have a more diversified set of mental abilities than the monolinguals.

Lambert, Just, and Segalowitz[11] conducted a longitudinal study of middle-class English-speaking children who were taught French, which was also used as the medium of instruction. After two years of instruction in their weaker language, general improvement was experienced by the bilingual children. Even though the children were instructed in French, their weaker language, they demonstrated an optimum level of skills in both the productive and reproductive aspects of French, and a generally excellent control of their home language, English. The investigators reported that socioenvironmental variables were accounted for in the study, and that if conflict occurred between the children's two languages, its negative effect was minimal.

In another study conducted in Sweden, bilingual children were organized into two groups.[12] The experimental group of bilingual elementary-school children received an initial ten weeks of reading instruction in Pitean, the local dialect, after which they were advanced to classes conducted in literary Swedish. The control group of bilinguals, who were also Pitean-Swedish speakers, received all reading instruction in literary Swedish. At the end of the first ten weeks the Pitean-taught group had progressed further in reading than the Swedish-taught group. At the end of the school year, the experimental group performed significantly better than the control group on word recognition, speed, fluency, and accuracy of reading in literary Swedish. Beginning reading instruction in the vernacular and then switching to the school dialect had positive effects in this study.

Like results were reported in similar studies conducted in Mexico.[13] The test data in these studies indicated that the bilinguals, who were initially taught in the vernacular, read with greater comprehension than those initially taught in the Spanish of the school. These studies also reported that bilinguals initially instructed in the vernacular achieved literacy in both languages within two years. Studies in the United States on bilingualism report that Spansh-English bilingualism does not negatively affect the Mexican American's syntactic language development. Peña[14] conducted a study to ascertain whether Mexican American first graders could control basic syntactic patterns of Spanish and English. Peña reported that the bilingual first graders could utilize basic Spanish and English syntactic patterns, and that the bilinguals had little or no difficulty generating transformations in Spanish and English. Garcia[15] conducted a study to identify and compare the oral English syntactic sentence patterns of bilingual adolescent lower-class and middle-class Mexican Americans. The results of the study indicated that the bilinguals used all of the patterns basic to standard English, and that they expressed a style consistent with their socioeconomic status. The Mexican Americans were found to be native English speakers in the syntactic sense because they used syntactic patterns much like monolingual English speakers. Kessler's study[16] on the syntactic acquisitions of Italian English 6- to 8-year-old bilingual children indicates that syntactic structures shared by the two languages develop in the same sequential pattern at approximately the same rate. Kessler's study, while thoroughly developed and executed, requires replication with a larger sample, but it points to the positive cognitive effects of bilingualism.

Are elementary school students, say in grades K–3, really very bilingual? Much depends on the student's home environment. Most elementary K–3 students are not fully literate in any language; the same holds true with bilingual students. Yet some K–3 students can speak two languages equally well. Others can speak a non-English language such as Vietnamese, but barely speak English. Some students can understand and speak a second language minimally, but speak English as well as any other K–3 student. Generally, K–3 bilingual students will control one of their two languages better. The bilingual instruction premise is that students should first develop literacy in their stronger language, and then develop literacy in their weaker language.

What about black students who speak Black English? Are they bilingual? If Black English were recognized in our society as a valid language, then black students literate in Black English and school English would be bilingual. Linguists recognize Black English as a valid dialect of American English, so black students literate in two English dialects would be "bidialectal." There probably is no essential difference between a bilingual and a bidialectal, except, of course, that they speak different languages or dialects.

Should black students receive bidialectal instruction? As with bilingual instruction, much depends on the wishes of the students' parents. There is no valid educational objection to black students developing full literacy in Black English and school English. Yet, racism is still so strong in our society that many black parents feel that their youngsters will be discriminated against if they speak Black English. Therefore, these parents stress learning school English for social uses and allow Black English only for informal occasions. Other parents feel that Black English should be taught along with school English. In my opinion, Black English is a valid American English dialect; some of it should be taught to all students. Elementary and secondary language arts curricula stress that there are three American English dialects: Eastern, Southern, and General American. The triad is no longer accurate; it should be abandoned and replaced with a paradigm that focuses on the dialectal diversity of American English.

FORMATS OF BILINGUAL INSTRUCTION

Because of U.S. bilingual education's diversity, a brief explanation of three major formats precedes the bilingual model:

Transitional format   The intent of this format is cultural assimilation. The intent is to assimilate foreign language speakers into the dominant linguistic and cultural group of the nation. Educators who implement the format perceive the nation as a monolingual melting pot which has one standard language; other languages or dialects of the standard are perceived as substandard. The student's "substandard" language or dialect is used as the medium of instruction to compensate for limited English-speaking abilities. Use of the "substandard" language-dialect is transitional. As soon as the student learns English well enough to receive instruction, then use of the student's language is discontinued and instruction is in English only.

Maintenance format   This format is based on a philosophy of pluralism. The intent is to allow different language/cultural groups to coexist within a nation, as well as to equalize schooling by using the student's home language and culture as the base of instruction. In this format, the non-English language group is perceived as a linguistic minority group that has a right to maintain its bilingual-bicultural status. Maintaining a group's language and culture is perceived as necessary to perpetuate the multilingual pluralism of American society. The language standard is egalitarian, that is, each language has its respective standard; American English dialects or non-English languages are perceived as having separate and equal standards.

Restoration format   This format is similar in philosophy to the maintenance format. However, the intent of this format is to restore or recover a language and culture that has been lost, stolen, or strayed. Examples of the format are the Window Rock Arizona Navajo bilingual program and the Cherokee, the Choctaw, and the Seminole Oklahoma bilingual programs.

BILINGUAL INSTRUCTIONAL MODEL

• *Goal:* To provide linguistic minority learners equitable educational benefits.

• *Operational assumption:* Optimal teaching and learning are possible when instruction is delivered in the learner's better-known language and culture.

• *Conceptual structure:* To provide optimal teaching and learning,

1. instruction should begin in the learner's stronger language;
2. instruction should begin in the learner's stronger culture;

3. instruction for basic literacy in the stronger language should precede formal instruction in the second;
4. instruction for full literacy in two languages and two cultures should be sustained until achieved.

BILINGUAL INSTRUCTIONAL METHODS

Bilingual instruction is more than language instruction; it is instruction by which the students' language or dialect is utilized to convey their culture to them. Generally, bilingual instruction is joined by "bicultural" instruction, which teaches students about their ethnic culture while providing them a background in the general American culture. In essence, the "bicultural" component is an ethnic studies component, since it focuses on the students' particular ethnic group. The purpose of bilingual instruction is to increase academic achievement by using the student's primary language as the dominant medium through which the student can develop appropriate academic attitudes, concepts, skills, and knowledge. Bilingual instruction entails the use of two languages as mediums of instruction for part or all of the activities within the classroom. One of the languages is English (in the United States), and the other language is the student's primary language(s), which is predominantly spoken in the student's home. It may be the only language spoken in the home, or it may be one of two languages spoken. Moreover, English is taught as a second language. Often the student is introduced to English for the first time upon entering school. In other instances, the student may begin school with minimum English language skills. Academic instruction in most school subjects is in the student's native language, if that language is the student's strongest language.

There are two distinct methods of teaching English to linguistic minority students: the native language method and the English as a Second Language (ESL) method. The native language method, also called the dominant method, uses the student's native language in all subject areas. After learning native-language listening and oral skills, the student is taught to read. After native-language mastery in listening, speaking, reading, and writing, the student is introduced to English as a second language (ESL). The native language method requires a bilingual teacher who is fluent and can teach the language arts and other subject areas in two languages. It is used to teach literacy in two languages. The method is based on the idea that the basic native language art skills—listening, speaking, reading, and writing—should be acquired before the student is formally introduced to the English language arts. Having mastered these skills, the student should have no difficulty transferring to English. At no time is reading of

English taught until the student masters native language listening and speaking skills, at least. The position assumes that the native language is the better medium of instruction for initial school instruction.

Criticisms of the method vary. One is that native language literacy is a waste of time since the student may have little use for the primary language in an English-speaking country. Others are that there aren't enough trained bilingual teachers, that the method actually requires two teachers, and that it delays learning English until the student is older and English is harder to learn. These criticisms are not serious. More bilingual teachers can be trained. The National Education Association and the American Association of Colleges of Teacher Education have recognized and supported bilingual teacher education programs. Federal money is available to assist the programs. The method does not require two teachers. The sophistication of the education profession—team teaching, programmed instruction, individualized instruction, paraprofessionals, and educational technology—has reached the point that a monolingual teacher could manage bilingual classes. Learning English is not delayed very long. By the end of the second year, the student is introduced to the formal study of English. Moreover, the student catches and absorbs English almost everywhere in school except in some of the classes.

The second method, English as a Second Language (ESL), is also called the direct method. ESL is a method to teach the student immediate English language skills which enable him or her to communicate and receive instruction in English. The ESL pull-out system takes the student out of the classroom daily for instruction in the English language arts. The student returns to the classroom for instruction in other subjects. In this system, the student plays catch-up all the time, trying to learn both a new language and new subject material. The ESL intensive system immerses the student in the English language for intense periods of time. Sentence pattern drills, vocabulary, and idiom exercises are structured so as to introduce the second language (English) gradually. When the student learns to speak the language, then reading is introduced. When the student reads in English, he is returned to the monolingual English classroom for instruction in all subjects. In this system, the student is segregated for long periods of time, but because length of time varies and the purpose of isolation is to meet special language needs, reasonable isolation for ESL instruction is allowed under desegregation regulations. However, in the past, school districts have isolated linguistic minority students without knowledge of or regard for their language needs. These students were deliberately segregated in school annexes and other remote areas of the school where they remained segregated. This latter practice violates desegregation regulations.

The major criticism of ESL is that it ignores the student's culture. ESL essentially teaches basic American English. It is a method to teach American English. While ESL uses American English words, phrases, idioms, it does not comprehensively teach about any specific cultural or ethnic group. Neither does ESL encourage or teach about the student's native language or culture. Minor idiomatic comparisons may be made between the student's language and English.

Both methods have distinct advantages. The native language method safeguards against cultural disorientation because the student understands instruction from the beginning. The ESL method does not require bilingual teachers.

Notes*

1. Ricardo Garcia. *Learning in Two Languages*. Fastback #84. Bloomington, Ind.: Phi Delta Kappa Education Foundation, 1976.
2. Meyer Weinberg. *A Chance to Learn*. New York: Cambridge University Press, 1977, pp. 178–229.
3. Weinberg, pp. 184–185.
4. Joshua Fishman. *Language Loyalty in the United States*. The Hague: Mouton, 1966, pp. 380–385.
5. Fishman. *Language Loyalty*, pp. 392–417.
6. John Macnamara. *Bilingualism in Primary Education*. Edinburgh: University of Edinburgh Press, 1966, Ch. 6.
7. John Macnamara. "Reading in a Second Language," *Improving Reading Throughout the World*. Newark, N.J.: International Reading Association, 1968, Ch. 5.
8. D. J. Saer. "The Effects of Bilingualism on Intelligence," *British Journal of Psychology*, (April 1923): 25–38.
9. Manila Department of Education. *The Relative Effectiveness of the Vernacular and of English as Media of Instruction*. Manila: Bureau of Public Schools, 1953, Ch. 14.
10. Elizabeth Peal and Wallace Lambert. *The Relation of Bilingualism and Intelligence*. Washington, D.C.: American Psychological Association, 1962, p. 27.
11. Wallace Lambert, J. Just, and N. Segalowitz. "Some Cognitive Consequences of Following the Curricula of the Early School Grades in a Foreign Language." *Monograph Series on Language and Literature*. James Alatis, ed., Washington, D.C.: Georgetown University Press, 1970, p. 259.
12. Tana Osterberg. *Bilingualism and the First School Language*. Umea: Vasterbottens TrychKeri AB, 1961, 85–103.

* Portions of material throughout Chapter 8 have been adapted from the following fastbacks, written by the author: *Fostering a Pluralistic Society*, no. 107, and *Learning in Two Languages*, no. 84 (Bloomington, Ind.: Phi Delta Kappa). They appear here with the kind permission of Phi Delta Kappa.

13. A. Barrera-Vasquez. *The Tarascan Project in Mexico: Use of Vernacular Languages in Education.* Paris: UNESCO, 1953, pp. 77–86.

14. Albar Peña. *A Comparative Study of Selected Syntactical Structures of the Oral Language Status in Spanish and English of Disadvantaged First-Grade Spanish Speaking Children.* Austin: University of Texas Press, 1967.

15. R. Garcia. *Identification and Comparison of Oral English Syntactic Patterns of Spanish-English Speaking Adolescents.* Unpublished dissertation, University of Denver, 1973.

16. C. Kessler. *Acquisition of Syntax in Bilingual Children.* Washington, D.C.: Georgetown University Press, 1971.

Chapter 9
Classroom Management and Human Rights Strategies

In the next two chapters we shift from instructional models to broader classroom management processes for teaching and learning in a pluralistic society. The ethnic studies and bilingual instructional models can be utilized with individual students or with an entire class, depending on the teacher's instructional needs. The models are thus limited because they do not focus on how a teacher can manage a class so much as on how pluralistic content can be conveyed to students. In this chapter, focus will be upon classroom management and human rights as a strategy to enhance cross-cultural and cross-ethnic relationships. Specifically, the classroom management-human rights strategy draws attention to the basic rights and responsibilities to which students are entitled, including, of course, the right to be culturally and/or ethnically different. The human rights approach provides a strategy to teach living in a democratic society.

BASIS FOR CLASSROOM MANAGEMENT

Teachers are responsible for maintaining a safe learning environment for their students. To manage a classroom effectively a teacher must understand how students are affected by the classroom's physical and human environments and by the teacher's choice of teaching styles. The three key factors, physical environment, human environment, and teaching style, are felt by the students in their totality: students enter a classroom; scan the bulletin boards and the seating arrangements; notice whether or not other students are visiting, studying, sitting casually or stiffly; and listen to their teacher. They soon sense the tone or catch the classroom climate. A drab room with empty bulletin boards, where desks are clamped to the floor, where students are compelled to sit without leaving for long periods of time, has the trappings of an oppressive learning environment. Yet, the teacher's choice of teaching styles in this room could greatly change the human environment so that these dismal trappings would have a smaller impact.

A classroom must be physically safe for students. Teachers should know all emergency procedures—what to do and where to go when fires, tornadoes, and other natural hazards occur. Teachers should be wary of all potentially dangerous school equipment or tools, and students should be coached in their proper usage. A sharp lead pencil, thrown across an aisle, could strike another student in the eye and cause serious harm. Adequate lighting, ventilation, heating, and cooling should be maintained whenever possible. Unnecessarily stuffy rooms, poorly lighted and overly hot or cold, affect the learning environment negatively. Further, the classroom's physical environment should reflect the nature of what is taught and what is learned in the classroom. Students' products, artwork, papers, posters should be displayed along with teacher-made materials and visual aids.

The teaching style can overcome the drabbest physical environment. In the reverse, the most tantalizing physical environment will not necessarily overcome overly oppressive or overly lax teaching styles. A teaching style can be thought of as the manner in which a teacher facilitates learning. A teacher's style reflects his or her personality and judgment about how best to facilitate classroom learning. Teachers develop styles compatible with their proclivities, toleration and frustration limitations, preferences, and idiosyncrasies. In other words, a teaching style is the manifestation of one's desire to teach something of value to oneself and to the student.

Teaching styles are usually categorized by the kind of leadership or governance techniques a teacher uses. The extent to which the teacher allows students to share in the decision-making process in the classroom identifies the type of teaching style utilized. The style can be located on a decision-sharing continuum as an autocratic, democratic, or laissez faire teaching style, as shown in Figure 9.1. Speaking in absolute terms, an autocratic style will not share the decision-

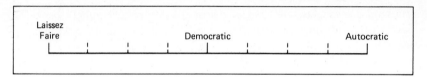

Figure 9.1   Decision-Sharing Teaching-Styles Continuum

making process. What is taught and how concepts are learned are determined by the teacher alone. The style is entirely directive, leaving little room for student involvement or input. The democratic style shares a good portion of the decision-making. While the teacher may reserve the responsibility to choose what will be taught (many times school boards or curriculum directors and committees make this decision for the teacher), the decision-making about how concepts are to be learned is shared with the students. The style is both directive and nondirective. The laissez faire style delegates most, if not all, of the decision-making to the students, so that at any given time they may select what to study and how to study it. In absolute terms, the style is nondirective. These are types of teaching styles, and by necessity they appear rigid and inflexible. They describe the degree in which teachers share the teaching and learning decision-making process. Therefore, an autocratic style is not necessarily an oppressive, overbearing, nonhumane teaching style. Neither is a laissez faire style anarchical, unstructured, or disorganized, or the democratic style kind, understanding, and humane. In fact, many teachers use the three styles interchangeably. A maxim for a good teaching style is flexibility— the ability to choose and use a particular style to bring about desired learning outcomes. The decision as to which teaching style to use may be made on the basis of the degree the teacher feels students should be involved in decision-making. Emphasis here is on the teacher's judgment of the degree of decision-making that is necessary or appropriate. If a classroom is on fire, the teacher had best use an autocratic style to get students out of the room safely. To get students to think creatively, a teacher may want to allow periods of time for free association and other divergent-thinking activities—activities in which students make most of the decisions on how and what to learn.

Teachers are instructional leaders appointed by a school board to achieve the school district's educational goals. Teachers may delegate their authority; they may decide when and how students will share authority; teachers cannot surrender their authority to students. The classroom is not a democracy. Students do not elect their leader. Teachers do not choose their students. By law, teachers are *in loco parentis*, which means that teachers act in place of the parents while students are in class. Acting as reasonable parents, teachers have the basic responsibilities of teaching academic skills and knowledge and socializing students to live in a pluralistic society. As instructional leaders, teachers can guide their behavior on the basis of the body of research on leadership.

Research studies on leadership behavior report that leaders operate within two broad dimensions: task orientation and people orientation. To lead requires both an orientation toward task achievement and good interpersonal relations. Hoy and Miskel define leadership as a

> set of functions, or behaviors, carried out by individuals . . . to assure that tasks, group climate and individual satisfaction relate to the organization's objectives. [Teacher] effectiveness . . . is student achievement in cognitive, affective, and psychomotor areas of development.[1]

The ideal teacher exhibits a high concern for task achievement and a high concern for the students. But under certain conditions, high task orientation may be more effective; under other conditions, high concern for students may be more effective. In other words, an effective leadership style depends upon the situation. Fiedler calls this approach "contingency" leadership.[2] His research on leadership styles shows that matching a leadership style with the situation influences a group's performance. If the leadership style and group's situation are appropriately matched, then high group performance can be anticipated. The opposite is also true; poor matching of leadership style with a group's situation can cause low group performance.

The laissez faire style shows high concern for students; the autocratic style shows high concern for task achievement; the democratic style shows high concern for students and task achievement. Which style is most effective depends on the classroom situation and on the dispositions of the students and teacher. Operating on a contingency basis, teachers need to match their teaching style with the group's situation. Successfully making the match is the challenge inherent in the art of classroom management.

CLASSROOM MANAGEMENT AND HUMAN RIGHTS

How does effective classroom management relate to human rights? In matters of human rights in the classroom, it is extremely critical that a climate of fair play be maintained if the human rights of everyone in the classroom are to be protected. There are times when the teacher may believe the majority of the class to be wrong (tyranny of the majority) in some matters pertaining to human rights. The teacher is then compelled to assume an autocratic style, directing rather than sharing decisions.

Consider the case of a student who is accused of cheating because answers to the test are written on his desk. Upon inspection, the teacher remembers seeing the writing on the desk during the previous period and also does not recognize the handwriting as that of the accused student. More than likely, the student is innocent of wrongdoing, especially since there is much reason to doubt his culpability. Should the teacher allow the class to decide his innocence or guilt? If he is unpopular or not well-known in the classroom, what chance does he have for fair play? The student may be wrongly accused. Other times the teacher may want to share the decision-making. Consider the case in which a Jewish fourth-grade girl slapped a fourth-grade boy for calling her a "kike" during recess on the playground. The boy complains to his teacher that she "beat him up" without reason and has three of his friends as witnesses. Should the teacher autocratically decide for or against either the boy or the girl? Should the teacher let the incident pass, allowing the students to decide for themselves the locus of wrongdoing? In my view, this case presents an ideal situation to teach all the students some lessons on human rights, such as due process and the rights of the accused, or free speech as a relative right and responsibility. To what degree does anyone have the right to insult someone else? What degree of rights does the insulted person have? Can one decide that the boy was irresponsible in the use of free speech, and thereby negated his right to free speech? In other words, that he deserved the slap because he insulted the girl? What about the girl's use of force to resolve a problem? Should violence be sanctioned or tolerated as a method to solve human problems? The list of ethical questions is endless. What is important is that this case presents a natural—and very real—situation in which human rights are threatened, and a good opportunity to teach how a community of people can share in the protection of rights.

NONVERBAL MODES IN A PLURALISTIC CLASSROOM

Some general considerations for management of a pluralistic classroom are factors such as the verbal and nonverbal messages conveyed by teachers and the message conveyed by the physical and human space relations within the class. The research on verbal and nonverbal communications[3] in classrooms reports that teachers talk more than they probably should, that they are unaware of the various verbal and nonverbal messages they convey, and that teachers verbally and nonverbally convey preferences for white, middle-class students over ethnic minority students. Instead of analyzing the above cited research, I should like to describe classroom verbal and nonverbal communication as it applies to teaching and learning in a pluralistic society.

Key to understanding verbal and nonverbal classroom communications is the answer to the question: How consonant is my denotative message with my connotative message? Or, is what I say, what I convey? I remember a teacher who would say "how interesting" every time we showed her something we had done. After a while, it occurred to us that she didn't mean what she said. Instead by that comment she meant to reject or ignore what we offered without appearing to reject or ignore. She apparently felt it less damaging to appear interested than to simply say, "I can't look now, I'm busy," or "I don't want to look now." To us, she was not an authentic person; she tried to convey the appearance of being interested in her students, but the dissonance between her verbal and nonverbal messages was high enough to cast doubt on her authenticity.

Nonverbal communications often convey unconscious cultural and ethnic biases. Anthropologist Edward Hall[4] devised a structural approach to understanding nonverbal communications between people of different cultural groups. He categorizes nonverbal communications into kinesics, proxemics, and haptics. These three nonverbal phenomena are popularly known as "body language" or "body talk." They do not include other aspects of nonverbal communications, such as paralanguage (intonational-connotational-tonal nonverbal messages) and olfaction (emission and reception of nonverbal odor messages). Because the complexity of a discussion on all aspects of nonverbal classroom communications would be book length, I will focus on the three aspects Hall identified and researched on a cross-cultural matrix as a way of sensitizing teachers to the nonverbal, cross-cultural dimension of classroom management.

Kinesics deals with the messages conveyed within and without different cultures by body movements. For example, now that female teachers are allowed to wear pantsuits or slacks in the classroom, many female teachers think it perfectly proper to sit on a table or on a desk in front of their classes. In *Latino* cultures, including the cultures of Puerto Ricans, Cubans, Mexican Americans, and other Central and South American cultures, women who sit on tables in public places are viewed as crude. Women teachers who sit on tables may convey by their kinesics a message of crudeness to their Latino/Latina students, and thereby embarrass the students. In other words, teachers should be aware that their kinesics are culturally conditioned, and that what may seem like perfectly natural body movement in one culture may be viewed differently in another culture. In U.S. Bureau of Indian Affairs schools, teachers have noticed that many Native American students don't gaze directly into the eyes of their teachers. Rather, when the teachers speak, the students turn their gaze downward, lowering their eye contact toward the floor. The teachers often interpret these kinesics as messages of "disrespect" and "shiftiness" because, in the teachers' cultures, indirect eye contact conveys distrust and disrespect. But, in the students' cultures, the opposite is true: direct eye contact with elders and adults in authoritative positions is viewed as "disrespectful." Thus, teachers misread their students' kinesics.

Proxemics deals with how people manage their life space, in particular how people interpret body space relationships. How close is too close when a stranger is standing near you? How far is too far when you are talking to a loved one? In a classroom, how do teachers manage the space relations between themselves and their students? How do they manage the body space between students? For example, in a desegregated classroom, do teachers manage classroom experiences so that minority and white students work together on projects? Or, do teachers manage the experiences so that these students rarely work together? Teachers may convey ethnic biases through their proxemics. For example, a white teacher may hover over a white student, many times touching the student's shoulder while explaining a math problem. Explaining the same problem to a black student, the teacher may stand erect, avoid physical contact, and explain the problem's operations from a distance. Provided, of course, that both groups of students like to be touched, this kind of proxemic behavior, if it recurs enough to reveal a pattern, conveys preference for the white student and nonpreference, perhaps rejection, of the black student.

Haptics deals with the quality of touch, especially stressing how people interpret touch. An apt illustration of haptics is how people interpret an embrace between adult men. In French, Spanish, Italian, and in other Latino cultures, an embrace is considered natural between adult males; this is not the case among Anglo-American males. In classrooms, how do students interpret the touches of their teachers? Teachers, especially elementary school teachers, are encouraged by their students to touch and to embrace them when students are happy, sad, or need reinforcement. But at the secondary levels, teachers are confronted by various interpretations regarding touch. Because haptics are culturally bound, how secondary students interpret their teachers' touch depends largely on their cultural or ethnic perspective. Conversely, some teachers don't like to touch their students. Even a light tap or approval on the shoulder is avoided by some teachers. Again, remember that students interpret nontouch or avoidance of touch according to their cultural and ethnic perspectives.

Teachers may reveal ethnic biases by the way they manage the space relations in their classrooms. In other words, they may move around their classrooms, approaching closely students of the ethnic group they feel most comfortable with and avoiding students from groups they are less comfortable with. Or, teachers may arrange the seating so that preferred students sit close to them and the nonpreferred sit further away. These are not far-fetched instances. In my experience with classroom spatial arrangements, I have seen classrooms in which all the minority students sat in the back of the class and the white students near the front. Another classroom had black students sitting at desks bolted to the floor and facing the walls, while the white students all sat at round tables in the center of the room. In each situation, the teachers were managing segregated spatial arrangements in their classes, and in my view, revealing their ethnic biases.

HUMAN RIGHTS APPROACH

Human rights have emerged from "natural law" doctrines. The moral basis of the natural law doctrines is in the universal ethics presumed to govern all human relations and transcend all cultures. These ethics exist in all of the great religions of the world—Christianity, Buddhism, Islam, Judaism, Hinduism—and are known as "golden rules," "categorical imperatives," or "dictates of the conscience." The Ten Commandments, the Magna Carta, the French and the American Declaration(s) of Independence are examples of moral codes that contain them. Ethics deal with the relationships between people; between man and man, woman and man, there exists a universally correct or right way to treat each other, as in the Christian ethic of "do unto others as you would have them do unto you."

Ancient Greek notions of the natural law were couched in the world view that the universe was organized in a harmonious order of which humans were an integral part. The universe is governed by its own laws, the natural law, and people as part of the universe are also governed by the natural law. The Greek stoic philosopher, Marcus Cicero, described the universe as a rational system in which people were governed by rational laws held in common by all. They were compelled to live in kinship with each other and with nature. The natural, human law bound them together as citizens of a community. Thus, the highest virtue in this system of natural law was to live according to the natural law of human nature.

The emphasis of the Greek natural laws was upon people as members of a human or a political community. People were viewed as social or political animals who could form groups to pursue the greater good of the group. During the latter parts of the Middle Ages in Europe there was a gradual shift in emphasis from viewing people as social beings to viewing them as individuals. Rather than stressing the social or corporate nature of humans, European scholars such as Machiavelli, Adam Smith, and later Thomas Hobbes and John Locke, stressed their individualist nature. Adam Smith's assumption about economics was that people, allowed to pursue their own self-interests within the constraints of the natural law, would attain well-being. The stress on individualism and self-determination also pointed to the need for protection from kings and rulers who would use their powers to abridge individuality and self-determination. The natural law, impeded by capricious kings and rulers, was dysfunctional; however, if people banded together and ruled themselves, then individual initiative and self-determination were possible and the natural law could work. Consequently, people were members of two societies or communities, a human society and a civil society. The human society was governed by natural laws, but since no mechanism existed to enact and enforce the natural laws, a civil society had to enact and enforce civil laws reflecting the natural laws as well as laws to protect individuals from the capriciousness of civil laws. Human rights were birthed by the union of the Greek world view of humans as social beings with the later European world view of humans as individual beings. Human rights, like the natural law, were presumed to exist in the nature of human relations. Within political or social bodies, these natural rights —for example freedom, liberty, individual ownership of property— were inalienable. To insure these rights, governments were formed and civil laws enacted, such as the amendments to the U.S. Constitution which guarantee the protection of human rights.[6]

Consider that we live in two communities, a human community and a civil community. In the human community everyone holds the right to life, liberty, and happiness. The greatest virtue is to use reason and justice to insure everyone the human rights to life, liberty, and happiness. The purpose of the civil community is to enact and maintain laws that preserve these rights for the human community. The rights in a human community are superordinate to the laws of the civil community. When the laws of the civil community violate, prohibit, or attempt to abrogate a human right, people are duty-bound to change, resist, or abolish the unjust civil law. Our fundamental duty is to reconcile the laws of the civil community with the rights of the human community. As Thomas Jefferson once said, "Eternal vigilance is the price of freedom."

The human rights strategy operates in a classroom on basic democratic principles which teachers and students should understand. The first principle is *rule by law* rather than by fiat or totalitarian ruler. The rules of a society are made by the people in the society or human community rather than by some elite group or individual who then imposes the rules on the society. The authority to make, change, or alter rules lies within the society. *Rule by law* is essentially democratic rule, or a rule by ideal democracy—that is, *demo* meaning "people" and *-cracy* meaning "rule" or "govern." The closest facsimile of ideal or pure democracy in the United States was the town hall meetings which were held in small New England communities in the late eighteenth and early nineteenth centuries. These meetings were called together whenever the community had a problem, faced a crisis, or needed to make a community-wide decision. In the meetings, everyone had an equal status because everyone was an equal member of the community. (Black slaves, Native Americans, and, no doubt, women were excluded from the meetings, or if allowed to attend, had no voting privileges. Note my earlier reference to the town hall meeting as a "facsimile" of ideal democracy.)

The group leader, usually the man who called the meeting, discussed the problem and sought consensus from the group on a solution. Because the problem at hand affected the entire community, individuals were compelled to consider both their individual interests and the collective interests of the community; any decision based upon a consensus was considered the collective will or decision which applied to the whole community. All differences of opinion were yielded when a consensus was reached regarding the solution. A consensus was not simply a 51 percent vote or a majority vote of the group; rather, a consensus was a general climate of opinion held by the plurality of the group, at least two-thirds of the group, that a particular course of action or solution should be followed by individuals in the community. Hence, rule by law is not rule by the majority (51 percent) or rule by fiat or a totalitarian ruler (1 percent); rather, it is rule by the plurality (75–100 percent) or the collective will of members of the community. In a town hall meeting it is apparent that not everyone gets his way; some individuals in the group will not be satisfied with the consensus of opinion. Consequently, through persuasion and appeals to reason, dissatisfied group members can attempt to change the climate of opinion; they can choose to accept the group consensus on a tentative basis, hoping that if the solution or consensus reached proves unworkable, their opinions will appear more reasonable. The town hall meetings call for community involvement, mutual respect, and mature, unselfish cooperation. The fate of the community is also the fate of the individual, as each individual is an integral part of the whole community.

Under a *rule by law* governing system *everyone has inalienable rights and responsibilities.* These rights and responsibilities cannot be earned, given, or taken from anyone. Simply because everyone is a human who consequently lives in the human community, everyone has inherent rights and responsibilities. No one, for example, has to earn the right to be free. Therefore, no one can buy, sell, or give anyone freedom. One presumably is born with the right to be free. Thus, human slavery of any kind is nonexistent when everyone has inalienable rights and responsibilities as a member of the human community.

There are two kinds of rights, substantive and procedural rights. *Substantive rights* are presumed modes of behavior individuals are allowed to use within the human community. For example, individuals have a right to practice a religion of their choice, and a right not to practice any religion at all. *Procedural rights* are presumed modes of behavior by which individuals are treated within the human community. Sometimes procedural rights are conceived of as the due process everyone is entitled to when accused or suspected of a crime. For example, if one is accused of committing a crime, one is presumed to be innocent until found guilty by a jury of peers. The jury must weigh and consider all the incidents and circumstances pertaining to the alleged crime so as to insure fair treatment of the accused individual.

Substantive and procedural rights are relative rather than absolute; that is, individuals do not practice rights in a social vacuum; they must practice their rights relative to the rights of other individuals and the rights of the total human community. Therefore, with every right there exists a concurrent responsibility. Or, everyone must practice rights responsibly, which means that everyone in the human community is required to consider the rights of others as well as the rights of oneself, if the individual and the human community expect to survive. The classic example of a relative, substantive right is freedom of speech: Do I have the right to shout "Fire!" in a crowded theater, when, in fact, no fire exists? Should my freedom of speech be abridged? If I do commit the act, should I be punished in any way? What is my responsibility to the people in the theater? Shouting "Fire!" would no doubt cause pandemonium and chaos. People would desperately try to get out of the crowded theater, jamming the exits and trampling each other; inevitably, many would be injured, perhaps killed. It's clear that my freedom of speech should be abridged; then everyone in the human community should be equally abridged or restrained.

Enacting specific laws to restrain freedom of speech in matters affecting public safety would not be possible. To prohibit yelling "Fire!" in a crowded theater does not prohibit yelling "Fire!" in a crowded terminal, church, or other building. Such laws could be cumbersome and in their final effect unjust in some way to someone. Instead, people are expected to use their rights responsibly, taking into consideration the rights of others. If individuals practice their rights responsibly, they can expect others to do the same. When they violate the rights of others by irresponsible action, they also violate their own rights, because, in the human community, the fates of all members are intertwined. For example, to prohibit protestors from freedom of assembly because their speech may incite a riot also prohibits other protesters on different issues from freedom of assembly. At the same time, protesters allowed freedom of assembly must act responsibly to prevent a riot and protect the public safety. If they do not act responsibly, people may be harmed, property damaged, and ultimately, their views may not be heard. If their goals are to harm others and damage property, they are clearly acting outside the better interests of the human community and outside the parameter of rule by law. In short, they are "outlaws."

What happens when the majority of the human community acts irresponsibly toward an individual or individuals? Unjust laws have been enacted by a majority of the community. The laws were unjust because they violated a categorical imperative or a universal ethic. The majority of a community can be unjust and thereby tyrannous to the human community. To prevent tyranny by the majority, the human community must allow individuals the *right to conscientious objection* or *civil disobedience*.[7] People must be allowed to attempt to change or disobey a law which they consider a violation of a universal ethic. But, the right to civil disobedience has a concurrent responsibility to the human community. If the law is unjust, then people have the responsibility to change the law through the established or agreed upon governmental means or to passively resist the law and thereby possibly effect its change.

The consequences of passive resistance, conscientious objection, and civil disobedience may be harsh. Imprisonment, fines, and social alienation are expensive prices to pay for one's minority opinions. For example, the conscientious objectors of the Vietnam war were of three types: those who fled to Canada and other countries, those who refused to be drafted and were jailed, and those who were drafted into noncombat roles in the armed forces. *Under the ethical code of civil disobedience*, those who fled to other countries were considered to be irresponsible to the human community. They practiced their right to civil disobedience but did not act responsibly to the human community by suffering the consequences of their disobedience. Had all those who fled the United States cluttered the jails and prisons along with others who in fact were imprisoned for their conscientious objection, public outcries and protests against the useless human costs of the war—both people in the prisons and people in Vietnam—might have ended U.S. military involvement much sooner. Those conscientious objectors drafted into noncombat roles also acted irresponsibly, because while they did not wage war directly on other humans, they indirectly assisted others in their war against humans, and thereby tacitly supported the war effort. If they believed that the war effort violated a universal ethic, and that the draft law was therefore unjust, they must have also believed that any support of the war effort was a violation of the universal ethic. By tacitly supporting the war effort, they violated their conscience and belief that the war was unjust. Also, their tacit support served to lengthen the war; withdrawal of their support might possibly have shortened it.

To prevent tyranny by the majority, everyone in the human community must practice at one time or another the rights and responsibilities of conscientious objection, passive resistance, and civil disobedience. By acting responsibly, by suffering the consequences of civil disobedience, individuals may change the climate of public opinion and thereby neutralize the laws of a tyrannous majority. Civil disobedience is not easy or popular, but it is necessary in a human community. The right to dissent, to challenge the majority, to attempt to change or disobey an unjust law (and suffer the consequences) are essential if a just, human community is desired. Civil disobedience is a categorical imperative.

Under the human rights strategy, the public school classroom is an involuntary civil community. Students are compelled to attend school. They by and large do not choose what they will be taught nor do they choose who will teach them. They may choose what they will learn by their attention or inattention. Teachers by and large cannot choose whom they will teach. They must teach anyone assigned to their classrooms, regardless of class, race, religion, sex, or physique. In the *realpolitik* of the classroom, teachers can and do show preference for nonminority students. This has been shown in studies conducted by the U.S. Commission on Civil Rights, such as the *Teachers and Students* study cited in Chapter 5, and other, more recent studies which report that minority students receive a disproportionately greater share of suspensions and other in-class punishment. In fact, teachers often express a preference for nonminority students.[8] The human rights strategy provides a nonpreferential method for classroom management, in which the public school classroom is a human community governed by the principle of *rule by law*.

In the human community classroom, everyone is a citizen with inalienable rights and responsibilities. All behavior, of both students and teachers, must be guided by the self-interests of the individual balanced by the interests of the group. Rules and regulations in the class must be devised to protect the rights of all students and teachers. Consideration must be given to the fact that as an involuntary community, the classroom will be constrained by imposed rules. State laws, city ordinances, and school policies may be imposed on the classroom. For example, some states prohibit bare feet in all public buildings; others prohibit smoking in all public buildings. Thus, in some classrooms students can't be barefoot; in some teacher lounges, teachers can't smoke. Teachers are ultimately responsible for providing a safe learning environment. If many of the imposed rules do impede upon human rights in the classroom, then teachers and students have the right to disobey, change, and alter the rules.

Within the classroom community, all citizens are governed by these natural law doctrines:

1. All humans have inalienable rights and responsibilities.
2. All humans live in communities governed by the natural law and the civil law.
3. The civil law is subordinate to the natural law.
4. Disobedience of civil laws that violate the natural law is both a right and a responsibility.

Following are some operational principles for the practice of natural law doctrines.

• *The principle of inalienable and correlative human rights and responsibilities.* The principle presumes that all humans, regardless of race, creed, or national or religious affiliations, have basic rights and responsibilities that cannot be taken away by other humans or by a government. The rights and responsibilities cannot be given away or abandoned. An example is the right to life. All people have the right to live and the responsibility to maintain healthy bodies. No person can arbitrarily kill another person (e.g., the commandment, "Thou shalt not kill"); no person can arbitrarily abandon the right to life (i.e., people have the responsibility of caring for the nourishment and health of their bodies). This is because we all live in a human community and are interdependent. In this example, maintaining healthy bodies allows people to practice their right to life and allows others to benefit from the skills, talents, and contributions healthy people can make to the community. Therefore, rights are correlative. If you have a right to privacy, you also have a responsibility to insist upon your privacy. In turn, I have the responsibility to honor your right of privacy. But, you must also respect my right to privacy.

• *The principle that all people live in communities governed by the natural law and the civil law.* The assumption here is that all people are citizens of two societies, a natural or human society and a civil society. The human/natural society consists of all living things in general and of all human beings in particular. People and the physical environment intertwine to form the basis of the society. The human society is the society referred to as the brotherhood and sisterhood of all people; it has no national boundaries, nor does it have governments. The natural society is governed by the universal ethics of human interaction. Within the classroom community, everyone is interdependent. It serves the greater good to pursue one's interests while also pursuing the interests of the classroom community.

• *The principle that the civil law is subordinate to the natural law.* The assumption here is that students and teachers are capable of knowing the natural law and able to operate under its guidance. Teachers and students cannot operate on natural or civil laws if they don't know the laws. They must be taught the natural and civil laws and they must be taught to practice them. What follows is a summary of this principle's assumptions and its civil laws which serve to protect human rights in the classroom community:

Human rights are basic to a democratic society.
Students must know what their rights are before they can practice them.
Human rights must be valued in a democratic society.
Majority rules should not quell individual students' rights.
Students have the right to be different.
Students have the right to a positive self-concept.
Students can learn to use their rights responsibly.

Phi Delta Kappa's Teacher Education Project on Human Rights is an exemplary human rights program. The preamble to the program follows:

THE HUMAN RIGHTS CREED IN EDUCATION

Preamble

As an educator in a democratic society, concerned with the human rights of people everywhere, I will exemplify in my behavior a commitment to these rights. Educators and the educative process must have a more significant impact in ensuring these rights for all people. Thus, I will translate my belief in basic human rights into daily practice. I believe in the right and its concomitant responsibility:

1. To Equal Opportunity for All in:
   Education
   Housing
   Employment
   The Exercise of the Franchise and Representation in Government
2. Of Due Process and Equal Protection Under the Law
3. Of Freedom of Speech and of the Press
4. To Dissent
5. To Freedom of or from Religion
6. To Privacy

    7. To Be Different
    8. Of Freedom from Self-Incrimination
    9. To a Trial by a Jury of Actual Peers
  10. To Security of Person and Property
  11. To Petition and Redress of Grievances
  12. To Freedom of Assembly[9]

• *The principle of civil disobedience as a right and a responsibility.* As with the other principles, teachers and students must know what the principle entails before they can use it. Civil disobedience is not to be taken lightly; rather, as with the other principles, it requires mature judgment as to the greater good of the classroom community and dictates of the conscience. Civil disobedience requires that teachers and students first attempt to change an unjust rule or law within the established governmental system. Second, if the governmental system persists in maintaining the unjust rule, then teachers and students are obligated to resist or disobey the rule and suffer the consequences within the established civil community. Third, if steps one and two do not achieve a change in the unjust rule, the objectors should take their plea to the public and attempt to sway the climate of opinion in the objectors' favor. If the public is unresponsive, then the objectors must continue dissension and passive resistance until the time the public acts on their pleas for justice. It is critical that teachers and students understand the value of civil disobedience; that is, civil disobedience serves as a check on tyrannous rule by the majority. Without civil disobedience, protection of the rights of minorities (any type of minority) is not possible.

    An organizational scheme for the human rights approach follows:

Philosophic bases
Natural rights doctrines: All humans have rights to life, liberty, and happiness, *ipso facto.*

Teacher needs
Values students as humans and their right to be human.
Knows when and how to apply differing teaching styles—authoritarian, democratic, laissez faire—to enhance student rights.
Knows when and how to apply civil disobedience.
Understands the complexities of rule by majority and protection of minority rights.

Student needs
All students need to know their human and civil rights with their concurrent responsibilities.
All students need to know how to use their human rights responsibly.

Content

Natural rights doctrines, for example: Magna Carta; Declaration
of Independence; Bill of Rights; United Nation's Declaration of
Universal Rights; Martin Luther King's "I Have a Dream";
Henry David Thoreau's "Civil Disobedience."

Method

Cycle 1. Formal approach to rights
  A. Teach students their rights.
  B. Teach students to understand principle of rule by majority
      and protection of minority rights.
  C. Teach students the balance principle, i.e., for every right
      exists a concurrent responsibility.
  D. Principle of civil disobedience.

Cycle 2. Informal approach
  A. Allow students to practice their rights.
  B. Hold students responsible for practicing or violating rights.
  C. Allow civil disobedience but follow through on its conse-
      quences.

Cycle 3. Loop to Cycle 1
  A. Review natural right doctrines.
  B. Discuss issues raised by students.
  C. Have students analyze and evaluate their practice of rights
      and responsibilities.
  D. Design (with students) mechanism to continue informal
      human rights practices as an ongoing process, e.g., grievance
      panel, human rights committee, "town hall meetings."

Evaluation

Determine the nature and degree to which students (and teacher)
  responsibly utilized their human rights.
Determine whether the classroom climate is conducive to the responsible utilization of human rights.

The challenge of the human rights approach is to balance the civil
rights of the group (e.g., senior class, homeroom) with the human
rights of the student. The teacher must balance "law" with "order."
The human right to be oneself may conflict with the group's civil rights
to an equal educational opportunity if one student insists on trumpet
practice during study sessions, for example. The teacher determines
which rights are to prevail at a given time. The teacher may want to
involve the whole class in making the decision. What's important about
the human rights approach is how the teacher handles conflicts of
rights, because it is more difficult to practice respect for human rights

than it is to merely espouse them. For example, in the case of a fire in a classroom, the teacher should take complete control of the group, insist on total conformity, and abrogate anyone's right to be different so that the group can be let out of the room to safety. But in the case of a student who is accused by the class of stealing the teacher's grade book, the teacher is challenged to handle the potential violation of rights of the class with discretion in order to foster respect for the rights of the accused—that is, the right to be considered innocent until proven guilty, or the right to face one's accuser. The teacher's approach has to be situational, assessing the incident carefully and then deciding upon an approach that would protect the rights of the students. Overall, the teacher is challenged to balance the group's and individual's rights in such a manner that a climate of respect for the rights of everyone predominates in the classroom.

The following are guidelines which suggest ways and means a teacher can govern a class with the human rights strategy. The guidelines are general, and while they may not specifically outline details for a class, they are sufficiently broad to be applicable to most public school classrooms:

1.0 The right to be different
   1.1 Teacher encourages students to assert their individuality.
   1.2 Teacher adapts lessons and instruction according to student cognitive learning styles.
   1.3 Teacher doesn't use large group instruction all of the time.
   1.4 Teacher enforces dress codes and hair style rules that allow for individual and group differences.
   1.5 Teacher doesn't ignore students who differ with respect to ethnicity, race, national origin, or linguistic background.
   1.6 Teacher fosters respect for divergent dialects and speech.

2.0 The right to fair, equal treatment
   2.1 Teacher doesn't have preferred students or "pets."
   2.2 Teacher doesn't show preferential treatment toward students of one ethnic/racial group.
   2.3 Teacher doesn't discipline more, or discipline more severely, students of ethnic minority or out-group affiliations.

3.0 Right to a safe learning environment
   3.1 Teacher doesn't allow students to physically harm each other.
   3.2 The classroom is well ventilated, well lighted, well cooled and heated for comfort of students.
   3.3 Classroom furniture is safe and nonhazardous.

4.0 The right to privacy
    4.1 Teacher does not reveal notes, term papers, or other confidential documents or expressions to the whole class without prior permission of the author.
    4.2 Teacher does not reveal grades on term papers or class projects, remarks on term papers, grades for a project or for a semester without prior permission of the respective students.
    4.3 Teacher does not directly search students, indirectly expect students to report deviant behavior—the tattletale —or unnecessarily embarrass students in the classroom.

5.0 The right to dissent
    5.1 Students are encouraged to agree or disagree with their teacher and their peers.
    5.2 The teacher fosters respect for student dissension as a means for rational understanding of opinions.
    5.3 Teacher allows discussion and dissension pertaining to class and school rules and regulations.
    5.4 Teacher fosters understanding of civil disobedience as a right and a responsibility.

6.0 The right to a safe emotional learning environment
    6.1 Teacher doesn't ridicule, tease, or publicly demean students.
    6.2 Teacher doesn't seat or arrange students in ethnically segregated arrangements.
    6.3 Teacher doesn't foster ethnic slurs, stereotypic, or racist expressions in the classroom.
    6.4 Teacher fosters classroom climate that discourages ethnic/racial disrespect.

Notes

1. Wayne K. Hoy and Cecil G. Miskel. *Educational Administration: Theory, Research, and Practice.* New York: Random House, 1978, p. 181.
2. Fred E. Fiedler. *A Theory of Leadership Effectiveness.* New York: McGraw-Hill, 1967, pp. 36–50.
3. Ned Flanders. *Analyzing Teacher Behavior.* Reading, Mass.: Addison-Wesley, 1970, pp. 14–38.
4. Edward T. Hall. *The Hidden Dimension.* Garden City, N.Y.: Doubleday (Anchor Books), pp. 3–48, 1966; see also, Hall's *Beyond Culture.* New York: Doubleday, 1977.
5. Cicero. *De Legibus.* Cambridge, Mass.: Harvard University Press, 1943; see also, Cicero. *De Re Publica.* Cambridge: Harvard University Press, 1943.

6. For an in-depth history of natural law and human rights, see Melvin Rader. *Ethics and the Human Community.* New York: Holt, Rinehart and Winston, 1964, pp. 15–52.
7. Henry David Thoreau. "On the Duty of Civil Disobedience," in *Walden.* New York: New American Library (Signet), 1963, pp. 222–240.
8. Betsy Levin. "Recent Developments in the Law of Equal Educational Opportunity." *Journal of Law and Education,* July 1975, p. 418; see also, David L. Kirp. "Student Classification, Public Policy, and the Courts." *Harvard Educational Review,* (February 1974): 7–52.
9. Glenn R. Snider, Phi Delta Kappa Commission on Education and Human Rights. "The Human Rights Creed in Education," in *A Guide for Improving Public School Practices in Human Rights.* Bloomington, Ind.: Phi Delta Kappa Educational Foundation, 1975, p. iv. Reprinted with permission of Glenn R. Snider.

Chapter 10
Intergroup Relations
Strategies

The intergroup relations approach will be analyzed as a strategy that can be used to foster cross-ethnic and cross-cultural understanding in most classrooms in the United States. Although promoting positive intergroup relations can be categorized as an instructional strategy, and while I had originally conceived of intergroup relations as an instructional model, it's clear that promoting intergroup relations is broader than an instructional strategy. Per se, it is neither an instructional strategy nor a classroom management approach. Rather, promoting positive intergroup relations can be categorized somewhere between the two. As such, the intergroup relations approach interfaces between a model and a strategy. Consequently, I will treat the process of promoting intergroup relations in this chapter as an instructional model and strategy but with the understanding that it lies in a middle range between a strategy and a classroom management approach, and with the understanding that its content is essential to good teaching.

THE PURPOSE OF INTERGROUP RELATIONS

The following poem is dedicated to one of my many students.

> He comes to my room,
> rather,
> he puffs to my room
> gasping and exhaling the air
> of a cigarette hastily wasted.
>
> So he puffs to my room
> slouched shouldered,
>
> caged
>
> and bound to learn.

What always struck me when teaching in New Mexico, Wisconsin, Colorado, Kansas, Oklahoma, and Utah is that students were strangers to each other. They came to class and fell into a role as student and often developed only a few real friends. Otherwise they were strangers. Also, the very role of being a student somehow precluded any chance of developing genuine relationships in the classroom, unless the teacher somehow intervened. The intergroup relations approach attempts to make friends out of strangers.

The intergroup relations approach has its origin in a nationwide project conducted by the American Council of Education (ACE).[1] In an attempt to alleviate the intense anti-Jewish and anti-racial minority feelings that existed after World War II, ACE infused the intergroup relations notion in teacher training programs and secondary and elementary schools in the United States. Throughout the country, teacher training programs[2] were chosen to implement an intergroup relations program for prospective teachers. At the public school level, classroom teachers and administrators were trained to use intergroup relations strategies. Special curriculum materials were developed by teachers which fit their respective intergroup relations needs.[3] The project officially started in 1945 and ended sometime in 1952. Its purpose was to reduce, if not remove, the level of conflict that existed between Christians, Jews, whites, and racial minorities. Much stress was placed on the similarities held in common by the various groups, although religious and cultural differences were also recognized as positive factors which needed understanding. Thus, the essence of the project was in the attempt to build religious and cultural understanding. The motives for the movement were honest. Based on the desire to increase communication between diverse groups, its ultimate goals were to reduce conflict and to foster harmonious intergroup relations.

The essence of the intergroup relations approach is empathy.[4] The approach provides a means by which students learn about the views, feelings, and perceptions of other students who may differ ethnically, racially, or culturally. Emphasis is upon building positive relationships between students who would otherwise know little about each other. Even in desegregated classrooms, white and nonwhite students many times are not encouraged to intermingle, sharing their views, feelings, or perceptions.[5] In fact, experience shows that many white and non-white students in desegregated classrooms rarely talk with each other, much less develop long-lasting personal relationships. The Native American adage that a person should walk in the mocassins of another for many days before judging that person best exemplifies the essence of the intergroup relations approach. As with the Native American adage, a person must get into the shoes of another and view the world from that stance in order to genuinely understand the other's actions and beliefs. The hope is that building empathy through planned and sustained interpersonal contact among ethnically differing students will lead to improved intergroup relations in the classroom and in society. What follows is a conceptual overview of the intergroup relations approach.

CONCEPTUAL OVERVIEW OF INTERGROUP RELATIONS

• *Goal:* To foster favorable attitudes among ethnic minority and majority students through interpersonal experiences.

• *Philosophic bases—ethnic pluralism:* Speaking generally, communication and understanding between ethnic minority and white ethnic groups have been limited, restricted, or nonexistent. Students need to develop positive, genuine interpersonal relationships with group members outside their groups through planned interpersonal relations.

• *Rationale:* Positive attitudes between ethnic minority and white students can be formed through interpersonal experiences if

1. ethnic minority and white students have equal status;
2. ethnic minority and white students have common tasks;
3. ethnic minority and white students' contact is sustained and on-going;
4. ethnic minority and white students' contact is facilitated by leadership stressing equalitarian norms.

The approach controls the nature of interpersonal contact between racially, ethnically, or culturally different students. But interpersonal contact and communication among students is essential. The approach is based on the equal-status[6] theory of interpersonal contact which posits that sustained, controlled contact between people of the same social status working at a task they hold in common can foster better understanding among the people, even though they differ racially, ethnically, or culturally. The key notion is that teachers can provide sustained, controlled contact among students so long as effort is made to provide equal status to all the students, something that is not always done in the *realpolitik* of the classroom. Mere contact alone, without conscious efforts to insure equal status among students, will not necessarily foster positive intergroup relations, as has been the experience of newly desegregated classrooms. Leadership on the teachers' part to control and sustain the interpersonal contact is therefore essential.

CRITICAL FACTORS

Teachers can foster genuine relationships between ethnic minority and white students by planning ongoing interpersonal learning tasks. Most critical is the teacher's leadership to insure that the interpersonal relationships, and the contact therein, are meaningful—that is, the relationships should foster better understanding of and empathy for students' feelings and beliefs. The contact must not be haphazard, contrived (fake), or arbitrary. Students as equals should be engaged in meaningful, common learning tasks which foster interdependence and cooperation. Also, the contact should lead to positive long-range behavioral changes which are assumed to be antecedents to cognitive and attitude changes. Once students begin to understand each other, form friendships, and in other ways relate to each other, their attitudes toward each other and toward their respective groups should improve.

INQUIRY GENERALIZATION FOR THE STUDY OF INTERGROUP RELATIONS

> Each person needs to belong or have a sense of belonging to a group.
> Ethnic groups have both similarities and differences.
> Separated or segregated people develop myths, prejudices, and stereotypes about each other.
> There is one biological race—the human race—but racial characteristics make a social difference.

These are generalizations about intergroup relations processes that students should be taught. All too often, students are not taught about group processes because much more effort is made to teach students their individual uniqueness. While individuality is important for students to know and practice, they should know that people live and function both as individuals and as members of groups.

STRATEGIES FOR FAVORABLE INTERGROUP RELATIONS

• *A study of family life patterns.* This strategy requires that ethnic minority and majority group students study each other's families. The study, if handled maturely, should provide students insight into the backgrounds and experiences of ethnic minority and majority group students. The study should include, but would not be limited to, an analysis of family roles, family livelihood, family problems and concerns, and family recreation patterns.

• *A study of ethnic minority and majority group communities.* This strategy includes a study of minority and majority group communities. The study would include, but not be limited to, an analysis of organizing generalizations:

    a. Communities have similarities and differences.
    b. Communities require interlocking relationships, i.e., human interdependence.
    c. Community conditions are results of current forces as well as the community's history.

• *A study of intergroup experiences.* This strategy gets at the crux of the intergroup relations approach because all students are taught to analyze objectively the intergroup relations process. The strategy answers this question: What happens when a minority group and a majority group come into contact?

    a. Students study in-group/out-group processes, stereotyping, ethnocentrism, prejudice, racism, discrimination.
    b. Students study attitudes, values, beliefs of peers through surveys, personal interviews, and panel discussions.
    c. Students study their own attitudes, values, beliefs as well as their ancestral ties through genealogies, historical lifelines, and "roots" family study.

• *A study of racism, prejudice, stereotyping in ethnically and racially homogeneous classrooms.* This strategy is intended for classrooms where no visible ethnic or racial mixture of students exists.

    a. Students experience in-group/out-group processes vicariously through open-ended stories, role playing, simulations.

b. Students visit and study ethnic minority community action agencies.
c. Students visit and study schools with high concentrations of ethnic minority students.
d. Resource speakers from ethnic minority groups are incorporated into courses of study.

• *A study of intergroup relations with emphasis on the nature of racism between in- and out-groups.* Such a study requires a serious study of the following characteristics of racist and prejudiced thinking.

Emotional racism This kind of racism ranges from slight distaste to extreme hate of ethnically and racially different out-groups.

Cognitive racism This kind of racism focuses on perceptions of meanings and understandings of what out-group people are like. Whatever the facts may be about the out-group people, the racist person has his or her stereotypes as "facts" about out-group peoples.

Action racism This kind of racism is observable; avoidance, discourtesy, exclusion, exploitation, and violence against out-group peoples are evident behaviors of this kind of racism. This is what is considered racial and ethnic discrimination.

Value racism This kind of racism focuses on the values a racist person wishes to maintain or preserve. Preservation of racist values insures material gain; it becomes necessary to maintain racist values to insure material gain and economic security.

The intergroup relations approach can be used to develop positive relationships between students who differ because of social class and religious affiliations. And, the model could be used to improve communications between male and female students. These uses of the model are equally valid.

INTERPERSONAL RELATIONS BETWEEN TEACHER AND STUDENT

Intergroup relations should not be confused with another important area of classroom interaction, "interpersonal" communications. In an attempt to improve teachers' abilities to communicate better with their students (both white, middle-class and culturally different students) various approaches have been developed. One of these approaches, "interpersonal skills training for teachers," developed and researched by Carkhuff and Berenson,[7] places emphasis upon attending behaviors for teachers. Under this approach teachers are encouraged to develop skills that show students they are interested in the students' concerns. For example, note these very probable classroom scenes:

STUDENT: But, Mr. Bissetti, I couldn't do the math problems 'cause I didn't have no paper to do them.

BISSETTI: Aw, come on! Who are you trying to kid? That's the same old story! You'll never pass this class with those excuses.

Or:

STUDENT: I couldn't do the math questions 'cause I didn't have no paper to do them.

BISSETTI: Let's see now, you're telling me you couldn't do the math problems because you didn't have any paper, right?

With the first situation, teacher Bissetti assumed that this student was lying; the teacher, operating on the assumption that this student couldn't be trusted, closed communications with the student by judging his response as a ploy to avoid doing the assignment. Yet the student may have been telling the truth. There are students who don't have paper readily at hand. And there are students who would rather spend their free time doing something other than math problems. In either case, Bissetti closed communications with his student by instantly judging his student's response as a lie. Bissetti, in the second situation, attempted to maintain communications by trying to understand the student's perspective. He did this by recapitulating the response. Once understanding the student's perspective, Bissetti was in a position to evaluate whether or not his student's answer was a cover-up for not wanting to do the math problems. In the second situation, the teacher maintained open communications with the student by attempting to understand the student's perspective and thus may eventually be able to discover why the student didn't do the homework.

What is important about interpersonal communications skill training is that it places emphasis upon maintaining communications between teacher and student. Teachers are encouraged to listen to their students without immediately judging the students' responses or behaviors; they are encouraged to attend to their students. In the pluralistic teaching-learning setting, it becomes important for teachers to consider when their students are genuinely acting from cultural orientations that may differ from their own. There are no easy answers to the question of when the student is "jiving" and when the student is really acting from a cultural orientation that differs from the teacher's. Students should not be allowed to use their ethnicity as a cover-up for refusing to learn fundamental skills. They are compelled to live in a highly technological society and fundamental literacy skills in math, science, and language are essential. All students should be expected to master literacy skills in math, science, and language without using the cop-out of ethnicity as a means to avoid the discipline that these academic areas impose. To my knowledge, no ethnic minority group is opposed to excellence for its children in math, science, or language. I implore teachers to be practical. They should teach what they know, and they should teach it thoroughly. Good teachers win over their students precisely because they teach well what they know. Because cultural and ethnic differences are real, it is necessary that teachers maintain communications with their students so as to determine when a student is acting from cultural differences or personal irresponsibility. Herein lies the importance of interpersonal communications skills. In the final analysis, teachers must come to know their students well enough to know when they are "jiving" and when they are legitimately acting from cultural and ethnic values that differ from the teachers'. There is no gauge or objective test which teachers can use to determine when students are acting out the truth of their cultural and ethnic experience. As adults, teachers must rely on their own understandings of students and their own threshold of trust in other humans, including their students.

The difference between interpersonal relations and intergroup relations as educational techniques is a difference of degree rather than kind. Both attempt to enhance communications between and among people. Interpersonal relations attempts to facilitate communication between individuals; intergroup relations attempts to facilitate communication between groups who are culturally or ethnically different. Both approaches work at building trust relationships among people.

Notes

1. Hilda Taba, Elizabeth Brady, and John T. Robinson. *Intergroup Education in Public Schools*. Washington, D.C.: American Council on Education, 1952.
2. Lloyd Allen Cook. *Intergroup Relations in Teacher Education*. Washington, D.C.: American Council on Education, 1951.
3. ———. *Elementary Curriculum in Intergroup Relations*. Washington, D.C.: American Council on Education, 1950.
4. Jean D. Grambs. *Understanding Intergroup Relations*. Washington, D.C.: National Education Association, 1973, Stock no. 387-11840.
5. ———. *Intergroup Education: Methods and Materials*. Englewood Cliffs, N.J.: Prentice-Hall, 1968.
6. F. James Davis. *Minority-Dominant Relations*. Arlington Heights, Ill.: AHM Publishing, 1978, pp. 56–57.
7. R. R. Carkhuff and B. G. Berenson. *Teaching as Treatment*. Amherst: Human Resource Development Press, 1976; see also, Carkhuff and Berenson. *Beyond Counseling and Therapy*. New York: Holt, Rinehart and Winston, 1976.

Chapter 11
A Synthesis of Pluralistic Teaching and Learning

This concluding chapter looks back at what's been said about teaching and learning in a pluralistic society, presents summative guidelines for pluralistic teaching, and then looks toward the future when ethnic and cultural pluralism will be a vastly different social reality.

This book's basic motive is to help teachers make a positive difference in the lives of their students. More than a histrionic platitude full of sound and fury signifying nothing, making a difference is a commitment to educate all students irrespective of their national origin, ethnic group, or social class affiliation so they may thrive in their work and play in a pluralistic society. Making a difference is inclusive of high expectations and excellence for all students and preclusive of negative expectations and mediocrity for lower-class and ethnic minority students. Teachers can provide mediocre instruction for minority and lower-class white students, consequently limiting their upward mobility; or, teachers can provide instruction grounded in excellence for minority and lower-class whites, increasing their chances for upward mobility. Teachers are faced with a simple choice (but this choice has profound ramifications): they may act as functionaries for the status quo, or they may act as agents of change for minorities and lower-class whites. Teachers in the former category—status quo functionaries—are inimical to a pluralistic, democratic society; teachers in the latter category—change agents—are indispensable for a pluralistic, democratic society. They will make a difference because they are committed to the education of all students. That it is possible to educate all of the masses is supported by educators who have assessed the educational systems of societies committed to the education of the entire populace. Hutchins concluded:

> Whatever can be said of the limitations of Soviet Education . . . it has knocked on the head the notion that only a few can understand difficult subjects. The compulsory eight-year school . . . demands that all pupils learn . . . the elements of mathematics, physical and biological science, and at least one foreign language. . . . [A]ccording to western standards the instruction in the subjects has succeeded.[1]

While Professor Hutchins was neither an apologist nor a proponent of Marxist, Soviet education, his assessment of the Soviet educational system as well as their subsequent scientific and technological advances validates the notion that a society can educate all of its populace. When the Soviets implemented the policy in the 1920s their people were predominantly poor and illiterate. Within a period of forty years Soviet society was transformed; by 1960 a sizable proportion were markedly less poor and literate. The motive was to build a strong, vigorous industrial society based on the precepts of Karl Marx. How much their society is based on the precepts of Marx is an ongoing debate, but that they built a strong, vigorous industrial society, with its predictable problems, is hardly debatable. The Soviet educational policy —a commitment to educate all students—served to elevate the nation from feudal disorganization to scientific, technological and military world prominence, an accomplishment not easily dismissed as communist propaganda.

In the United States, all students have the right to equal educational opportunities. The term "equal educational opportunities" means more than equal access to education. The term means that all students, irrespective of racial, linguistic, sexual, or ethnic background or physical condition, have a right to benefit equally from public education programs. Therefore, students should not be treated as though they have the same educational needs. Rather, they should be treated according to their specific, unique needs. In successive landmark U.S. Supreme Court decisions and federal legislation, *the U.S. government has affirmed a policy of equal educational opportunities for all students.* The *Brown* v. *Topeka Board of Education* decision, the U.S. Civil Rights Act, the *Lau* v. *Nichols* decision, Title IX, the Indian Education

Act, the Southeast Asian Refugee Children's Act, and the Education for All Handicapped Children Act all prohibit discrimination against special categories of students, establishing a federal policy aimed at educating all students irrespective of race, national origin, sex, language, or handicap. Even though the policy has the force of law and the U.S. Constitution to enforce its intent, the reality is that some educators are oblivious of the policy, refusing for reasons of ignorance or other spurious arguments, such as local autonomy or states rights, to translate the policy into educational programs and practices.

My experience shows that the federal policy exists because some state and local educators historically have not provided equal educational opportunities for lower-class and ethnic minority students. The need for the policy would be nonexistent were educational opportunities equitably provided all students. By tradition and law, educational policies have emanated from the state and local school officials. The policies have usually reflected the value and belief systems of the state and local communities. Thus, local and regional policies reflected their respective ethos and mores: some policies were pro-equal opportunity, others were anti-equal opportunity and simply ignored the issue. In communities hostile or complacent to equal opportunity, the school district officials have been unable or unwilling to rise above the level of their community's norms. Rather than asserting leadership by raising the equal opportunity issue and insisting that all students deserve equal opportunities, some educators have washed their hands of the issue. Indeed, they have ignored the issue, hoping it would go away, a ploy designed to satisfy local power groups without upsetting the status quo or improving the educational lot of the poor and ethnic minorities. Nonetheless, these educators—quite adept at evading the federal policy—act in violation of the law of the land. An anomaly of American life is that one can be both a respectable citizen and an outlaw.

Some educators view with jaundiced eyes or, even worse, cynically scoff at the idea of making a difference as liberal do-goodism and other idealistic nonsense. Students are the ultimate victims of these views, but teachers are the immediate victims. All too often, teachers become the disenchanted functionaries of an educational system that serves to select, distribute, and place lower-class and ethnic minority students into low academic and vocational career tracks. In this context, teachers are no more than intermediaries who are forced to have a negative impact on the daily lives of students. Indeed, within this context teachers are replaceable gears in an automated system of meritocracy that destines students to life positions that perpetuate the social caste system of U.S. industrialized society.

All students need to know and learn from committed teachers. Our society demands it. Now more than ever before in our history, students are required to excell as a matter of national survival. The nation can ill afford to miseducate any of its youth, as the youth are one of the few remaining renewable resources.

Currently, we are witnessing the closing of a frontier—the frontier of inexhaustible national resources. The experience of the nation, and the North American continent, has been an experience of bountiful forests, fertile soil, and abundant mineral resources. But, the unbridled scalping of forests in the early decades of the twentieth century and the last decade of the nineteenth century left hills and prairies studded with tree trunks; many have since eroded. The problem was so grievous that the federal government felt it necessary to establish national forests and reserves to protect the nation's forests from future scalping. The federal government showed great foresight when it nationalized much of the country's forests, yet there have been recurring movements to denationalize the forests in some western states. The latest movement, the so-called sagebrush revolution, proposes to dismantle the national forest system and thereby create conditions conducive to further scalping of the nation's forest lands. The Dust Bowl of the 1930s decimated crops, livestock, and the small family farm as an American institution when large sections of midwestern and southwestern topsoil blew away. John Steinbeck, in *The Grapes of Wrath*, sensitively recorded the human plight of those most directly affected by the Dust Bowl. Dispossessed of their land and their pride, many Oklahoma farmers migrated to California where they experienced rejection and violence. These farmers were not viewed as agricultural resources; rather, they were viewed as expendable blight. In the 1970s the insatiable thirst for petroleum fuels and the awareness that U.S. petroleum demand far exceeds its production precipitated skyrocketing oil and gasoline prices as well as estranged relations with oil-rich Third World countries.

In all of these national crises the human factor—the idea that humans are renewable national resources—has been grossly underestimated. Rather than mourning the depletion of mineral resources, we should place stock in people as natural resources (especially since we now realize that our natural resources are exhaustible) and seek viable alternatives for petroleum fuels. Just as the closing of the American pioneer frontier precipitated cultural changes, the closing of the natural resources frontier is imposing fundamental changes in American attitudes, values, and behaviors.

We face an era of depleted resources, perplexing economic problems, and pessimism about future prospects. The noted educator, Clark Kerr, reported in a recent Carnegie Foundation study entitled "Giving Youth a Better Chance: Options for Education, Work and Service,"[2] that one out of every three youths is ill-employed, ill-equipped, and ill-educated to succeed in U.S. society. The report stipulated further that without vast educational improvements, the country faces the danger of producing a permanent lower class, and, even worse, a self-perpetuating poverty culture. Clearly, prudence in the utilization and conservation of all resources—including the education of all youth—is the challenge of the hour for the nation. Education of all youth is so important that making a difference is more than platitudinous rhetoric; it is the essential test of good teaching.

A SUMMARY OF PLURALISTIC TEACHING CONCEPTS

There is absolutely no educational reason why teachers cannot make a difference in the lives of students, especially if they keep a perspective on two societal constants that render effective teachers indispensable: (1) the generic problems of hunger, disease, poverty, and ignorance common to most cultures and nations, and (2) the specific realities of ethnic, racial, and cultural diversity in U.S. society. Teachers, irrespective of who or where they teach and irrespective of their cultural or ethnic backgrounds, can commit themselves to the eradication of ignorance, disease, or poverty. Teaching a Navajo reservation youngster to read and teaching a white, suburban youngster about Navajos are equally liberating because both teaching acts, by minute but potent degrees, can serve to eradicate ignorance and poverty. Students in public school classrooms represent a vast array of ethnic, racial, religious and cultural groups, which, of course, is reflective of the diversity of U.S. society. To live well in the society, students need both direction and guidance to successfully interact within the diverse society. To keep a perspective on these societal trends I have proposed that teachers take a posture of cultural relativism within their teaching-learning universe.

Just as the astronomer Copernicus broadened human understanding of the physical universe, I attempted by analogy to broaden our understanding of the current teaching-learning universe of the U.S. public school classroom, placing white, middle-class culture within the galaxy of our multiple ethnic, social and cultural groups rather than at the center. I have argued that teachers should perceive the teaching-learning universe from the vantage point of cultural relativism—the notion that cultures should be perceived from their own perspective rather than compared with white, middle-class U.S. culture. In the wrong hands, cultural relativism could be a destructive force because it could allow bigoted or racist teachers to present their cultural positions as valid and thereby justify their acts of racial or ethnic discrimination. Since I am aware of this difficulty with cultural relativism, I have argued that bigoted, racist, or in any way narrow-minded teachers have no place in the education profession. In the right hands, cultural relativism could be a constructive force because it releases teachers from the skewed perceptions of learner's cultural and linguistic deprivations and allows them to perceive students as culturally-whole, educable humans.

Cultural relativism operates on several important assumptions. First is the assumption that teachers can understand and respect cultural differences. Just as teachers in the past have been required to learn the "new" math, the "new" English and various other academic innovations, teachers can learn about different cultures within the United States and, given appropriate training, can learn to respect differing ethnic and cultural groups. The second assumption is that teachers can teach students to understand and respect cultural differences. The pluralistic instructional models—ethnic studies and bilingual education—and the pluralistic instructional strategies—human rights and intergroup relations—analyzed in the second half of this text provide teachers some ways and means by which they can teach students to understand and respect cultural differences. *These models and strategies are applicable to any U.S. public school classroom in any social, cultural, or regional setting. They are not intended only for ethnic minority student populations or desegregated schools. Rather, they are intended for suburban, white schools and student populations, as well as for urban and rural white and nonwhite school populations. The bottom line of these models and strategies is that they provide all teachers in all settings means to teach cultural understanding and respect.*

The third assumption is that students are not mere data bank receptors of knowledge (the cultural monistic posture). Rather, cultural relativism operates on the assumption that students can be self-initiating, learning beings if they are directed and allowed to pursue their cultural and personal curiosities. This third assumption is not a call for permissive "do your own thing" ideologies, but rather the assumption challenges teachers to take leadership in their teaching-learning universe by creating for students the culturally correct set of circumstances so that students can spring from their curiosities to even greater depths of knowledge and understanding.

Embracing cultural relativism is not enough. Teachers should understand important sociocultural notions that impinge on teaching and learning. The most fundamental notion is that of "culture." All students have a culture—that is, all students have a culture (even though they may not be conscious of it!) inclusive of a system of values, beliefs, and behaviors. There is nothing mysterious about culture. It is not necessarily an exotic rite that occurs in the hinterlands

to the beat of frenetic drums, nor is culture a high-brow concert re-
sounding in some Philadelphia or New York symphony hall. Culture
is much more than exotic rites or lofty rhapsodies. Culture is the complex of values, attitudes, behaviors, and materials that provide humans
the sustenance for social existence. While rites and symphonies may be
a part of a student's culture, they are not the entire culture.

Students learn their culture and are socialized to live through their
families, their peer groups, their communities, and schools. Other socialization agents are the mass media and the church. Students also
learn their culture from the communal context into which they are
thrust. In U.S. society, students are bound to be thrust into one of three
communal contexts (or some combination thereof): (1) an Anglo-
conformity, racial exclusion context, (2) a biological melting pot or
ethnic synthesis context, or (3) an ethnic or cultural pluralistic context. These communal settings, reflected for example in local and regional cultures such as the Southwest or the Deep South, will influence
the attitudes and perceptions of students. Teachers cannot ignore
prevalent local or regional cultural attitudes and beliefs. Instead, they
need to understand the attitudes and beliefs so as to better reach and
thereby teach their students. Teaching and learning in U.S. public
schools is ultimately a community affair.

Students also learn their culture through their heritage, be it
ethnic, religious, national, or racial. In the United States, it's possible
for students to have a nationality, "American," and an ethnic group,
"Japanese," affiliation. Some students may identify only with their nationality and consider themselves primarily American. Others may
identify with their nationality and ethnic or racial group, thereby considering themselves both ethnic and national, as in black American or
Mexican American. The impact of ethnic, racial, or national group heritage upon the student's culture largely depends upon the social status
and role ascribed to the student's particular group. Nonetheless, for
many students, ethnic, racial, or national group membership and affiliation are formative aspects of their social identity. And last, students
learn racism, ethnic biases, and cultural stereotypes the same way they
learn their culture—at home, in schools, among peers, in communities,
in the mass media, and even in churches. Now we are ready to turn
our attention to guidelines for pluralistic teaching.

GUIDELINES FOR PLURALISTIC TEACHING

Teachers do have guidelines and broad power to implement them.
What follows are guidelines for teaching in a pluralistic society. Teachers are charged to provide equal educational opportunities for all of
their students. Equal educational opportunities require that all stu-

dents will benefit equally from the school experience. When certain facts are considered, it is obvious that schools and teachers tradition-ally have not provided equally beneficial educational experiences for all students. Poor white and ethnic minority students drop out of school at a much higher rate than white, middle- and upper-income students. The attrition rate for Native American students is as high as 95 percent in some regions in the country. Only about 60 percent of Spanish-speaking students graduate from school.[3]

Guideline I

• *Teachers should be aware of their own biases toward ethnic minority students.* Many teachers, regardless of their ethnic identities, have built-in biases against ethnic minority students.[4] Also, teachers may at times have lower expectations of ethnic minority students.[5] A teacher's lower expectations when coupled with linguistic and cultural differ-ences of ethnic minority students can effectuate lower academic per-formance.[6] Teachers may confuse cultural differences as motivational or cognitive deficits. For example, a Native American student who does not like certain competitive learning tasks may be exhibiting a cultural orientation toward cooperation rather than "laziness" or "passiveness." Spache[7] analyzed studies which tested the effectiveness of instructional approaches and found all of the approaches helpful for teaching read-ing. The critical factor for reading achievement was the teacher's at-titude toward the student's learning capabilities. Therefore, if the teacher has a built-in bias against the academic capabilities of ethnic minority students, then that bias more than likely will be reflected in the students' lower academic performance. One way of attempting to overcome ethnic group biases is to study a group's history, literature, or language. These disciplines can provide new knowledge and insight into a group's culture and can increase a person's ethnic literacy (see the ethnic studies model).

Guideline II

• *Curriculum materials and instruction should reflect the ethnic diversity in the United States.* This guideline requires permeation of instruction and materials with multiethnic themes and experiences. The intent is to expose all students to the cultures of Asia, black, Native, and Spanish-speaking Americans, as well as to the cultures of white ethnic groups. It's not satisfactory to simply add ethnic lessons to an already crowded secondary program, nor is it satisfactory to add a few minor characters representing ethnic groups to the children's literature of an elementary program. The additive approach—adding a few token lessons in ethnic group historical events, persons, or cultural contributions —perpetuates the notion that ethnics are not an integral part of society.

Are the curriculum materials permeated with multiethnic themes and concepts? For example, what image of Chinese Americans is evoked in reading materials? If students learn nothing about the courage, resourcefulness, and endurance of the Chinese American, then students probably will know only stereotypic images about the Chinese learned outside of school. Worse yet, Chinese American students may internalize the image as appropriate for their self-concepts and adapt their classroom behavior to fit the stereotype.[8] Differing family patterns—for example, interracial families, single parent families, extended families, matriarchal families—should be portrayed in curricular materials. Also, key to sustaining interest in materials are follow-up discussions conducted with students. For example, the book *Graciela* is about a young Mexican American girl who lives in an extended family.[9] Graciela learns to share her things with all members of the family. Sharing becomes critical to the family's maintenance. After reading the story, students should be encouraged to discuss the different feelings they have about sharing personal property (see the intergroup relations strategy). Are they encouraged to share? Do they share with grandparents? Do grandparents or godparents live in their homes? Students learn as part of their comprehension exercises something about minority cultures, enriching their lives with positive experiences about minority people.

Guideline III

• *Curriculum materials and instruction should exhibit the linguistic diversity of the United States.* Teachers are charged with developing a policy of linguistic pluralism. Traditionally, students who spoke a nonstandard dialect or a foreign language were prohibited or discouraged from using their dialect or language. In recent years, bilingual education legislation, the *Lau* v. *Nichols* decision, and professional education organizations have endorsed policies of linguistic pluralism. The National Council of Teachers of English has issued a policy statement supporting the student's right to speak a nonstandard language or dialect. The International Reading Association has published articles and texts which advocate retention of nonstandard dialects.

Linguistic chauvinism—the attitude that one's dialect is inherently superior to other languages and dialects—is the heart of the problem. Studies on teachers' attitudes toward the dialects spoken by Mexican Americans and urban black students indicate that the teachers' negative attitudes toward the dialects are of greater importance than other cognitive factors for producing low reading performance; that is, teachers generally view nonstandard dialects as substandard and deficient, and therefore inferior to standard English.[10] This attitude, when felt by the nonstandard speaker, has a negative impact on the student's expectations and motivation. To counter standard-English chauvinism, a student's dialect should be incorporated into curricular materials. Or, students should be encouraged to read standard English using their preferred articulation and pronunciation. A policy of linguistic pluralism is proposed—one that places emphasis on acceptance of a student's language or dialect regardless of the degree to which it deviates from standard English. It is certainly important that students learn to understand and read standard English as a tool for living and working within U.S. society; it is equally important that teachers emphasize and students understand the notion that while language or dialects may differ, they are not necessarily inferior to standard English. Thus, standard English should be taught as an alternate dialect necessary for communication in American life; it should not be taught as a dialect to replace the student's dialect. Legal support for this position was established with the U.S. District Court ruling in *Martin Luther King Junior Elementary School Children* v. *Ann Arbor School District*[11]: ". . . this court finds it appropriate to require the defendant Board to take steps to help its teachers to recognize the home language of the students and to use that knowledge in their attempts to teach reading skills in standard English. . . ." In this case, a group of black parents, on their children's behalf, filed suit against the Ann Arbor school district. The suit's essence was that many black elementary youngsters in the district were not learning to read well because teachers were failing to consider the effects that the youngsters' home dialect, Black English, had upon their learning to read standard English. The court ruled that if these black students were to benefit equally from a public school education, then their teachers must take into account and utilize the students' Black English to teach them standard English.

There is a strong belief among many minority parents, especially blacks, that the school should teach their children standard English and simply allow them to use their dialects elsewhere. This belief is predicated on the fear that if their children do not learn standard English, their upward mobility and social status will be inhibited. To a large extent, this fear is well-founded. Schools have often failed to teach their students basic standard English reading, writing, and speaking skills. Consequently, I am not advocating that black youngsters, or any other group of students, be taught only in their dialect. Rather, I am advocating that the student's dialect be respected and allowed to coexist with standard English. For nonminority students to understand Black English, for example, they would have to know a little about it. As a former high school English teacher, it always struck me as curious that we taught about prestigious English dialects such as "Bostonian English" but ignored the English dialects of poor and ethnic minorities. Resistance to teaching small segments of Black English to nonblack students, merely as a means to teach about the dialect, strikes me as curiously chauvinistic.

PLURALISTIC TEACHING AND
FUTURE CONSIDERATIONS

A lesson of singular significance taught by a study of teaching and learning within a culturally relative universe is that hardly anything ever stays the same. Living things and beings, plants, humans, and other animals continually confront alteration and adaptation. These are the dynamics of biological and cultural evolution; living things and beings must change to live. While these dynamics are older than the biologist Darwin and the astronomer Corpernicus, still they affect the future of pluralistic teaching and learning. And, while there are obstensibly no facts in the future, it is probable that many of the students currently enrolled in elementary schools will live and work in the twenty-first century. Since it would be pretentious for me to assume the powers of a Cassandra, predicting the future and forecasting human destinies, I ask you instead to envision with me a world vastly changed from the one to which we are accustomed. Envision with me a world in the future that we can understand with what we know today. Project with me what seems to be a feasible future. For example, assume it is a fact that the knowledge, attitudes, and values needed for group and human survival in the 1980s will be obsolete in the twenty-first century. The question then arises how can we best prepare students to live in that century, if all we know is grounded in past customs and traditions? At best, we can look at the present and, based upon that, we may realistically devise a course of action that rationally deals with the future.

By looking rationally at our current social situation (a most difficult thing to do) we can better plot our future course. We live in an ever-changing society. Both national and international events impinge upon us, forcing us to make changes; obviously, this is a permanent factor in American life. Since this text deals with teaching and learning, we should focus on changes that will affect future teaching and learning. The most fundamental question is what will be good teaching in the future pluralistic society? The answer to the question's first part, "what is good teaching," has evaded generations of teacher educators primarily because many of them have not analyzed the question's second part, "good teaching in a pluralistic society." A clear understanding of future pluralism mandates an assessment of the probable nature of that society. So what lies in store for the future? Technological change will continue incessantly. When coupled with the information explosion precipitated by computers and other data retrieval systems, technological changes will greatly modify the substance as well as the process of teaching and learning. Current teaching practices as well as their knowledge base will soon be obsolete— and thereby curtailed in effectiveness as well as relevance. Hence, teaching practices and academic content will experience continual modification and adaptation.

The notion of cultural relativism is responsive to technological change. Recall that cultural relativism operates on the assumption that students are more than data bank receptors of knowledge. In Chapter 1 cultural monism is contrasted with cultural relativism to emphasize that learning is an analytical, thinking process requiring skills to interpret and evaluate phenomena and data. This text's two instructional models and strategies place emphasis upon learning as a process to foster analytical and reflective thinking habits about fluid and volatile issues pertaining to race, culture, and ethnicity—learning habits that should not be made obsolete by technological innovations.

The demography of the United States is changing rapidly. By slow but deliberate degrees, black Americans are entering the mainstream of American political life, holding powerful political and economic positions. The Spanish-speaking population is ever increasing; it is the fastest growing population in the United States. At current projections, by the turn of the century the Spanish-speaking population will be a much larger ethnic minority group. Both the Asian American and Native American groups are expanding in numbers, although not at the rate of the Spanish-speaking. Other non-European peoples are making their presence felt, especially peoples from the Middle East and Southeast Asia. All these groups are to a greater or lesser degree solidifying their economic and political resources, building toward a future when their participation in American life will have greater impact on critical activities and institutions. For example, in the future their votes will perhaps swing presidential and congressional elections. Conversely, the white population is not expanding at its former growth rate. What this all means is that twenty-first century American demography will be vastly different because a much larger number and percentage of U.S. citizens will be culturally and racially nonwhite.

Just as our society's complexion is changing, so is its language. Increasing international communication and trade, the emerging bilingual education movement within the United States and the awakening of U.S. citizens to the fact that the English language is a minority language in the American hemisphere will catapult the new society toward bilingualism and perhaps multilingualism. English will remain the de facto national language, but unlike the past reign of English-only for Americans, other languages will become accepted, respected, and taught in the schools.

Recently, a presidential Commission on Foreign Languages and International Education[12] reported to former President Carter that Americans were embarrassingly monolingual and recommended that comprehensive foreign language and international education programs be federally funded in the public schools, colleges, and universities. For those familiar with the politics of language, the commission's report is reminiscent of the Sputnik scare of the late 1950s (the Russians managed to orbit the first space satellite) which caused many Americans to doubt U.S. supremacy in math, science, and languages. Under the National Defense Education Act, federal monies were appropriated to train more scientists, mathematicians, and foreign language specialists. Once these specialists were trained, federal priorities changed and interest in continuation of the programs declined, along with the federal support. What is different about the current commission report is the realization that the U.S. government cannot continue a crisis management approach toward foreign languages and cultures. One lesson garnered from World War I, World War II, and the Korean and Vietnam conflicts was that the United States cannot continue a course of aloofness and isolationism. We are compelled by world events to learn other languages and cultures. Yet another lesson learned from the wars is that the road toward international involvement has proved to be rocky and hazardous. Regardless of our stance on U.S. involvement in Vietnam, for example, we are recoiling from its shock. Our wounds are not entirely healed and discussions on the topic are still heated debates. The current commission's report calls for a comprehensive, rational approach to internationalization of American culture. Rather than a piecemeal, crisis inspired program, the current report is a declaration of a nonaggressive wager against American monolingualism, a wager whose consequences would be nondestructive, as Americans could begin to communicate with other nations and cultures.

The future society will need a formulated policy of linguistic pluralism, adopting U.S. English as the national standard but proposing national multilingualism. The business of government, the mass media, and most other daily activities will be continued predominantly in English. Yet schools will be supported through state and federal funds to teach elementary and secondary students a second language as a basic academic subject. Thus, instead of prohibiting non-English languages in the public schools, the policy will encourage if not mandate their instruction. Bilingual teachers may become the rule rather than the exception, especially those who are trained in a non-English language as well as in elementary pedagogy.

The impact of the ethnic revitalization movement of the 1970s will be felt as ethnic and cultural awareness increases within the next decades. Some people will continue the search for their roots, seeking and discovering the uniqueness of their ethnic or cultural heritage. They will also become acquainted with the unique contributions made by other U.S. ethnic and cultural groups. Thus, the future society will be pervaded by a novel type of ethnic pluralism, becoming increasingly complex and more equitable than the Americanization and melting pot notions of early twentieth-century America. Ethnic minority groups will participate on an equitable basis in the new ethnic pluralistic society. Fears and stereotypes about their racial stock will decrease, and their participation will be more amenable to their ethnic and cultural values, heeding less the offer of the Statue of Liberty, "Give me your tired, your poor," and heralding more the promise of the dream of Martin Luther King, Jr.

The twentieth century's last decades will witness a decline of rugged individualism and self-reliance as a viable ethos. Doctrines emphasizing social interdependence, social cohesion, and social action will replace individualism as the societal ethos. Some aspects of Marxism will become obsolete as we evolve into a postindustrial society. Yet, collective notions and ideologies will emerge, pleading for a greater sense of community and greater industrial and corporate social responsibility. Within this societal transformation, all ethnic and cultural groups will need to recognize the inevitability of interdependent social action, *e pluribus unum*. In the rhetoric of the civil rights movement, the society will need to "hang together" if it is not to hang separately. All ethnic and cultural groups will be compelled to go beyond culture and ethnicity to address broader issues of human survival within an increasingly complex and hazardous postindustrial society. As all the movements of the 1970s accelerate into the next decades, synergism— shared, collective, regenerating energy—rather than rampant competition for limited resources should be the rallying cry. Thus, a trend toward a more communal society is in the offing, one in which cooperative planning and pooling of human and natural resources will be the rule rather than the exception. Rugged individualism as an operating principle will lose its mystic power, thereby leading to the demise of the laissez faire, individualistic society. What this all means for good teaching in a pluralistic society is that educators at all levels of public and higher education will be challenged to provide people the means to release their creative, ever-renewing energies, making ethnic and cultural differences amenable to the pluralistic communal society.

Notes

1. R. M. Hutchins. *The Learning Society*. Baltimore: Penguin Books, 1970, p. 22; see also, V. T. Thayer. *The Role of the School in American Society*. New York: Dodd, Mead, 1960, pp. 334–335; see also, Levitas. *Marxist Perspectives*. London: Rutledge and Paul, 1974, pp. 63–71.

2. Clark Kerr. "Giving Youth a Better Chance: Options for Education, Work, Service," *A Report of the Carnegie Foundation for the Advancement of Teaching*. Berkeley, Cal., November 1979.

3. Ricardo L. Garcia. *Fostering a Pluralistic Society Through Multi-Ethnic Education*. Bloomington, Ind.: Phi Delta Kappa Foundation, 1978, p. 20.

4. Geneva Gay. *Differential Dyadic Interactions of Black and White Teachers with Black and White Pupils in Recently Desegregated Social Studies Classrooms: A Function of Teacher and Pupil Ethnicity*, Project No. 2 F 113. Washington, D.C.: Office of Education, January 1974.

5. D. T. Entwisle and M. Webster. "Raising Children's Performance Expectations: A Classroom Demonstration." *Social Science Research, 1* (January 1972): 147–158; see also, R. C. Rist. "Student Social Class and Teacher Expectations: The Self-Fulfilling Prophecy in Ghetto Education." *Harvard Educational Review 40* (1970): 411–451.

6. Romily Enoch. "The Relationship Between Indian and Non-Indian Teachers' Perceptions of Indian First-Graders' Achievement in Reading." *BIA Education Research Bulletin 6* (January 1978): 23–28.

7. George Spache and Evelyn Spache. *Reading in the Elementary School*. Boston: Allyn & Bacon, 1969.

8. Theresa Chang. "Asian American Identity and School Curriculum," in James Boyer and Joe Boyer, eds., *Curriculum and Instruction after Desegregation*. Manhattan, Kan.: AG Press, 1975, pp. 99–104.

9. Joe Molner. *Graciela: A Mexican American Child Tells Her Story*. New York: Franklin Watts, 1972.

10. Victoria Seitz. *Social Class and Ethnic Group Differences in Learning to Read*. Newark: International Reading Assn., 1977, p. 23.

11. *Martin Luther King Junior Elementary School Children* v. *Ann Arbor School District Board*. East Lansing, Mich.: United States District Court, July 1979, p. 41.

12. "Strength Through Wisdom: A Critique of U.S. Capability," Commission on Foreign Languages and International Education. Washington, D.C.: U.S. Government Printing Office, October 1979.

Part III
EXERCISES
AND ACTIVITIES

Part III provides critical-thinking exercises and activities to stimulate thought about issues in pluralistic teaching. Self-analysis exercises, human rights exercises, communal theory exercises, and self-study activities are presented. The exercises and activities can be used as springboards to indepth analysis and assessment of value issues pertinent to pluralistic teaching.

SELF-ANALYSIS EXERCISES: *SIMPATICO*

Experiment with the following exercises I call *simpatico*, which is the Spanish word for a sympathetic person, a person who feels as you do. How do you feel about your values, attitudes, beliefs? Are you in sympathy with your group? Can you be *simpatico* with other cultural groups? These exercises were suggested by the writing of Dr. Wilma Longstreet in her text *Aspects of Ethnicity*.[1] The exercises have been used in pre- and in-service workshops to introduce teachers and other educators to their attitudes toward culture, ethnicity, and, in some exercises, cultural differences. By examining personal feelings toward various aspects of culture, a person can begin to understand his or her feelings about cultural differences. The following diagram gives an overview of the *simpatico* process.

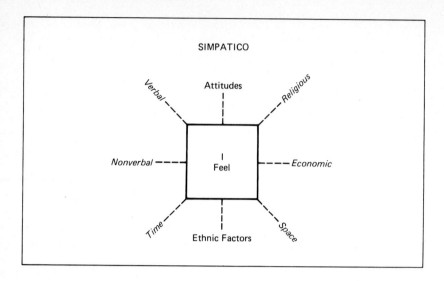

The purpose of the *simpatico* self-analysis exercises is to increase awareness about ethnic factors. The exercises are intended as introductory and are by no means intended as indepth consciousness-raising exercises.

EXERCISE I   NONVERBAL

During cross-cultural communication at least two-thirds of the message is conveyed nonverbally. Gestures, facial expressions, word connotations, and social distance among people who differ culturally are interpreted differently. In some cultures, for example, it's considered rude to stand too close to another person while conversing; in other cultures, it's considered rude *not to* stand close while conversing. Rather than attempting to categorize nonverbal do's and don'ts, the following questions and activities are intended to heighten awareness of nonverbal cross-cultural communications.

1. If someone smiles while making an apology, what does the smile mean?
2. How does a light tap on the shoulder by a teacher make you feel? How much touch by a teacher is too much touch to you? Should a teacher touch students ever?
3. In a classroom, what distance do you like classmates and teachers to keep? How close is too close? How far is too far vis-à-vis you and a teacher?
4. *Paired activity—Nonverbal Trustwalk—sensing nonverbal, nonvisual cues:* Two persons assist each other. Taking turns, one as a guide, one as blind person (close eyes), do the following: take a drink of water, walk

up and down a staircase, shut and open a door. Be careful and be sensitive to nonverbal cues both when receiving and transmitting.

5. *Role playing:* Role playing, unlike simulations, is open-ended. Players are given rules and roles and are to act out the roles within the rules. Conclusions are unpredictable because people will act out the roles according to their experiences and imaginations.

  a. Read the following roles carefully, selecting four people to act out the roles. Two people should be short, and two should be tall.

  b. Assign the role of "Americans" to the two tall people. Give them their role sheet and tell them to study it.

  c. Assign the role of "Largos" to the two short people. Give them their role sheet and ask them to study it. Ask the rest of the class to fish bowl (watch the players), observing their nonverbal communications. Or you can organize all the students into groups of four and have them all role play.

  d. Role players are to be told only their roles; they are not to be told the roles of their opposites.

  e. After the role playing is resolved—some conclusion is reached— discuss the nonverbal nuances and feelings that the players experienced, and the observations of the fish-bowlers.

ROLE I: You are Americans on vacation in the country of Largo. The nation is noted for its tall people—7 feet, six inches is the populace's mean height—everything in Largo is tall or large to accommodate tallness. Shortly after arriving, you lose your money and need to borrow some to catch a train, the only means of transportation, to return for help to the U.S. embassy in another town in Largo. It's late in the evening in the train terminal, and only two other persons are there. They are Largo people but both of them are 4 feet tall. You decide to ask them for a loan. They speak English. You must obtain the loan.

ROLE II: You are 4-foot tall Largos. In Largo people 5 feet and under are a minority group called "Shortos" who formerly served as slaves. Recently, they were emancipated and given full Largo civil rights. At one time they were considered half human and were treated that way in language and action. Now it is considered offensive to glance down at them when conversing with them. Rather, taller Largos must bend their knees or sit down, conversing with Shortos on a horizontal plane. Also, words that draw attention to their shortness, such as "low," "down," "under," "less than," "don't have any," "please" (begging), "diminutive," "shorty," "midget," "punk," "short," "little," "understand," "ground," "tall," "big," "large," "bottom," "squatty," "downtrodden," are considered offensive. Shortos are considered generous with people who need help, but they are extremely sensitive. You have the money to lend if you so desire.

EXERCISE II VERBAL

Everyone speaks a dialect that is standard to him or her. The question is, when speaking the same language in the same society, should a particular standard be imposed on all members of the society? In the United States, standard school English is informally (rather than legally) imposed on students. Yet students have a right to speak their own dialects. This exercise's purpose is to clarify the issue of standard versus nonstandard English. Read the following passages, and then discuss the questions below.

> Your spirit goin' to hell anyway, good or bad. Cause you see, doesn' nobody really know that it's a God, y'know, 'cause, I mean I have seen black gods, pink gods, white gods, all color gods, and don't nobody know it's really a God.

> And look, by the camp, *dos hombres*, they are fighting with two skunks, *que va*. They're eating all the food on the men's camp, *como cochinos*, but the men, those two, they are afraid they'll be sprayed, ha! *Pues*, I guess I would be afraid if these skunks were at my camp. And then there is the other man, he's alone, *muy triste*.

> I like the way he's dressed. He's got that belt, you know? And I think it's attractive, but you know? It's hard to say why I like the way he's dressed, but uh, maybe it's, oh, you know what I mean!

> There is something about the way he's dressed that I like, but I can't really identify what it is. It might be something about the way he matches his clothing which is to say that he has a color and fashion sense; yet, one is never sure exactly what that means. I'm really not at all certain but that I know what I mean because it's a matter of feeling that presupposes that he is an attractive dresser.

1. What do you think about the above dialect samples? Substandard? Different? Valid or invalid communication media?
2. Do you speak a "standard" dialect? Where did you learn the standard? For purposes of communication, is there such a thing as a "standard" English dialect?

EXERCISE III ECONOMIC

Economic relations are not always "strictly business." In some cultures, borrowing and lending money from friends and relatives is acceptable; in other cultures it is not. Also, attitudes about where one should be paid differ in different cultures. The following questions can serve as a springboard to understanding cross-cultural economic attitudes.

1. If you had one hundred dollars to use freely, would you spend it immediately? invest it in stocks? put it in a savings account? lend it?
2. If you needed a small loan, would you go to the bank for a loan? go to a savings and loan association? a credit union? a friend?
3. Would you rather be paid by the hour? by the day? by the week? by the month? no salary? by commission?

EXERCISE IV   RELIGIOUS

Religious beliefs about basic conditions—birth, death, the meaning and purpose of life—influence a person's way of behaving. Analyze how answers to the following questions might influence a teacher's behavior and a student's behavior.

1. To what extent does a person have control over his life? Do you consider life to be a trial period? one part of a natural cycle? the only important consideration?
2. Is it possible to believe in the Golden Rule of "Love thy neighbor" and compete for a position? Explain your answer.

EXERCISE V   TIME

Everyone has a sense of time. However, one's sense of time may be influenced by cultural, economic, and geographic life experiences. Analyze the following questions in terms of how they might influence a teacher's behavior and a student's behavior.

1. What are the three natural means people have used to describe time? Which of these do you use?
2. Why is the calendar you use square? Are there round calendars? What might this signify?
3. React to the following: You have traveled to New Mexico to attend a Native American Pow Wow that was advertised to start on a certain date at 9:00 A.M.; you arrive there ahead of time, but notice that no one is there. After 9:00 A.M. on that date, other people are there but the Native Americans have not arrived. Actually the Native Americans began to arrive sporadically after 1:00 P.M. They finally all arrive by 9:00 P.M. that evening. Since you paid to see the event in the morning, do you have a right for a refund? Should you remain for the Pow Wow at a lower rate? Just forget the whole matter and go home?

EXERCISE VI   SPACE

Different cultures prefer different spatial relations. Teachers prefer certain types of seating arrangements, room arrangements, and room shapes according to their cultural orientations. Also, teachers prefer to stand or sit in certain areas within their classes. The following diagram can provide a quick check on your preferences.

Classroom space arrangement: X = teacher; : : = students

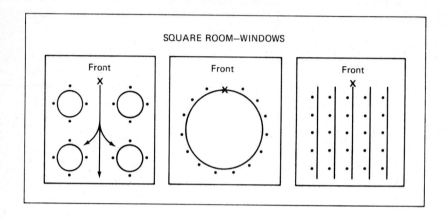

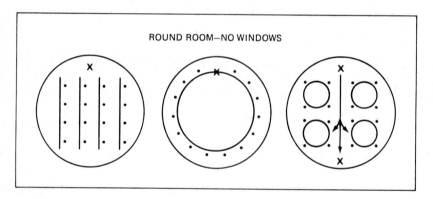

Discuss which space arrangement you prefer. Which do you dislike? Why do you like or dislike certain arrangements?

HUMAN RIGHTS EXERCISES

The following exercises involve incidents which have occurred in U.S. public schools. Work through these exercises to sharpen your perceptions on human rights classroom management.

EXERCISE I

Incident

In a ninth-grade social studies class, a student makes the comment, "the problem with blacks is that too many of them are on welfare." The comment was made during a session on the contemporary status of black Americans.

Questions

1. What are the facts about black dependence on social welfare programs?
2. How might the facts change the student's opinion? Or would the facts reinforce the student's opinion?
3. What are the students' rights to know? To hold an opinion unsupported by evidence?
4. What might the perspective of an expert be pertaining to the issue at hand? What might be the perspective of a black expert on this issue?

EXERCISE II

Incident

A certain state passed a law years ago prohibiting bare feet in all public buildings. The law was passed to insure public health at a time when communicable diseases were uncontrollable and were being transmitted in various ways, including bare feet. Recently, a student from a very poor Puerto Rican home was kept from attending school whenever his one pair of shoes was being repaired. His parents could not afford another pair, nor were they willing to solicit public welfare funds to buy the shoes. So their son stayed home whenever his shoes were at the shoe shop because it was against the law to attend class barefoot. Clearly, the parents were in violation of the compulsory school attendance law, but had they sent their son to school barefoot, they would have been in violation of the public health law. Further, there existed strong ethnic biases against Puerto Ricans in the community because of the belief that too many Puerto Ricans were on welfare programs. Consequently, the parents felt that it would be demeaning to use public assistance money to buy more shoes.

Questions

1. What human rights are involved here? Students' rights? Puerto Rican students' rights? Parents' rights?
2. How might civil disobedience apply in this incident?

EXERCISE III

Incident

Just as a fourth-grade class was leaving the classroom, a student accused Marie Z., a Japanese American, of stealing his lunch. Her desk was searched by the teacher, who found his lunch in it. The teacher asked the classmates (all in a hurry to eat their lunches) how to punish Marie. The majority felt she should be punished by classroom confinement for a week rather than eating lunch in the lunchroom with her classmates.

Questions

1. What human rights are threatened in this incident?
2. What about the dangers of rule by majority?
3. As the teacher, how would you handle the incident?

EXERCISE IV

Incident

The word "nigger" is commonly used in the local all-white community to connote any tricky or devious person. A black youngster moves into the community. During a soccer game, a white friend of the black child calls him a nigger for executing a tricky play. The black student, angered by the remark, beats up the white student.

Questions

1. What human rights are involved?
2. Was the black student's rage understandable?
3. Was the white student's *faux pas* understandable?
4. What intergroup relations strategies might be used to prevent such incidents?

EXERCISE V

Incident

A Native American student is told to wash off the brown grease smeared over his arms. He does. The next day his sister dies. According to this Native American's religious belief, oil mixed with brown soil should be smeared on the arms of all family members when a family member is ill. Removal of the "grease" can do harm to the ill person. The parents pull the student out of school.

Questions

1. What human rights are involved?
2. Should the teacher have known better? Was the teacher acting out attitudes about hygiene and cleanliness? Was the teacher acting out an attitude against "silly" superstitions?
3. How much should a teacher know about a student's culture?
4. How might a study of the school's community prevent similar incidents?

EXERCISE VI

Incident

A Jewish American organization feels that Jewish students should be allowed vacations during certain Jewish holidays; arguing that Christians are allowed Christmas and Easter vacations, so should Jewish students be allowed, without penalty, time off for their holidays. A bandwagon is begun: other ethnic groups join the Jewish thrust—Mexican American, Polish, and Islamic—insisting on free time for religious holidays other than Christmas and Easter.

Questions

1. What human rights are involved?
2. In a pluralistic society, are schools able to accommodate all ethnic group holidays? Or should schools become more secular and less Christian?
3. How might a study of the school's community have prevented this incident?

EXERCISE VII

Incident

A group of teachers feel that a teacher does not provide her third-grade students an acceptable language model because she speaks with a thick Latino accent. The students can all understand her and their parents are pleased with her teaching performance, but the other teachers feel she should be dismissed or transferred.

Questions

1. What human rights are involved?
2. Is this a case of linguistic chauvinism? Should teachers be required to speak in some standard of American English?

EXERCISE VIII

Incident

Maria Martinez was caught by her teacher passing answers to a friend during an exam. Maria explained that she was not cheating, because in her family, she was taught to share her things with brothers and sisters. She claimed to be sharing answers.

Questions

1. What human rights are involved?
2. Did Maria act out a cultural preference? Or did she use "culture" as a shield to justify "cheating"?
3. How might the ethnic studies model be used to create better cultural understandings in this incident?

COMMUNAL THEORIES EXERCISES

Following is a summary of the three primary U.S. communal theories. Read the summaries, and then discuss the questions and quotations provided for analysis of the theories.

MELTING POT I: ANGLO-CONFORMITY

To assimilate into the Anglo-conformity society, a person had to conform to Anglo-Saxon (New England English) Protestant values, conform to a laissez faire, free enterprise economic system, conform to a theory of white racial superiority; racial minorities were not to be assimilated. Rather, they were to be deported, enslaved, or exterminated. The theory consisted of a racial hierarchy: the "whiter" a person was the better and more superior he or she was:

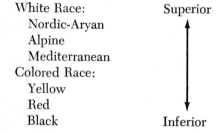

White Race: Superior
  Nordic-Aryan
  Alpine
  Mediterranean
Colored Race:
  Yellow
  Red
  Black Inferior

The society was held together by having one race (white), on religious denomination, and one type of economic system.

MELTING POT II: ETHNIC SYNTHESIS

To assimilate into the ethnic synthesis society, a person had to abandon his former culture, language, and nationality, had to adopt "American" ways of dressing and speaking English, had to adopt constitutional democracy, and had to intermarry with persons of different cultural and national affiliations. Within this society, a new biological "American" race would evolve, having a new white culture in common. Racial minorities were excluded from this society. The issue of what was the place (status/role) of racial minorities was not addressed. This society was held together by a common, "new" white race, a "new" culture based on the American (U.S.) English language and core culture, and an economic system and democratic government held in common. The volatile issues of interracial and interreligious marriages and mixtures were ignored.

CULTURAL PLURALISM: MOSAIC ANALOGY

To assimilate into the cultural pluralism society, a person had to adopt constitutional democracy, accept a laissez faire, free enterprise economic system, speak English, and accept cultural differences. But, a person could choose his or her cultural, ethnic, or religious affiliation. A person could be bilingual. Because of the resilience of religion, the assumption existed that the cultural pluralistic society would be sort of a "triple" melting pot (Protestants, Jews, Catholics) held together by general Judeo-Christian values and constitutional democracy. The society was perceived as a mosaic in which each part kept its identity and yet each part contributed to an overall pattern. This society is also described as a "salad bowl" society. Racial minorities were included in this society if they adhered to Judeo-Christian values.

Exercises for Group Discussion

1. What elements of the three social theories are similar? Why?
2. What elements of the three social theories are dissimilar? Why?
3. Read the following passages. Discuss which social theory they best describe.

> Female and male, Indian, Negro and White, Irishman, Scotchman and Englishman, German and Spaniard and Frenchman, Italian and Swede and Pole, Hindu and Chinaman, butcher, baker and candlestick maker, workingman and gentleman, rich man and poor man, Jew and Quaker and Unitarian and Congregationalist and

Presbyterian and Catholic—they are all different from each other, and different as they are, all equal to each other.[2]

What . . . is the American, this new man? He is either an European, or the descendant of an European, hence that strange mixture of blood, which you will find in no other country. I could point out to you a family whose grandfather was an Englishman, whose wife was Dutch, whose son married a French woman, and whose present four sons have now four wives of different nations. He is an American, who leaving behind him all his ancient prejudices and manners, receives new ones from the new mode of life he has embraced, the new government he obeys, and the new rank he holds. He becomes an American by being received in the broad lap of our great Alma Mater. Here individuals of all nations are melted into a new race of men, whose labours and posterity will one day cause great changes in the world.[3]

The [immigrants to America] come to a life of independence, but to a life of labor—and, if they cannot accommodate themselves to the character, moral, political and physical, of this country with all its compensating balances of good and evil, the Atlantic is always open to them to return to the land of their nativity and their fathers. To one thing they must make up their minds, or they will be disappointed in every expectation of happiness as Americans. They must cast off the European skin, never to resume it. They must look forward to their posterity rather than backward to their ancestors; they must be sure that whatever their own feelings may be, those of their children will cling to the prejudices of this country.[4]

Our progress in degeneracy appears to me to be pretty rapid. As a nation, we began by declaring that "all men are created equal." We now practically read it "all men are created equal, except negroes." When the Know-Nothings get control, it will read "all men are created equal, except negroes, and foreigners and Catholics." When it comes to this I should prefer emigrating to some country where they make no pretense of loving liberty. . . .[5]

The people of the United States, considered as a whole, are composed of immigrants and their descendants from almost every country. The principal portion of them, however, derived their origin from the British nation, comprehending by this term the English, the Scotch and the Irish. The English language is almost wholly used; the English manners, modified to be sure, predominate, and the spirit of English liberty and enterprise animates the energies of the whole people. English laws and institutions, adapted to the circumstances of the country, have been adopted here. . . .[6]

To our reproach it must be said, that though for a century and a half we have had under our eyes the races of black and of red men, they have never yet been viewed by us as subjects of natural history. I advance it therefore as a suspicion only, that the blacks whether originally a distinct race, or made distinct by time and circumstances, are inferior to the whites in the endowments both of body and mind. It is not against experience to suppose, that different species of the same genus or varieties of the same species, may possess different qualifications. Will not a lover of natural history then, one who views the gradations in all the races of animals with the eye of philosophy, excuse an effort to keep those in the department of man as distinct as nature has formed them? This unfortunate difference of colour, and perhaps of faculty, is a powerful obstacle to the emancipation of these people. Many of their advocates while they wish to vindicate the liberty of human nature are anxious also to preserve its dignity and beauty. Some of these, embarrassed by the question "What further is to be done with them?" join themselves in opposition with those who are actuated by sordid avarice only. Among the Romans emancipation required but one effort. The slave when made free, might mix with, without staining the blood of his master. But with us a second is necessary unknown to history. When freed, he is to be removed beyond the reach of mixture.[7]

These new immigrants were no longer exclusively members of the Nordic race as were the earlier ones who came of their own impulse to improve their social conditions. The transportation lines advertised America as a land flowing with milk and honey and the European governments took the opportunity to unload upon careless, wealthy and hospitable America the sweepings of their jails and asylums. The result was that the new immigration . . . contained a large and increasing number of the weak, the broken and the mentally crippled of all races drawn from the lowest stratum of the Mediterranean basin and the Balkans, together with hordes of the wretched, submerged populations of the Polish Ghettos. Our jails, insane asylums and almshouses are filled with this human flotsam and the whole tone of American life, social, moral and political has been lowered and vulgarized by them.[8]

We live in a diverse society held together by dynamic democratic principles and economic values based on the ethic of individual free enterprise. While some elements of white ethnic groups have blended and melded, and while legal segregation of racial minorities is unconstitutional, we still live in a society in which individuals discriminate against others for religious, economic, and racial preferences. Vestiges of the past percolate into the present.[9]

SELF-STUDY ACTIVITIES

To develop a broader background and wider experience with ethnic group cultures or current situations, education students may want to pursue the following list of suggested activities:

1. Enroll in an ethnic studies course or a course that treats culture and ethnicity.
2. Tune in to whatever ethnic student activities occur on campus.
3. Check local schools and public libraries for films, books, and other media that treat ethnic groups.
4. Check state and federal agencies for information pertaining to ethnic groups, especially the State Department of Education in your state.
5. In the campus library, read and analyze the state and federal legislation that treats ethnic groups, e.g., Bilingual Education Act, Ethnic Heritage Act, U.S. Civil Rights Act, Emergency School Assistance Act, Indian Education Act; also read and analyze key U.S. Supreme Court decisions, e.g., *Brown* v. *Board of Education, Lau* v. *Nichols.*
6. Visit the affirmative action office on campus. Find out their goals and activities.

Notes

1. Wilma Longstreet. *Aspects of Ethnicity.* New York: Teachers College Press, 1978.
2. Horace Kallen. *Americanism and Its Makers.* New York: Bureau of Jewish Education, 1944, p. 8.
3. Hector St. John Crevecoeur. "Letters from an American Farmer," in Gordon, *Assimilation in American Life.* New York: Oxford University Press, 1964, p. 116.
4. John Quincy Adams. *Niles Weekly Register*, v. 28, April 29, 1820, pp. 157–158.
5. Abraham Lincoln, quoted in Benjamin Thomas, *Abraham Lincoln.* New York: Knopf, 1952, pp. 163–164.
6. Jesse Chickering. *Immigration into the United States.* Boston: Little, Brown, 1848, pp. 79–80.
7. Thomas Jefferson quoted in Gilbert Osofsky. *The Burden of Race.* New York: Harper & Row, 1967, p. 55.
8. Madison Grant. *The Passing of the Great Race.* New York: Scribner, 1916, p. 92.
9. Ricardo Garcia.

Index

88   89   10   9   8   7